Praise for
Looking for the Hidden Folk

"Nancy Marie Brown reveals to us skeptics how rocks and hills are the mansions of elves, or at least what it takes to believe so. *Looking for the Hidden Folk* evocatively animates the Icelandic landscape through Brown's past and present travels and busts some prevalent clichés and myths along the way—this book is my reply to the next foreign reporter asking about that Elf Lobby."

—Egill Bjarnason, author of *How Iceland Changed the World: The Big History of a Small Island*

"Using ideas and stories about the hidden folk in Iceland as a stepping stone into the human perception of our homes in the world where stories and memories breathe life into places, be it through the vocabulary of quantum physics or folklore, Nancy Marie Brown makes us realize that there is always more to the world than meets the eye. And that world is not there for us to conquer and exploit but to walk into and sense the dew with our bare feet on the soft moss, beside breathing horses and mighty glaciers in the drifting fog that often blocks our view."

—Gísli Sigurðsson, Research Professor, The Árni Magnússon Institute, University of Iceland

"Nancy Marie Brown is a scholar and a pilgrim, and Iceland (plus much more) is illuminated here through her knowledge and passion."

—Thomas Swick, author of *The Joys of Travel*

"This is a sweeping and moving journey across time and space—through myth and theory, language, and literature—into the world of wonder and enchantment. Beautifully written, *Looking for the Hidden Folk* offers a compelling and surprising case for the recognition of forces and beings not necessarily 'seen' in everyday life but nevertheless somehow sensed, exploring their complexity and why they matter."

—Gísli Pálsson, Professor of Anthropology,
University of Iceland

"Astonishing, lyrical, and thought-provoking. Yes, I am a scientist, but this book makes me consider a new reality. I am captivated."

—Pat Shipman, author of *Our Oldest Companions*

"A love song to the living landscape of Iceland and the cultural history in which it is clothed, inspired by the author's numerous encounters with the country and its people over the last decades."

—Terry Gunnell, Professor of Folkloristics,
University of Iceland

"Nancy Marie Brown's *Looking for the Hidden Folk* is an elegantly written and wonderfully individualistic exploration of Icelandic culture through the ages, combining a shrewd appraisal of traditions with an acute interest in the modern world and all its intellectual quirks."

—Ármann Jakobsson, author and scholar

"In this fascinating book Nancy Marie Brown shows how the stories of Iceland's hidden people are a natural human response to the island's extraordinary landscape, and makes the reader question whether dismissing such beliefs as irrational is itself irrational."

—Michael Ridpath, author of the
Magnus Iceland Mysteries

LOOKING FOR
THE HIDDEN FOLK

LOOKING
FOR THE
HIDDEN FOLK

How Iceland's Elves Can Save the Earth

NANCY MARIE BROWN

PEGASUS BOOKS
NEW YORK LONDON

LOOKING FOR THE HIDDEN FOLK

Pegasus Books, Ltd.
148 West 37th Street, 13th Floor
New York, NY 10018

First Pegasus Books paperback edition September 2023
First Pegasus Books hardcover edition October 2022

Interior design by Maria Fernandez

Library of Congress Cataloging-in-Publication Data is available.

Paperback ISBN: 978-1-63936-574-6
Hardcover ISBN: 978-1-63936-228-8

10 9 8 7 6 5 4 3 2 1

Printed in the United States of America
Distributed by Simon & Schuster
www.pegasusbooks.com

For the family at Helgafell and all the other Icelanders
who have shared stories with me.

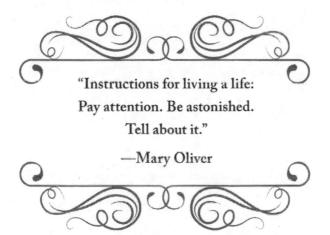

"Instructions for living a life:
Pay attention. Be astonished.
Tell about it."

—Mary Oliver

Contents

A Note on Language   xiii

ONE

1. The Elf Lobby   5
2. Icelanders Believe in Elves   15
3. Otherworlds   24

TWO

4. The Island That Likes to Be Visited   41
5. Thought and Memory   54
6. Walking Withershins   67

THREE

7. Windows   87
8. Seeing Is Believing   100
9. The Volcano Show   115
10. Send Cash, Not Ash   129

FOUR

11. Elf Stories   147
12. Doors   160

13. The House of the Steward   173
14. A Kind Troll   188

FIVE

15. Wonder   205
16. A Soul Clad in Air   218
17. A Sense of Place   229
18. Everyone Is an Artist   241

Acknowledgments   255
Notes   257

A Note on Language

⟨⟩

I n this book, I have anglicized the spellings of most Icelandic words and names, changing the letters ð (eth) to *d*, þ (thorn) to *th*, and æ (ash) to *ae*, and omitting all accents. I have retained the nominative endings (as in Hjortur) for most modern Icelandic names; for saga characters, I have dropped the endings (turning Gudridur into Gudrid) to be consistent with most saga translations. Icelandic words in italics are correctly spelled. Since an Icelander's last name is generally their father's name plus son or daughter (spelled *dóttir*) and not a family name, I follow Icelandic style, using first names for all Icelanders. Some of our conversations were conducted in Icelandic, although my notes were taken in English. Such quotations, therefore, are both translations and reconstructions. I apologize to any Icelanders whose words I might have misunderstood.

ONE

"Pay attention to what
they tell you to forget."

—Muriel Rukeyser

Galgahraun

The Elf Lobby

On the outskirts of Iceland's capital lies a lava field called Galgahraun. The name comes from a large basalt feature like a sleeping giant's open maw: two opposing lava waves that crested and froze into peaks or, more likely, a single lava bubble that domed, cracked, and collapsed when the volcano Burfell, some seven miles distant, erupted eight thousand years ago. A wooden beam was balanced from one peak of this feature to the other, from the giant's upper jaw to his lower; affixed at the midpoint was a noose from which outlaws were hanged, as if to plummet in death down the giant's gullet. *Gálgi* means gallows, *hraun* means lava field. No written texts attest to any hangings here, but people have found human bones in the *hraun*, according to a placard set up by Friends of the Lava and the Environmental Agency of the nearby town of Gardabaer, though this story of the board, the rope, and the bones is also attached to a different Galgahraun in a different part of Iceland, hundreds of miles away, by Sagnagrunnur, the geographical database of Icelandic folklore established by the University of Iceland in 2010.

The giant's maw is my own fancy. It takes little suggestion to find huge, ugly faces in Icelandic lava rocks.

As we walked for an hour in Galgahraun in June 2016, I also imagined trolls turned to stone by sunbeams. One troll we strolled by rode a trollish steed. Another watched us, fascinated, transfixed, as if its head had just popped from the surface of the lava waves, like a curious seal's will pop from the sea to watch people wander along the seashore. I knew about trolls' fatal sensitivity to the sun from J. R. R. Tolkien's *The Hobbit*. Early in the book, when Bilbo Baggins and his dwarf companions are caught by the huge and ugly Bert, Bill, and Tom, the wizard Gandalf's trickery keeps the three trolls bickering—are dwarves tastier roasted, or squashed to jelly?—until the sun comes up and "Dawn take you all, and be stone to you." I knew, as well, that Tolkien took the troll-and-sunbeam motif from Icelandic folktales, taught to him by an Icelandic au pair, who told such tales to Tolkien's children.

Ragnhildur did not encourage me in my trollish fancies. In fact, we didn't speak about trolls at all, as I recall, and only a very little about elves or the *huldufólk*, the Hidden Folk, which was odd, since Ragnhildur Jonsdottir is a famous elf-seer. Just how famous was underlined by a call she accepted on her cell phone as we walked. A foreign journalist wanted to know if the elves had anything to do with Iceland's unexpected success that summer in soccer's Euro Cup.

Instead, we photographed lava crags and stacks and pillars, pillows of silver-green moss, caves and clefts and individual lichen-splashed rocks. It was by turns warm and sunny and cloudy and cool, a fine summer's day. The breeze was light—just enough to keep the gnats at bay. The land smelled of peat, with hints of salt and sea. We wandered about pointing out plants. I didn't keep a list, but two hours later, back at my hotel when I wrote up my recollections, I remembered blueberry, crowberry, stone bramble, violet, dandelion, mountain avens, buttercup, butterwort, wood geranium, wild thyme, willow shrubs with pale fluffy catkins, and several kinds of grass, including sheep's sorrel, which we tasted—it was sour as limes. Elves' cup moss was the only sign of elves I saw. We listened to the wind sighing in the knee-high willows and the incessant cries of seabirds: black-backed gulls barking *now! now! now!* and arctic terns, many terns, with their piercing *kree-yah* cries. It was the terns' nesting season, so we'd wandered away from the bay, where the birds lay their eggs on beach stones and black sand. Once Ragnhildur waved me down to ground level to watch a wet, black slug, fatter than my thumb, with a mouth like an anus.

Ragnhildur is a grandmother, with grandmotherly long silver hair. She wore a long silk scarf in a bright tie-dye pattern, a blue jacket, a leopard-print shirt, blue jeans, and sturdy black sandals. Her eyeglasses had gray-blue frames; her sunglasses were stuck on top of her head like a hair band. In a news photo from October 2013, she likewise wears a long scarf, that one gray wool, and her gray-blue eyeglasses. A wool hat covers her silver hair. The rest of her grandmotherly figure is hard to make out, as she is prone, facedown as if planking, and being carried by policemen who look anything but happy about it. She and her family had camped in the path of the bulldozers hired to destroy the parts of Galgahraun that were in the way of a new road. Like other demonstrators, they had pitched a tent, rising early to enjoy their morning coffee on a lava cliff and to witness the sunrise. It was beautiful fall weather, Ragnhildur remembered. The police tried to carry away her husband, Larus, too; he is quite large and they soon gave up. But eventually all the demonstrators were evicted and jailed. And the bulldozers began their work.

Rising from her perusal of the slug, Ragnhildur gestured toward the cityscape looming beyond the lava. Near that edge of Galgahraun, from 1945 through the 1960s, she informed me, Johannes Kjarval liked to come and paint en plein air—or even in pouring rain, which splashed his canvases in ways he liked. Kjarval's Cliffs, the formations are now called; I have seen several paintings in Reykjavik's Kjarval Museum titled *From Galgahraun*. Internationally, Kjarval is Iceland's best-known painter. In *The Idea of North*, Peter Davidson calls his art "an art of slowness, of unhurried meditation on northern place," adding, "He is absolute master of minute and exquisite gradations of gray." Kjarval left his paint cans in a lava cave nearby. When a house was built beside the cliffs, the cave was cleaned out. Organizing protests against the new road, Ragnhildur thought to capitalize on Kjarval's name. She called in artists to protect Kjarval's Cliffs. They held a "paint-in": like a sit-in, except everyone painted.

The aesthetics of the *hraun*, those minute and exquisite gradations of gray, did not move the Icelandic Road Administration.

Nor did the environmental slant of the lawsuit filed by Friends of the Lava, which argued that the road building was illegal: Galgahraun had been listed as a protected natural area since 2009.

Defeated in district court, the Friends were appealing their case to Iceland's Supreme Court—the tent city was taken down, the bulldozers were back at work—when, thanks in large part to Ragnhildur, the plight of Galgahraun's Hidden Folk catapulted this little local road fight into international media fame. "I wrote a letter," she told me. "I wrote a letter on behalf of the elves and *huldufólk* in Galgahraun. I sent it to the mayor of Gardabaer and all the council members. I sent it to the president of Iceland and several ministers of parliament."

News of the Icelandic "elf lobby" trying to stop progress was reported by the Associated Press in December 2013 and picked up by the *North Dakota Insider*, the *Denver Post*, the *Salt Lake Tribune*, the *Pueblo Chieftain*, and the *Buenos Aires Herald*. The phones in Iceland's Road Administration rang and rang. The *Guardian* ran the story, as did the *Huffington Post*, the *Daily Beast*, PBS, NBC, Fox News, Breitbart News, and *The Wire*, whose reporter accused the AP of unfairly focusing on the "loony elf 'seers'"—who claimed to have identified a spectacular twelve-foot-long rock formation as an elf church—just to get laughs.

The elf-seer named in the AP story was Ragnhildur; she was also a leader of the Friends of the Lava environmental group. Seeing the Hidden Folk, and speaking to (or for) them, is not a joke to her. After our walk in Galgahraun, she quite naturally described the moment she saw her first elf, when she was two years old. Ragnhildur had just walked home with her mother, and when her mother closed the door, Ragnhildur burst into tears: Her mother had shut the door in the face of an elf. That elf was named Pulda. She was, and still is, Ragnhildur's friend. From Galgahraun,

Ragnhildur drove me to a small public park beside her childhood home in the town of Hafnarfjordur and pointed out the rock in which Pulda lives. I saw only a rock.

Ryan Jacobs, writing for the *Atlantic Monthly*, understood that Ragnhildur was neither loony nor out for laughs. He writes: "Both she and another seer visited the field separately and came to the same conclusion about the spot. 'I mean, there are thousands or millions of rocks in this lava field,' she said, 'but we both went to the same rock or cliff and talked about an elf church.' She knows about the elf church because she can see it, she says, and also sense its energy, a sensation many Icelanders are familiar with." Later in the article, Jacobs presents more of Ragnhildur's point of view: "As industry has encroached, Jonsdottir insists, many humans have forgotten about 'the inner life of the earth' as they bend it to their will. When elves act out, they are doing more than just protecting their own homes, they are reminding people of a lost relationship. 'They're . . . protectors of nature, like we humans should be,' she said."

The Icelandic Supreme Court halted work on the Galgahraun road, citing both its environmental and its cultural impact—"including the impact on elves," reported an Icelandic newspaper.

The mayor of Gardabaer arranged to meet Ragnhildur in the lava field. With him came another town official, two men from the Road Administration, and two from the firm contracted to build the road. "I took them on an elf walk," Ragnhildur told me. "I described the big elf church with its amazing energy and all the powerful beings there working with the Light. There was also this smaller rock, which is a sort of chapel." The words *church* and *chapel* were metaphors, she explained: "We have to use human terms so that we can understand." The men asked Ragnhildur how they could preserve this sacred area and still build a road. With Ragnhildur speaking for the elves, they agreed on a plan.

This "pact between men and elves," as Ragnhildur called it, was kept. The new road narrows where it passes the elf church. In March 2015, a large crane took six hours to move the seventy-five-ton elf chapel, in two pieces, to a spot next to the church—or, according to a press release from the Road Administration, "next to other beautiful and similar rock formations, thus creating a unified whole." Having had over a year to prepare, Ragnhildur told the newspaper, the elves were satisfied and would no longer "act out" and block the road.

Yet as the bulldozers began again to level Galgahraun, Ragnhildur could not restrain her tears. She screamed at the bulldozer operators—later she apologized, telling them how hard it was for her to see the elves' kitchens being destroyed and their sofas tossed about; even though the elves had already left the area, it was still a home being wrecked. She said the young men driving the machines were very affected by her grief and her stories. "They won't forget it," she told me. "It wasn't their fault. They were just doing their jobs. But still, they need to take responsibility for destroying something beautiful. They need to think about it."

The new road connects the suburb of Alftanes (population 2,500) and Bessastadir, the official residence of the Icelandic president, with the suburb of Gardabaer (population 17,000), and thence with Iceland's capital city of Reykjavik (population 130,000). The new road is wider than most roads in Iceland, wider in most places than Highway One, the Ring Road, Iceland's main artery, which circles the country. With two full lanes, and shoulders, plus a bike path, the new Galgahraun road is one of the best roads I've seen in Iceland, where many minor byways are unpaved and frighteningly narrow, and where shoulders—even on the Ring Road—are generally nonexistent. Bicyclists throughout most of the country teeter on the edge of the one lane, "sharing" it with cars, campers, trucks, and buses that rarely slow down for them. On the European Road Assessment Programme's five-star scale, nearly three-quarters of Iceland's roads are rated unsafe.

"Clearly," Ragnhildur said, "they needed a shoulder here so people didn't slam into the lava in a crash."

"But roads in the West Fjords," I objected, "have no shoulder and drop straight into the sea."

"Yes," she said, "there's that."

The new road angles toward an older road that connects the same settlements. That Alftanes road is also wide and paved, with a shoulder. According to Friends of the Lava, of forty-four roads in the greater Reykjavik region, twenty-one were more dangerous than the old Alftanes road. Of the 1,427 roads in Iceland, 301 had more accidents.

The day we walked in Galgahraun, the wind and the birds were louder than the sounds of the new road—it was very lightly traveled. There was no traffic hum, no noise of human voices except our own. It was a good place, a place I would choose to sit and write, a place of inspiration.

What is inspiration? Why do some places attract artists and spark creative thought? Why are some places beautiful—and how do you define beauty?

Ragnhildur and I talked over these questions as we walked out of Galgahraun, past the grassy ruins of an ancient farm, heading for her car. What about this landscape inspired Kjarval? If you asked him, would he have said that an elf woman brought him here and showed him the view he tried to capture on canvas so many times in his exquisite gradations of gray? Kjarval often included elves in his paintings, or spectral faces in the rocks. Did he see spirits in the landscape the way Ragnhildur does? After she received her art degree from the Icelandic Academy of Arts and Crafts, she explained, she felt freed to do what she had always wanted to do. Being an artist gave her permission to use her "inner eye."

I said the role of the artist in society has always been to make us see things differently. I told her she was a performance artist. I thought she took that well—though in hindsight I wonder why, just about then, we started talking about crazy ladies. Is Ragnhildur a crazy lady because she talks to elves? Are Christians crazy because they talk to God? What immaterial beings are we allowed to believe in, and who is allowed to do the believing? Ragnhildur may be serious about seeing elves, but she can also joke about it. Once a Christian journalist confessed to her that he couldn't believe in elves because there were no elves in the Bible. Ragnhildur replied, "There are no cats in the Bible either, and yet I have five cats."

We had just reached her car and were chuckling over the cats when another car zoomed into the parking lot, screeching to a halt beside us. The driver flung open her door and screamed at us in Icelandic—something about our dog disturbing the arctic terns' nesting site.

"We don't have a dog," Ragnhildur replied.

The woman continued berating us. Ragnhildur answered her calmly, in a soft, pleasant voice.

But the woman was beside herself, gesticulating and crying, almost incoherent.

"We saw a dog, but it was on a leash," Ragnhildur said.

The woman began a passionate description of the fight for Galgahraun, and the tiniest crack appeared in Ragnhildur's shell of politeness. "Yes, I know," she said. "Do you know who I am? I am Ragnhildur Jonsdottir." The name meant nothing to the incensed bird lover. Ragnhildur looked at me, and we got into our car. As we began to pull out, the other woman gunned her vehicle and came roaring up next to us, apparently intending to ram us, or at least to cut us off. Ragnhildur slammed on the brakes. Out of the corner of my eye I saw the other car leap into the air and come down hard. It stalled out. Steam burst out of its engine.

"Oh dear," Ragnhildur said.

We got out of our car and went to look. The woman had driven over a boulder the size of a basketball. It was firmly fixed between the front and back wheels of her small sedan—there was no possibility of moving the car without a wrecker. The woman froze in shock.

"Let me drive you home," Ragnhildur said, taking her elbow. "Where do you live?"

Her house was close by, in sight of Galgahraun, though a little too far to walk in the house slippers she was wearing. Ragnhildur coaxed her into the back seat of our car, and we drove her home in silence.

As soon as we were back on the road, the bird lover safely delivered, Ragnhildur turned to me with a smile. "Now do you believe in elves?"

Icelanders Believe in Elves

O n my first trip to Iceland, in 1986, my husband and I visited the families of three Icelandic graduate students we knew from Penn State University, where I worked: an economist, a seismologist, and a mathematician. Driving us to her house outside of Reykjavik, the mathematician's mother, Thyri, pointed out a cluster of rocks in the middle of a small fenced lawn at a bend in the road. "Elves live there," she said.

Thyri was a teacher, her English was excellent, but I was never quite sure when she was joking. One night she served us a formal dinner—white tablecloth, flowers—and out from the kitchen, with a flourish, she brought a platter of singed sheep's heads. Whole heads—eyeballs, teeth in the jaws—blackened to burn off the fleece. The eyes and ears are the best parts, she said. She mimed plucking out an eyeball and popping it into her mouth, rolling it about, licking her lips. Seeing me barely pick at my head, she took pity on us and brought out a second platter of broiled lamb steaks. (The family, on the other hand, devoured the sheep's heads.) Was she likewise teasing about the elves in the rocks?

Maybe, maybe not.

"Practically every summer," writes Icelandic ethnologist Valdimar Hafstein in the *Journal of Folktale Studies*, "a new legend is disseminated through newspapers, television, and radio, as well as word of mouth, about yet another construction project gone awry due to elven interference." Unlike most urban legends, these are based on "the experience of real people involved in the events." That the news reports "are often mildly tongue-in-cheek" does not, in his opinion, "detract from the widespread concern they represent."

In August 2016, for example, an Icelandic newspaper printed the story "Elf Rock Restored after Its Removal Wreaks Havoc on Icelandic Town." The previous summer a mudslide fell on a road in the town of Siglufjordur. While clearing the blockage, the road crew dumped four hundred cubic feet of dirt on top of a large rock known as the Elf Lady's Stone. The Elf Lady (illustrated on the paper's English-language website as Cate Blanchett in the role of the elf queen Galadriel from The Lord of the Rings films) was not happy, and a series of mishaps ensued. A road worker was hurt. A TV newscaster "sank into a pit of mud, right up to his waist and had to be rescued." The river flooded the road, and the constant rain caused further mudslides. A bulldozer operator reported: "I had just gotten into the vehicle when I see a mudslide coming toward me, like a gigantic ball. When it hit the river flood it exploded and water and rocks went everywhere. We fled." Then the bulldozer broke down. The Siglufjordur town council officially asked the Icelandic Road Administration to unearth the Elf Lady's Stone. They complied. They also power hosed it clean.

Icelandic elf stories light up the internet: I found that one in the *New York Times*, *Travel and Leisure*, the *Daily Telegraph*, the *Minneapolis Star Tribune*, the CBC, Yahoo.com, and as far afield as the *Philippine Daily Inquirer*, among others. Many media outlets justify their interest by citing a series of surveys proving that, in Valdimar's words, "elves are alive and frisky in modern day Iceland." In 1974, Icelandic psychologist Erlendur Haraldsson conducted a fifty-four-question survey on spiritual matters. Of those who responded, 15 percent considered elves likely to exist, 7 percent were certain they existed, and 5 percent had seen an elf. "A third of the sample," Valdimar points out, "entertained the possibility of their existence (33 percent), neither affirming nor denying it." A church historian in 1995 sought out people "with an interest in mysticism": 70 percent of this sample thought elves existed, while only 43 percent believed that space aliens visited Earth. An Icelandic newspaper polled its readers on politics and government in 1998, slipping in the sly yes-or-no question, "Do you believe in elves?" Nine out of ten respondents answered the question. Of them, 54.4 percent replied yes.

In 2006 and 2007, the University of Iceland's Department of Folkloristics entered the debate, with technical help from the university's Social Science Institute. Their survey's fifty questions were based on those of Erlendur in 1974, adapted for "a modern society that had been in contact with New Age thought," according to folklore professor Terry Gunnell. Again, 5 percent of the thousand respondents said they had seen an elf, while more than 50 percent "entertained the possibility of their existence." While outnumbered by the percentage who had received an omen (55 percent), dreamed a prophetic dream (40 percent), or felt the presence of the dead (40 percent), the number of elf-seers (5 percent) was still higher than those who said they had seen a UFO (2 percent).

Let's put those numbers into context: 2 percent of the Icelandic population at that time was about 6,600 people. In July 2016, 6,500 people went to see the 1970s-era hard-rock band Kiss perform in the Taco Bell Arena in Boise, Idaho.

Compare that number to the 10 percent of Americans who said they had seen a UFO, when polled by Kenyon Research in 2012 at the request of National Geographic. Ten percent of the American population is over 30 million people, more than the entire population of the state of Texas (29 million). A 2013 poll by the *Huffington Post* and YouGov found that 48 percent of Americans "are open to the idea that alien spacecraft are observing our planet," while a previous *HuffPost*–YouGov survey found that 25 percent of Americans "think alien visitors have come to Earth." Now who looks silly?

For Gunnell, the most striking result of the Icelandic surveys is that "in spite of the radical changes in Icelandic society" between 1974 and 2006, the Icelanders' traditional beliefs about elves had "remained near static." They were, he concludes, "deeply rooted."

The 2016 accounts of the Elf Lady's Stone, for example, match a story first printed in 1862: According to a goldsmith named Vigfus Gislason, in 1808, when he was a boy of ten, the farm of Stadarfell, some ten miles from his own home, burned to the ground after an elf stone was tampered with. Vigfus explained:

Just below the farm, on a cliff jutting out to sea, there was a large rock in which it was said that an elf woman lived, but since the cliff was crumbling this rock half overhung the water; however, it was firm enough if no one interfered with it, and it might have stayed like that for a long time, because everyone was warned not to play the fool with this rock. But shortly before the fire, the farm workmen had sent the rock crashing into the sea, just for fun; and the next night old Benedikt Bogason dreamed of the elf woman, and she told him he would be the worse off because his men had had their fun with her house. And shortly afterwards the farm burned down, and so the prophecy was fulfilled.

Another striking result of the Icelandic folklore surveys, Gunnell says, is that he can now tell the coming of summer by the arrival of two things: gnats and foreign journalists who want to ask him about Iceland's Hidden Folk.

Icelanders believe in elves! If you've read anything about Iceland in the last twenty years, you've read this. It was already a cliché in 2004, before Gunnell's survey came out. Speaking with Alex Ross of *The New Yorker*, the singer Bjork joked, "A friend of mine says that when record-company executives come to Iceland they ask the bands if they believe in elves, and whoever says yes gets signed up." The Icelandic Tourist Board was trading on elves in 2000: An advertisement in that same magazine claims that "In such a mystical lunar environment, one begins to understand why 41 per cent of Iceland's population"—I'm not sure where that number came from—"believes in gnomes, fairies, and elves. The rocks and hills, where these fantastic beings are reputed to make their homes, are carefully preserved, with public roads going around, rather than through, the haunts of the Hidden People."

Brad Leithauser, writing about Iceland in the *Atlantic Monthly* in 1987, casually links the elves to light (or darkness): "Perhaps because the island lies just south of the Arctic Circle, where it endures some twenty hours of unbroken darkness during the shortest days of winter, the pull of the supernatural remains strong. Farmers still routinely leave patches of hay unmown where 'hidden folk' are thought to live, and a few years ago a road was rerouted in order to leave an elf colony undisturbed." In *Smithsonian*, too, the elf meme crops up. Robert Wernick remarks there in 1986 on the Icelanders' "matter-of-fact acceptance of supernatural presences," which he ascribes not to the lunar landscape or the lack of light but to the wind: "Iceland is virtually a treeless land and the wind blows freely—in the long winter nights it blows perpetually. This makes a good breeding ground for ghosts, elves, trolls."

After the economic crash of 2008, Iceland's elves made the big time, thanks to Michael Lewis. Writing in *Vanity Fair* about "What led a tiny fishing nation, population 300,000, to decide, around 2003, to re-invent itself as a global financial power"—accruing debt approaching 900 percent of the nation's gross domestic product—Lewis blames the male bankers' Viking-like love of risk and their unwillingness to listen to the (few) female bankers who tried to rein them in. He comes to this conclusion after visiting the waxworks Saga Museum in Reykjavik, "in which a blood-drenched Viking plunges his sword toward the heart of a

prone enemy." Lewis writes: "This is the past Icelanders supposedly cherish: a history of conflict and heroism. Of seeing who is
willing to bump into whom with the most force. There are plenty
of women, but this is a men's history." There's much Lewis missed
about the Icelandic sagas. But he may have a point: Icelanders
themselves compared their bankers to Viking raiders. What's
pertinent here, however, is that his ten-thousand-word piece held
three sentences about elves. Three, in general, respectful sentences
told in the context of two problems Alcoa had establishing an
aluminum-smelting plant in Iceland. "The first was the so-called
'hidden people'—or, to put it more plainly, elves—in whom some
large number of Icelanders, steeped long and thoroughly in their
rich folkloric culture, sincerely believe," Lewis writes. He cites
an anonymous Alcoa spokesman who said they had to "pay hard
cash to declare the site elf-free." The second problem was that the
Icelandic male "took more safety risks than aluminum workers in
other nations did."

The elves, for Lewis, were a throwaway line, a little bit of local
color, a way to work up to his main point about men and risk. They
were also, according to the *New York Times*, the part of his article
that "may have drawn the most attention on the Internet" (not to
mention among my own friends, one of whom emailed me to ask
if there really was a "Department of Elf and Human Services" in
Iceland). Commenting for *New York* magazine, Jonas Moody, an
American living in Iceland, writes, "I've heard the elf thing mentioned in tired travel articles (normally wedged between paragraphs
on the beauty of waterfalls and tips for eating ram testicles), but
I personally know no one on this island who believes in elves.

Not one." The Alcoa spokesman was referring to the Icelandic environmental-impact assessment, Moody explains. "The assessment includes an archaeological survey to ensure no important artifacts or ruins are destroyed, and the site's history is surveyed to see if it was ever named in any Icelandic folklore. And yes, some of that folklore involves elves." Which would seem to make Lewis's point that Alcoa did have to certify the site was "elf-free," except for one caveat: The only folklore that counts toward the assessment are written tales at least a hundred years old.

Matt Eliason, an American writing for *Iceland Magazine* in 2014, thinks "the Icelandic people continue to acknowledge the existence of the nonexistent elves to drum up business for their growing tourist industry." And it's true that you can pay $64 to go to Elf School to learn, as writer Jessica Pan puts it, that "elves fuck, and dress, better than you."

Arni Bjornsson, long the head of the ethnology department at the National Museum of Iceland, reached the same conclusion as Eliason in 1996. He "finds that contemporary elf-tradition in general reeks of money," reports Valdimar Hafstein in his *Journal of Folktale Studies* paper. "If I have understood him correctly, he claims that modern elflore is to a great extent fabricated to defraud tourists." Yet when asked point-blank by Sarah Lyall of the *New York Times* in 2005, Arni refused to deny the existence of elves. Instead he reframed her question: "If you were to ask me, 'Are you sure there are no supernatural beings?' I would say I don't believe there are. But I wouldn't rule it out."

Supernatural beings, as a class, includes much more than elves. Arni could be referring to ghosts. Or aliens from outer space. Or

God. His evasion reveals our critical mistake when we laugh off an Icelander's belief in elves. We assume we agree on what each of us means by *belief* and *elf*. Those terms are tricky. What they signify shifts with our point of view.

Until I met Ragnhildur Jonsdottir, I might have agreed with Matt Eliason that the Icelanders who spoke of elves were playing tricks, poking fun, talking tongue-in-cheek, telling tall tales. Yet after our stroll through Galgahraun and our encounter with the outraged bird lover, Ragnhildur's question—*Now do you believe in elves?*—grew to obsess me. I found myself wondering. Then I found myself wandering through history, religion, folklore, and art, circling back to explore theology, literary criticism, mythology, and philosophy, stopping along the way to dip my toes into cognitive science, psychology, anthropology, biology, volcanology, cosmology, and quantum mechanics. Each discipline, I found, defines and redefines what is real and unreal, natural and supernatural, demonstrated and theoretical, alive and inert. Each has its own way of perceiving and valuing (or not) the world around us. Each admits its own sort of elf.

Otherworlds

⚬⚬⚬

"The hidden people, or *huldufólk* as they're known in Icelandic, have caused me no shortage of grief," writes Stefan Jonasson, a Unitarian minister and editor of an Icelandic-Canadian newspaper. It's not because they hounded him out of his home, as they did his great-great-grandfather, he writes. No, it's due to a sermon in which he expressed his "disbelief" in elves to his largely Icelandic congregation in Canada. "Some considered it heresy, and, as I recall, a couple of people never returned to church."

He's not, he insists, "devoid of any sense of wonder." Elf stories "are woven into my thought and speech," and he's printed several in the newspaper, including the one about his great-great-grandfather, Elias Kjaernested. From 1856 to 1860, Elias lived on the farm of Holaholar, beneath the glacier Snaefellsjokull in western Iceland. He was breaking up rocks on a craggy hillside to clear space for a new sheep pen when he began having ominous dreams. A woman came to him repeatedly in these dreams, and asked him to leave the crags alone. He ignored her. His wife began having the same dreams; still, Elias ignored the warnings. One morning, the horses grazing in a pasture by the sea cliffs were found dead. Another day, seventy sheep grazing along the shoreline suddenly died. The livestock deaths continued until "Elias was driven away from Holaholar, an impoverished man." He emigrated to North America. His descendants, including Stefan Jonasson, came back to visit Holaholar in 2012 and 2016. "We saw some of the roughest lava-strewn terrain imaginable and wondered why Elias thought he could carve out a living there," Jonasson writes. "We weren't bothered by *huldufólk*, but perhaps they were simply watching and laughing from afar. Still, there was something magical about standing on this ancestral ground and imagining what life must have been like for our ancestors there."

Despite feeling the magic, Jonasson "thinks that the *huldufólk* belong to the realm of imagination," he writes. (I have not had the nerve to ask him, a minister, if God, too, belongs to "the realm of imagination.") Reviewing a book by Alda Sigmundsdottir, he announces, "I have found an author who, like me, takes the *huldufólk* seriously, but not literally. *The Little Book of the Hidden People* challenges the assertion that most Icelanders believe in elves in the same way they believe in gravity"—and there I stopped reading.

How do most Icelanders believe in gravity?

How do *I* believe in gravity, for that matter? What first comes to mind, of course, is Sir Isaac Newton sitting in his English garden when an apple bonks him on the head and he discovers the force of gravity, inventing calculus along the way to describe it. The apple story is more or less true. As an old man, Newton told his first biographer, William Stukeley, who wrote it down many years later, that "the notion of gravitation" came to him while he was sitting in his garden, drinking tea, and saw an apple fall. The apple did not hit his head. That part's a fairy tale, which is why I remember it: It's vivid. Newton's equations, published in his *Principia* in 1687, are (to me) not vivid. Besides the apple story, all I could remember about Newton's theory, before checking an encyclopedia, was that Albert Einstein proved it false.

Newton's theory of gravity was panned in his lifetime as "action at a distance." Even he admitted that the idea of two bodies, like Earth and the moon or even an apple and the ground, being able to push and pull each other without touching and "without the mediation of anything else" was absurd. (Rene Descartes went further: He called it "occult.") Newton could not explain what the "anything else," that is, the "force" of gravity, was. "And I feign no hypotheses," he declared in the second edition of the *Principia* in 1713. "It is enough that gravity does really exist and acts according to the laws I have explained, and that it abundantly serves to account for all the motions of celestial bodies."

If that phrase read "It is enough that elves do really exist," would you let it pass unchallenged? Is it the mathematics that make gravity believable, or is it Newton's bluster? For his theory of gravity does not, as he claimed, account for "all the motions of celestial bodies." It is accurate enough for most day-to-day calculations. It explains how apples fall from trees and how to place a satellite in a geosynchronous orbit. But if you want to understand the orbit of Mercury around the sun, for example, Newton's theory does not work. The sun is too massive and the planet is too close. You need Einstein.

As described by Einstein's general theory of relativity, published in 1915, gravity is not a force. It is, says the very helpful Wikipedia page, "a consequence of the curvature of spacetime." And if you're not lost yet, read on a bit:

> Einstein proposed that spacetime is curved by matter, and that free-falling objects are moving along locally straight paths in curved spacetime. These straight paths are called geodesics. Like Newton's first law of motion, Einstein's theory states that if a force is applied on an object, it would deviate from a geodesic. For instance, we are no longer following geodesics while standing because the mechanical resistance of the Earth exerts an upward force on us, and we are non-inertial on the ground as a result.

The word *geodesic* is permanently paired in my mind with *dome*, leaving me struggling with the unfortunate image of myself standing atop a yurt-like pimple on the globe and not processing this explanation really at all. Fortunately, there are books written for people like me. Two are by Carlo Rovelli, a physicist who writes like a poet. In *Reality Is Not What It Seems*, he allows Einstein to be human. He is "a rebellious twenty-five-year-old" who studied physics but hadn't yet found a job. He was working at the patent office in Bern and essentially staring off into space when he formulated his first groundbreaking theory. Rovelli writes:

> If we attentively observe very small particles, such as a speck of dust or a grain of pollen, suspended in still air or in a liquid, we see them tremble and dance. Pushed by this trembling, they move, randomly zigzagging . . . It is as if the small particle is receiving blows randomly from each side. No, it isn't "as if" it were being hit; it really is hit. It trembles because it is struck by the individual molecules of air, which collide with the particle, at times from the right and at times from the left.

From this dance of dust motes Einstein mathematically proved the existence of atoms—first posited by Democritus almost 2,500 years ago, but, until 1905, not thought to be real because (like elves) they couldn't be seen or otherwise detected.

A second paper Einstein published in 1905 described his theory of special relativity, which, as Rovelli explains, "does not fit with what we know about gravity, namely, with how things fall." (It also predicts time travel, but let's overlook that.) Either Einstein's relativity was wrong or Newton's idea of gravity was. Einstein spent the next ten years disproving Newton—disproving, in Rovelli's words, "what we know." The result was Einstein's theory of general relativity, on which modern physics is based—even though key parts of the theory, such as the existence of black holes, were not proved until 2016, in a set of experiments that required a thousand scientists, fourteen years, and over $475 million.

In *Seven Brief Lessons on Physics*, Rovelli writes that "there are absolute masterpieces that move us intensely: Mozart's *Requiem*, Homer's *Odyssey*, the Sistine Chapel, *King Lear*. To fully appreciate their brilliance may require a long apprenticeship, but the reward is sheer beauty—and not only this, but the opening of our eyes to a new perspective upon the world. Einstein's jewel, the general theory of relativity, is a masterpiece of this order." Unlike Mozart and the others, however, Einstein cannot be appreciated much at all without that apprenticeship. Rovelli describes his own initiation into its beauties in romantic terms. He learned "as if by magic: as if a friend were whispering into my ear an extraordinary hidden truth, suddenly raising the veil of reality to disclose a simpler, deeper order." It was "a deeply emotional experience."

To Newton, space was an empty box. To Einstein, it was a gravitational field, analogous to the electromagnetic field discovered by Michael Faraday and James Maxwell in the first half of the nineteenth century. Rovelli writes:

It is a moment of enlightenment. A momentous simplification of the world: space is no longer something distinct from matter—it is one of the "material" components of the world. An entity that undulates, flexes, curves, twists . . . The sun bends space around itself, and Earth does not turn around it because of a mysterious force but because it is racing directly in a space that inclines, like a marble that rolls in a funnel. There are no mysterious forces generated at the center of the funnel; it is the curved nature of the walls that causes the marble to roll. Planets circle around the sun, and things fall, because space curves.

Despite the beauty of Rovelli's language, I'm not sure I understand him any better than I do the anonymous Wikipedia editors. Nor am I sure I can *believe* in the gravity that Einstein's theory of general relativity presents. Do I *believe* Earth is a marble in a funnel? That space undulates, flexes, curves, and twists? Frankly I find it easier to believe that elves appear to Icelandic farmers in their dreams and warn them away from backbreaking and ultimately pointless labor.

But I'm also intrigued. Within Einstein's equation, Rovelli promises, "is a teeming universe." The theory is "magical." Like a door into another world, it "opens up into a phantasmagorical succession of predictions that resemble the ravings of a madman but have all turned out to be true." My reward for further study, he says, "is sheer beauty and new eyes with which to see the world." Here is language I understand: In Rovelli's hands, physics sounds like an elf story. So I read on.

Rovelli's next brief lesson is on quantum mechanics. In 1900, Max Planck, studying electricity, imagined that energy came in lumps, or quanta. Einstein took up the idea, proving that light was made of these energy packets; we now call them photons. Pioneered by Niels Bohr and proved (in part) by a pair of scientists at Bell Telephone in 1927, the year my mother was born, quantum theory brought us the computer technology that has altered my lifestyle a quantum leap from hers (pun intended).

Quantum theory concerns not atoms, but bits of atoms. Hundreds of these subatomic particles have been detected, from photons and electrons (whose jumps from one energy level to another are the original quantum leaps); to the tinier quarks, which are whimsically named up, down, strange, charm, bottom (or, originally, beauty), and top (truth); to the long-predicted Higgs boson, first detected in 2012 by CERN's Large Hadron Collider. Promoted as "the largest machine in the world," this twenty-seven-kilometer circular tunnel of magnets beneath the Swiss and French countryside took thousands of scientists decades to build, at a cost of about $5 billion.

Progress in the science of subatomic particles is not always linear. At Fermilab, near Chicago, in 2021, scientists fired muons—also known as fat electrons—through a magnetic field and perceived a wobble that was "slightly but firmly inconsistent with the known rules of modern physics," according to a *New York Times* report. The experiment, writes Dennis Overbye, "suggests that there are forms of matter and energy vital to the nature and evolution of the cosmos that are not yet known to science." (Shall we name them "elves"?)

Even what is "known to science" takes some effort to believe, for key to quantum theory is Werner Heisenberg's uncertainty principle, also dating to 1927. According to Rovelli, "Heisenberg imagined that electrons do not *always* exist. They only exist when someone or something watches them, or better, when they are interacting with something else." (Iceland's elves, it's said, only exist when they want to.) You can't simultaneously measure the position and the motion of an electron, Heisenberg concluded, not even in theory. The same is true of all subatomic particles.

Quantum mechanics, writes Rovelli, presents the world as "a continuous, restless, swarming of things, a continuous coming to light and disappearance of ephemeral entities."

Einstein thought the uncertainty principle absurd, panning it as "spooky action at a distance." And we still can't explain it, Rovelli admits. Is it a "dive deep into the nature of reality?" he wonders, or a "blunder that works, by chance?" As he reminds us, "before experiments, measurements, mathematics, and rigorous deductions, science is above all about visions. Science begins with a vision. Scientific thought is fed by the capacity to 'see' things differently than they have previously been seen." Steeped in elflore as I am, I can't help but hear the echoes. Rovelli's physics is like Ragnhildur's art, a way "to 'see' things differently"—only a whole lot more time and money have been spent detecting the predictions of these scientific theories than has ever been spent investigating the possibility of elves or the ability of some Icelanders to sense their presence.

Nor, just because they are expressed in equations, can we say that the theories of general relativity and quantum mechanics reflect the "real" world, the world which denies the existence of elves. Both theories have spawned extraordinary technologies. They are undeniably useful. But they're not something you can *believe* in. They are contradictory. Both cannot be true.

And both lead to bizarre predictions that have not been, and might never be, proven true, such as the existence of dark matter and the multiverse.

I chanced upon a special edition of the magazine *Nautilus* as I was trying to fathom these fantasies. "General relativity tells us that galaxies would fly apart if not held together by unseen matter," writes Oxford University cosmologist Joseph Silk. Without dark matter, agrees Joel Primack of the University of California, "there would be no galaxies, no stars, no heavy elements, no rocky planets, and no life."

Look up at the sky on a crisp, clear night somewhere without light pollution—try a lava field in Iceland—and once your eyes adjust to the dazzle of the Milky Way, you'll notice the universe is mostly dark. Even what the Hubble Space Telescope can see amounts to only 0.5 percent of the matter Einstein's calculations call for. Some of the missing matter (another 4.5 percent) is ordinary hydrogen and helium molecules spread too thin to emit light. But "about 27 percent is mysterious dark matter, which is not made of atoms or any of the parts of atoms and does not emit or absorb light," says Primack. "The remaining 68 percent is even more mysterious dark energy." Mysterious because while we can mathematically predict this "double dark universe," we can't detect it.

Astronomers "routinely" map out dark matter, says Silk. "We conceive of galaxies as lumps of dark matter with dabs of luminous material." Yet no one has ever detected dark matter directly; we see only "the shadow it casts." Silk frames that failure as an existential crisis: "Eighty-five percent of all matter is unknown. Our greatest fear is that it will always remain so." And to assuage scientists' fears, he suggests spending $25 billion on a dark-matter detector.

If, as Primack says, dark matter is not "made of atoms or any of the parts of atoms" (sorry, no dark quarks), then quantum mechanics does not apply. Lisa Randall, a theoretical physicist at Harvard, calls this assumption "hubris." "We of course care more about ordinary matter because we are made of the stuff," she notes. But science needs to be open to the idea of dark particles, she argues—not only dark quarks, but even dark creatures. "You have no idea how cute dark matter life could be," she teases, "and you almost certainly never will. Though it's entertaining to speculate about the possibility of dark life, it's a lot harder to figure out a way to observe it—or even detect its existence in more indirect ways." We didn't detect gravitational waves from black holes—thus proving true that bizarre part of Einstein's theory—until 2016, and black holes are enormous. Says Randall, "We stand little to no chance of detecting the gravitational effect of a dark creature, or even an army of dark creatures—no matter how close all of them might be." If only she had called these dark creatures "elves," I could imagine it.

The even more mysterious dark energy, for its part, supports quantum theory's weirdest prediction: the multiverse. "The world we observe," writes Paul Davies in *Other Worlds*, "is a slice through, or projection of, an infinite dimensional superspace—a vast collection of alternative worlds." I hear more echoes: In Norse mythology, as recorded in Iceland in the Middle Ages, there are nine overlapping worlds, one being the home of the elves. According to quantum theory, our world "depends in a crucial way on all the other worlds that we don't see," explains Davies. "Without the other worlds of superspace, the quantum would fail and the universe would disintegrate; these countless alternative contenders for reality help steer our own destiny."

Now that's mind-boggling. Can you *believe* it? The multiverse is not a fairy tale, not Norse mythology. It's the physics of the twenty-first century. You can do the math.

"Even physicists find the multiverse faintly disturbing," writes Tasneem Zehra Husain in *Nautilus*. A theoretical physicist who did her postdoc at Harvard, she acknowledges that most of her peers won't admit it. Physicists aren't emotional; they are "hard-nosed, quantitative, and empirical." (But you're talking about *other worlds*, for heaven's sake.) Husain, indeed, can do the math, "but while I understand the multiverse as a mathematical construction, I cannot bring myself to believe"—there's that word again—"it will leap out of the realm of theory"—or, as Stefan Jonasson might say, the "realm of imagination."

The debate over the multiverse is not about math, Husain continues. "It is a fight about identity and consequence," she writes, "about what constitutes an explanation, what proof consists of." It matters, she argues, because "we are molded by the spaces we inhabit." If we find out that our universe "is just one pocket in the multiverse, the entire foundation upon which we have laid our coordinate grid shifts." It's the same existential crisis we'd face if aliens did, without question, visit Earth. Or if you came face-to-face with an elf. Or with God.

The multiverse "obliterates God" as an explanation for why the universe is as it is, some scientists say. Mary-Jane Rubenstein, a professor of religion at Wesleyan University, disagrees. The theory might instead help us redefine God as "an all-governing dark energy," she says. If God is, in this way, diffused throughout the world, Rubenstein asks, "might we be more inclined to care for it?"

Or, as Ragnhildur Jonsdottir might put it, if elves are, in this way, diffused throughout the world, alive in every rock, would we be less apt to bulldoze new roads?

TWO

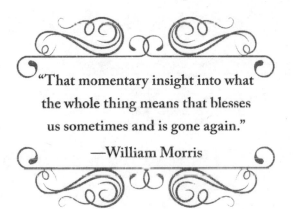

"That momentary insight into what
the whole thing means that blesses
us sometimes and is gone again."

—William Morris

Helgafell

The Island That
Likes to Be Visited

One summer, flying to Iceland for the seventeenth time, I read a luminous essay, "Summer in the Far North," in the magazine *Mother Jones*. It began, "One summer some years ago, on a peninsula jutting off another peninsula off the west coast of Iceland, I lived among strangers and birds." The author, Rebecca Solnit, loved the birds, especially the arctic terns. She wove a story out of these birds, who migrate from the Arctic to the Antarctic each year, flying from the north's summer to the south's, living their entire lives in light. Solnit wrote so evocatively about Iceland's birds, I wondered what she'd say about the strangers.

I bought *The Faraway Nearby*, from which the essay was excerpted, and in early December, missing Iceland's unending summer light, I opened it. I wanted a book about light and darkness and arctic terns and Icelanders. What I got was a book about

Alzheimer's, a failed romance, breast cancer, fairy tales, a heap of rotting apricots, Che Guevara, Wu Daozi, Peter Freuchen, and Buddhism. I liked the "wild mash-ups," to use the *New York Times*'s phrase. I liked Solnit's "frenetic energy." But it seemed to me as if she had never reached Iceland. Sure, she resided on the island for a time. But she never entered its Otherworld. Her Icelanders remained strangers.

J. R. R. Tolkien, in a footnote to his essay "On Fairy-stories," expressed a similar disappointment in J. M. Barrie's play *Mary Rose*. "It was as if Barrie, expending his art in making a notion of Celtic fantasy 'credible' in the centre of the stage, and enchanted with his elvish heroine, had simply ignored the torment in the wings. Taken as a diabolic drama it is moving; that is if the producer says: the sufferings are the thing, cruel, valueless, purposeless; the fairies do not matter."

As a child, Mary Rose hears the call of the Island That Likes to Be Visited. Vacationing there with her family, she disappears for twenty days. Once recovered, she remains a little odd, a little abstracted: "curiously young for her age," in Barrie's phrase. "You know how just a touch of frost may stop the growth of a plant and yet leave it blooming," says her mother in the play. "It has sometimes seemed to me as if a cold finger had once touched my Mary Rose."

Barrie is the author of *Peter Pan, or the Boy Who Wouldn't Grow Up*. Childhood and time concern him. As does the question of how we learn to think. His whimsicalities "comprise deliberate errors of cognition," writes Rosalind Ridley in *Peter Pan and the Mind of J. M. Barrie*. They are the means of exploring "perception, memory, reasoning, judgment, and so on."

Peter Pan folds up a shadow and stores it in a drawer, making something ethereal behave like something solid.

He distinguishes between solid objects and socially constructed ones—something science didn't manage until 1995, Ridley notes. She cites an example from *Peter Pan in Kensington Gardens*, published in 1906. There, Peter Pan is marooned on an island (he's forgotten how to fly), when an origami boat washes ashore. Instead of paddling it away, he unfolds it and finds it's made of money: a British five-pound note. So he cuts it into smaller strips, convinces the thrushes that these are money, too, and uses them to buy a bird's nest boat. "Here Barrie recognised that money is not only a piece of paper, but is also a socially constructed object that only exists as currency so long as everyone believes in it," Ridley writes. "Similarly, fairies are socially constructed objects, who only exist if you and your friends believe in them." Is money real? Are fairies (or elves) real? Are gravity and dark matter real? What do we mean when we say something is real?

"There are also occasions," Ridley writes, "when art tells us something that science only recognizes at a later time."

Ridley is a neuroscientist; she retired from the University of Cambridge in 2005. Scientists like herself divide the mind into three parts, she explains: the unconscious mind, the subconscious mind, and the conscious mind. The unconscious mind contains "knowledge about how to do things," like ride a bicycle. The subconscious mind "contains information that can be called to mind"—languages, facts, or knowledge based on simple logic. The conscious mind "includes perceptions, our train of thought, and the feeling that it is *me* that is having this experience and that it is *me* that is in control of my actions. This latter feeling is known as having a *sense of agency.*"

Barrie knew, well before science described it, that you are born without a feeling of *me*. Unburdened by a sense of agency, as a child you are free to live moment to moment. You know how to do things. You gather information. But facts, languages, and logic alone do not create a self. To grow up, you need to learn how to think. You need to learn to interpret the world around you. And how you interpret the world—how you apply your memories, fears, hopes, and thoughts to the things around you—defines your self, the "you" you eventually become.

Barrie's fantasies underscore psychology's rule that "we encounter the outside world only as experiences"—as interpretations of what our senses perceive. Yet he hopes also to remind us, says Ridley, that "there is something of Peter Pan in all of us: the child who lives in the heart of the adult; memories that we carry with us throughout our life but which do not themselves age; dreams that disobey logic; the private world inside our head and those moments of exceptional experience that we rarely talk about."

Exceptional moments like our glimpses of the Otherworld. In the play *Mary Rose,* the mother mentions her daughter's Otherworld adventure to warn off a suitor, but he marries Mary Rose all the same. They have a baby and take him picnicking on the mossy rocks, under the rowan trees of a picturesque island. It's the Island That Likes to Be Visited, of course, and again Mary Rose is lost. She remains in the Otherworld twenty-five years this time, and when she returns, still girlish, still odd, no one knows her. Her father is, in the words of theater reviewer Alexander Woollcott in 1920, "bent and querulous," her mother is "faded and worn," her handsome suitor is now "grizzled," "a little paunchy," and an admiral in the navy "eager for the war." Her son, well, he ran off when he was twelve. When he appears in the play, "a coarse, swaggering, hairy man," Mary Rose does not recognize him—and he hopes she never will, for he knows he is "grotesquely different from what her prayers for him had been." All this because the island likes to be visited.

Elfland, Tir na nOg, Faërie—by whatever name, the Otherworld "is a perilous land," writes Tolkien. "In that land a man may (perhaps) count himself fortunate to have wandered, but its very mystery and wealth make dumb the traveller who would report. And while he is there it is dangerous for him to ask too many questions, lest the gates shut and the keys be lost."

Like Mary Rose, I have disappeared into an Otherworld; not for twenty-five years, but for a hundred weeks spread across thirty trips over thirty-five years. I have been absent when others needed me. I have returned from my island—Iceland—a little abstracted, a little odd, a little off-balance. It's not always easy returning to real life. For although my island that likes to be visited is "real"— it's on the map, you can fly to it—my island is not the island you will likely find. My Iceland, for example, is nothing like Rebecca Solnit's Iceland. On my Iceland, I can't think about nature (birds) without thinking about culture (strangers) as well. The nature/culture divide, so ingrained in our American way of life, does not apply in my Iceland.

Solnit was the first writer-in-residence at an art museum called the Library of Water in Stykkisholmur, a fishing village on the north side of the Snaefellsnes peninsula in western Iceland. She writes:

> The farthest point I could reach on foot was Helgafell, the sugarloaf hill around which stories were wrapped like clouds, and where Gudrun Osvifursdottir was buried a thousand years before, the proud woman at the center of the *Laxdaela Saga* and all its slaughter and loss.
>
> Once a farmer who spoke only Icelandic gave me a ride back from Helgafell in a rain; and cashiers spoke brusquely to me about money in the low-ceilinged, fluorescent-lit den that was the chain supermarket; and there was a librarian with some responsibility for the Library of Water who provided practical aid every now and again. Otherwise no one spoke to me because Iceland was not good at strangers.

I can guess who the "farmer who spoke only Icelandic" might be, since I have been friends with the farmer at Helgafell, Hjortur Hinriksson, for thirty-five years. It's something he would do, give a stranger a lift. If Solnit had tried a few words of Icelandic on him—even the few words she includes here, "Gudrun Osvifursdottir" and *"Laxdaela Saga"*—he would have tried to speak with her. I know, because I did and he spoke with me.

On my first trip to Iceland, in June 1986, my husband and I backpacked the four miles from Stykkisholmur to Helgafell.

There'd been an inch of snow that morning. In my journal, I reduced the walk to "rain, bones, sheep dung, mud; some birds: Iceland gull, snipe, geese low overhead."

Helgafell means Holy Mountain. It is a long, low hill that does not seem to grow larger as you approach it, only more distinct. The hill's south side is gentle and grassy, its north abrupt: a fluted black basalt wall that glows golden in the midnight sun. According to volcanologist Haraldur Sigurdsson, who grew up in the vicinity and, after retiring from the University of Rhode Island, established the Volcano Museum in Stykkisholmur, Helgafell is a volcanic plug. Deep beneath Iceland, he told me, magma is "pushing, pushing, always pushing up." It forms in Earth's mantle, partly molten, spongy, the consistency of wet sand on the beach, but hot and under enormous pressure. Less dense than solid rock, "it's always looking to come out." As molten magma pushes its way up from deep underground, it prises the rocks of Earth's crust apart. It carves itself a channel, a tube. When the eruption ends, the tube "won't close up, it will stay there with the magma in it," Haraldur explained. "In a few years it will harden and become a plug." The magma that made Helgafell is ten million years old. The rest of the volcano has eroded away. Only the plug—the mountain's heart—remains.

According to Iceland's medieval records, the hill was named in 884 by Thorolf, a chieftain hounded out of Norway by King Harald Fair-Hair. Iceland was nearly empty at the time—there were no indigenous Icelanders—so Thorolf, in the first wave of settlers fleeing Harald's unification schemes, had his choice of house site. Sailing up Iceland's west coast, he'd reached a broad bay when the wind failed. Throwing overboard a wooden post bearing an image of Thor, he declared he'd settle wherever the thunder god came ashore.

That turned out to be Solnit's fractal "peninsula jutting off another peninsula," where she found the birds and the long summer light more engaging than the strangers. Thorolf named it Thor's Ness.

"On this ness," says one of the Icelandic sagas, "stands a hill. To Thorolf, this hill was so holy that no one should even look at it without washing first. Nothing on the hill was to be killed, neither animals nor humans, unless they came down from the hill of their own will. Thorolf named the hill Helgafell and he believed that he would go into it when he died, as would all his family there on Thor's Ness."

Thorolf established his farm and built a temple to Thor about two miles from the Holy Mountain, on the west side of Thor's Ness. His son, Thorstein Cod-Biter, moved to Helgafell after his rivals desecrated the original temple grounds; they refused, they said, "to wear out our shoes walking to those rocks offshore" (still on the map as Shit Skerry) whenever they needed to, in the euphemism of the day, "drive away the elves" or, as we still say, answer the call of nature.

At Helgafell, Thorstein Cod-Biter "ran a magnificent farm. He always had sixty free men with him and was generous with food, so they were constantly rowing out to fish" among the uncountable islands in the Breidafjord, the broad bay to the peninsula's north. One evening in the autumn of 918, his shepherd "saw the whole north face of the hill open up. Looking inside, he saw great fires burning. He heard a drinking bout going on, amid raucous merriment. And as he listened, trying to catch what they were saying, he heard someone greet Thorstein Cod-Biter and his crew, and tell him to take a seat on the bench opposite his father." The news came from the islands the next morning: Thorstein Cod-Biter had drowned.

In 1986, when I arrived, Helgafell was a dairy farm. Dropping my backpack in the dirt of the lane, I went up to one door of what turned out to be a duplex and knocked. To the formally dressed old man who answered, I said, *"Snorri goði búa hér?"* He understood, despite my grammatical fault, that I was asking about a former tenant—the grandson of Thorstein Cod-Biter—who had moved out in the year 1008. I did not understand what the old man answered, but at that moment his son stepped out of the cow barn, his coveralls streaked with cow dung, a stocking cap tight over his ears. With the younger man, my husband tried a more practical approach: *"Tjalda?* Tent? Here?" The farmer nodded and led us back up the lane to a large stack of fertilizer bags, which he made us understand, using gestures and easy words like *vindur* (wind), would provide a windbreak. He pointed out walking trails up the hill and around it and out between the fields, introduced himself as Hjortur, son of Hinrik (the old man I had originally approached), shook both our hands, and went back to work.

We settled in, had lunch, and traipsed all over the farm in a drizzle, up the hill (without remembering to wash first), down to the lake, out to the farthest skerries edging the shallow bay, collecting sparkling stones and wisps of sheep's wool, taking photos, and watching the birds—black-backed gulls, greylag geese, arctic skua, redshanks, whimbrel, ringed plover, golden plover, red-throated diver, loon. On the north side of Helgafell itself, I spied a raven, hunched up in the corner of two basalt columns. The bird flew out, cawing, as I came up. A second raven took up the racket, perched on an outcrop. As I walked on, I glanced back at the first bird's perch and spied the nest: two young ravens, almost full-grown, sitting motionless, head-to-tail, in a tangle of twigs and feathers and white sheep bones.

Back at the tent, when Hjortur and his children walked by with fishing poles, we waved our empty water bottles and asked for more. They waved us to the house. Two women answered the door. *"Átt þú meiri vatni?"* I mumbled. "You need more water?" replied one of the women. She was the local English teacher and had lived in Rochester, New York, for five years. We told her about the raven's nest. The farmwife, Kristrun, wanted to see it, so we traipsed back around the hill (with our interpreter) and studied the birds with binoculars. Kristrun was delighted and insisted we come home for coffee. She had been searching for that nest.

The English teacher soon left, but the oldest daughter, Johanna, who was learning English in school, lost her shyness and helped us out. We had tea (when I asked for it they went next door to the grandparents to get some, as they drank only coffee), a chocolate cake, a raisin cake, and crackers with cheese. The whole family—mother, father, five children, mother's mother—and a hired man crowded into the little kitchen to meet us. They asked us to come back the next morning. At eleven, they fed us tea and sandwiches and more cake. At twelve thirty they fed us fresh-caught lake trout with drawn butter. We did not have much luck talking, though I managed to say that the fish was very good. My husband took out our Icelandic-English dictionary and entertained them by trying to pronounce Icelandic numbers.

After lunch, they showed us pale violets and made us understand that the whole hillside was covered with purple wood geraniums in the summertime. They showed us the church built in 1903—most likely on the site of the first church, from the year 1000, when Iceland became Christian by law. They showed us the grave of the saga character Gudrun Osvifursdottir, or at least a modern stone with her name carved on it that had been set on someone's grave in 1917; the English writer and painter W. G. Collingwood had dug up and then reburied that someone's bones—he claimed they were Gudrun's—in 1897.

Ravens are the wise god Odin's birds. Two sit on his shoulders, named Thought and Memory. Says Odin in the ancient Icelandic *Lay of Grimnir*:

> Thought and Memory
> Fly every day
> The wide world over.
> Thought, I fear,
> May never return;
> I worry more for Memory.

Folklore tells how the ravens gather each autumn to divvy up Iceland's farms: two birds to each, a male and a female, to become their house ravens, bringers of luck, as these ravens were for me. That day at Helgafell, my life changed. Like Mary Rose, I heard the siren call of the Island That Likes to Be Visited. Yet unlike

Barrie (in Tolkien's reading, at least), to me the fairies mattered. If Iceland was my Otherworld, then the fairies in this analogy were my new friends at Helgafell. Leaving them made me cry for reasons I could not articulate—as if the gate might be shut, the key lost, and I would be locked out of their world. Back in America, I saw them and their lucky ravens as, somehow, less real, as if time moved differently for the two of us, as if their lives were paused in that mysterious other world where hills were holy and stories held such power.

I wrote them long letters in Icelandic, with the help of the Icelandic graduate students at Penn State University, where I worked. One letter per season, winter, spring, summer, fall. It was my way of tackling the language. Perhaps they read like school papers, for I received few replies. I got a Christmas card with photos, once, when the twins were born, Oskar and Osk, bringing the number of children on the farm to seven. Each time I visited, for a day or two every other year or so, I was warmly welcomed. And then—*astonishment! joy!*—one day in 2009, I got an email from twenty-two-year-old Osk: "Are you on Facebook?"

I signed up. My friends at Helgafell are no longer Hidden Folk; our worlds now overlap, the gates of time and distance dissolved. I've seen Osk's sonograms for each of her three children. I saw when the footers were poured for Oskar's new house beside the lake, when the horses were bought and saddled, the lambs born and rounded up, when the siblings traveled to Tenerife, when Hjortur retired from dairying. I *tsk*ed at photos of the path up the Holy Mountain churned to mud by busloads of tourists. I cheered at photos of Hjortur crouched down, arm uplifted, directing the gaze of two grandsons to the two black heads in the bundle of sticks and bones wedged into the sheer black cliff: the lucky house ravens.

Iceland may not be "good at strangers," as Rebecca Solnit found, but I never felt like a stranger at Helgafell. Hjortur and I shared few words at first, but we held in common a way of interpreting the world around us, a way of defining the self. I knew the sagas of Snorri Godi and Gudrun. I knew the raven lore. I knew why the Holy Mountain was holy—and what that meant to the people it sheltered. Just as money is not only a piece of paper, Helgafell is not only a hill.

Thought and Memory

I n 1937, the American poets W. H. Auden and Louis MacNeice went to Iceland. They wrote about it in *Letters from Iceland*, a collection of poems, prose, photographs, charts, graphs—you name it. Auden also took time to chat with poet and newspaper editor Matthias Johannessen, providing him with three sentences that have echoed in my mind ever since I read them in *Iceland Review* magazine in 1987: "For me Iceland is holy earth. This memory is background for everything I do. Iceland is the sun which colours the mountains without being there, [having] gone over the horizon."

In a 2012 essay in the *New York Times*, Eric Weiner extols "thin places"—places where the barrier between two worlds is so thin it's see-through—"places that beguile and inspire," places where "we're able to catch glimpses of the divine, or the transcendent or, as I like to think of it, the Infinite Whatever." He traces the phrase "thin places" to Celtic Christianity. George Macleod, founder of the Iona Community on the Scottish island of that same name, is generally credited with bringing the concept into modern times—to the extent that you can now take thin places tours to catch glimpses of a divine that is decidedly biblical. I'm more interested in "the Infinite Whatever." I catch glimpses of it regularly in Iceland, often while sitting on the hillside at Helgafell—on the roof of the thunder god's Otherworldly feast hall—stories from the sagas unreeling in my mind.

Saga derives from the Icelandic verb *to say*. It implies neither fact nor fiction. Some sagas could be shelved as history, others as fantasy. Over 140 medieval Icelandic texts are named sagas. Most date from the thirteenth century or later, two hundred years after Iceland converted to Christianity and missionaries introduced the technology of books: an alphabet for expressing the sounds of Icelandic; ink made from berries, soil, and sticks; feather-quill pens; parchment pages from sheepskins or calfskins; boards and sinews for binding them; and the concept of stringing tales together chronologically. *Eyrbyggja Saga*, set at Helgafell, with its cliffs that open like doors, is most like magical realism, its realistic, multi-generational tale infused with the occult. But whether Thorstein Cod-Biter and his father truly feast forever beneath the hill is, to me, immaterial. It's the stories themselves that make Helgafell holy earth, that make it my thin place.

Carol Hoggart, a saga scholar and writer of romance novels, published a short paper in 2010 that helped me understand why these stories mattered so much. She discusses three ways the sagas "inscribed cognitive maps over Iceland." She takes as her starting point a notion developed by social scientists that "humans cannot understand their environment until it is cast in human terms. Space needs to be 'mapped,' named, understood through (past) human interaction with it." By explaining place-names, by setting actions geographically, and by asserting that evidence of these acts can "still be seen today," the sagas, says Hoggart, "portray a gradual filling up of landscape with human meaning," in which "saga and land act to magnify each other's impact."

Despite describing it so clearly, Hoggart seems strangely averse to the idea. "So convincing has this process been," she writes, "that people still look to find a medieval saga-landscape in modern Iceland."

People like me, hiking up to the door at Helgafell in 1986 and asking, "Does Snorri Godi live here?"

Emily Lethbridge, a scholar at the Arni Magnusson Institute for Icelandic Studies in Reykjavik, finds a deeper connection between saga and place. True, the "rootedness" of the sagas contributes to our sense that they are, indeed, true. True, most of the place-names in the sagas "still exist and are in use today," making it "dangerously seductive and compelling," as she puts it, to imagine *Eyrbyggja Saga* truly happening right here at Helgafell—in spite of the fact that, rationally, I know the farm has changed in a thousand years, through plowing, planting, grazing, grading, draining, deforestation, sedimentation, construction, erosion, and road building, though not (as in many parts of Iceland) through volcanic eruptions and glacial outburst floods.

But sagas and saga sites remain tied in our minds.

Think of the way anthropologist Tim Ingold describes human life as "wayfaring." We don't live *in* places, Ingold argues in *Being*

Alive, "but through, around, to, and from them." Each path we tread from place to place is a thread, each place is a knot, "and the more that lifelines are entwined, the greater the density of the knot." A knot of what? "Every place," Ingold says, "is a knot of stories."

Our simple word *text*, Lethbridge reminds me, derives from the Latin *texere*, to weave or thread or knot together. Imagine walking or riding a horse through the Icelandic landscape with the sagas on your mind, as I have done—or driving about in a converted Land Rover ambulance, as Lethbridge did for a year, visiting saga sites and rereading the sagas in situ—allowing the reaction between land and text to proceed. As you hike south from Stykkisholmur, through the rain and the mud, your backpack heavy, greylag geese honking mournfully overhead, and your eye catches sight of the sheer north face of Helgafell, itself catching a low glimmer of sunlight slipping between the leaden clouds, it's impossible not to imagine, if you've read *Eyrbyggja Saga*, the side of the hill opening up like doors.

Place-names, continues Lethbridge, "are the equivalent of hyperlinks." They are "receptacles for stories, prompts and vehicles for the telling of them." They are expressions of cultural identity, of belonging, of ownership, and of how to interpret the world.

For saga pilgrims like me, says Hoggart, rather dismissively, "The terrain is seen positively to glow with an identity sourced from medieval texts."

It does. It glows. I've seen Helgafell glow: Its sheer black basalt side, the side of the doors, glows in the long, slanting rays of summer sun, especially near midnight. But it also glows with meaning. Helgafell is a thin place to me not because the first settler, Thorolf, saw its immanent holiness or was buried there. Helgafell is a thin place to me because it connects me to an Otherworld of story.

Stories from the sagas drew me there: The time the whole north face of Helgafell opened up like doors. Stories of Snorri Godi, who, unlike most Viking heroes, won his battles with strategy (and trickery), not brute strength. Or of Gudrun Osvifursdottir, the equal of any man when it came to plotting (or thwarting) revenge; one time she even outfoxed wily Snorri Godi himself.

But stories from the last thirty-five years keep me coming back: The times we went to the islands to watch puffins or collect eiderdown. When we put up the hay, rode the horses, rescued the injured sheep, found the raven's nest. The time I came back from a walk with my pockets filled with sparkling stones and my hair braided with ravens' feathers. The time we sat around the kitchen table telling stories from the sagas about the time the whole north face of Helgafell opened up like doors. The time I wrote a story about the mother's illness in a vain hope to magically heal her.

What is a story? It is a way to make sense of the chaos of existence. In the late 1970s, I studied creative writing at Penn State University with S. Leonard Rubinstein. "We can be clear about confusion. It is wild, random energy," he says in *Writing: A Habit of Mind*. "We can use that energy. We can convert it into force. We can make it into sense. Writing makes sense. It makes experience into form." He defines *experience*:

> We are born and we die. An unbroken line stretches
> from one to the other. Yet we are able to say, "I had

a strange experience the other day." What enables us to take a segment of that unbroken line and call it an experience? What enables us to make a point on the line and call it the start? What enables us to make a point and call it the end? . . . Any instant in your life consists of an infinity of stimuli. If you were to register and react to every stimulus in that simultaneous, endless number, you would go crazy, you would be crazy, you would explode, you would disintegrate, you would evaporate . . . To survive, we select.

To survive, we remember some things and forget others.

And the stories we tell based on those memories reflect—and shape—how we interact with the world around us. The stories we tell protect a place, or permit its destruction.

Kristrun Kjartansdottir, named for her grandmother who loved the lucky ravens and who died much too young, had not yet been born when I arrived at Helgafell in 1986. In 2015, she sent me a copy of a school paper she had written, "The Saga of Helgafell." She told how Helgafell got its name. She told how the whole north face of Helgafell opened up like doors. She told how Gudrun Osvifursdottir, the steel-minded romantic heroine of *Laxdaela Saga*, came to Helgafell in 1008, saw the ghost of her drowned husband, dug up a witch's grave, died in 1060, and was buried beside the church. Gudrun married four men and loved a fifth; she caused the deaths of four out of five. Pressed by her son, in old age, she expressed one of the most famous lines in the sagas: "I was worst to those I loved best." All these stories of Helgafell's first two hundred years I knew. But Kristrun's "Saga of Helgafell" also included a story new to me, a story that illustrates how stories—thoughts and memories—can be erased and our interpretation of the world changed. For Kristrun also wrote of the 350 years during which Helgafell was the site of a monastery, the 350 years of which we know almost nothing.

In 1184, the Augustinian monastery that had been established on an island in the Breidafjord twelve years earlier was moved inland to Helgafell. A note from 1186, preserved in a fourteenth-century manuscript, mentions five priests and two deacons, along with a library of 120 books. More books would soon be in production, including, perhaps, *Eyrbyggja Saga* and *Laxdaela Saga*. Translators Hermann Palsson and Paul Edwards think the two sagas were written by two of Helgafell's monks "and that they used each other's work. This would explain why Helgafell becomes the focal place of *Laxdaela Saga* precisely at the point where it ceases to be [the focal place] of *Eyrbyggja Saga*," they write.

Sixteen manuscripts made at Helgafell remain. One is "an exceptionally lavish work," writes paleographer Lena Liepe, the "richest in decoration of all Icelandic manuscripts." The book contains the law code issued by King Magnus the Law Mender in 1280, sixteen years after Iceland lost its independence and became a colony of Norway. The book is quite large, measuring nearly fifteen inches tall by eleven inches wide, with an "unusually large script and wide margins, indicating that the scribe was instructed to make unsparing use of the high-quality parchment on which it was written," Liepe notes. The writing was completed in 1363, the decorations—on nearly every page—somewhat later. The illuminator painted backgrounds that look "like tapestries with cross-shaped leaves, vine leaves, lilies, and fleurs-de-lis," Liepe says, vegetation found nowhere in Iceland. "The colouring as a whole is dominated by olive green, verdigris green, light blue, and bright and dark red, supplemented by yellow and yellowish brown," the pigments for which were most likely imported. The artist's style is a little old-fashioned compared to similar books from England: "Several of the younger male figures are manifestly elegant, wearing tight tunics that emphasize their long spool-shaped trunks and standing with legs crossed and feet pointing downwards in an attitude of courtly refinement." There are monsters with animal heads and human bodies, hunting scenes, bearded faces framed with curly hair that peek out in surprise from the bodies of letter forms. There's even a dragon—introducing the section on marriage. It's the work of a rich and well-run monastery with foreign cultural and trade connections, one that lasted until 1543, then vanished without a trace. Not even the most modern archaeological techniques can prove it ever existed.

"We've been successful at many monastery sites," archaeologist Steinunn Kristjansdottir told me, "but Helgafell is a big mystery. We've been going again and again and again, and we can't find anything. Maybe there's something we missed, but we have been searching so much."

Steinunn, a professor at the University of Iceland, is the expert on Iceland's medieval monasteries. In 2000, she was asked to excavate one in the East Fjords—about as far from Helgafell, in the west of Iceland, as you can get. The site had once been owned by one of Iceland's most popular twentieth-century writers, Gunnar

Gunnarsson, famous for his novel *The Good Shepherd*, a Christmas story about a shepherd who goes out in a blizzard to rescue lost sheep. Gunnar's farm, Skrida, was to be a museum, and funds were available to research its early history, including the monastery run there from 1493 until the Protestant Reformation shut down all such Catholic establishments about fifty years later. According to the "sacred legend" of Skrida—a legend very much like an elf story—in the waning years of the fifteenth century, a cleric traveled down the valley to visit a dying parishioner. On the way he dropped his chalice and paten, the holy cup and plate he needed to say Mass. "A man was sent to look for them and found them on a knoll . . . The chalice was filled with wine and the paten laid neatly on top, with bread on it," Steinunn writes. "This event was viewed as a miracle and was commemorated with the construction of a chapel" and, a little later, a monastery. Ruins of the chapel, which became a Lutheran church that stood until 1793, could be clearly seen. But the monastery, like that at Helgafell, had vanished.

Most people assumed its buildings were hidden under the later farmhouses. Iceland has no brick or building stone; its mud lacks binding clay, and its ubiquitous basalt is difficult to shape. Few native trees grow tall enough to provide structural timbers. Most buildings before the twentieth century were ephemeral constructions of uncut stones, dried turf blocks, and driftwood. If well maintained, these Icelandic turf houses can be snug and handsome; they are wonderfully ecologically sound. But their practical nature means most were rebuilt on the foundations of older homes, the stones and timbers recycled, the discarded turf tamped down to create the signature Icelandic "house mound." Dutifully, Steinunn surveyed the outskirts of the modern farmhouses at Skrida. She found no signs of the monastery. Then she surveyed—using various forms of remote sensing, soil testing, and the digging of small trenches—the hayfields around the chapel site. She discovered a rectangular complex covering more than 14,000 square feet. Her excavations over the next twelve years revealed the classic quadrangular plan of a medieval European monastery, with the church linked to a chapter house, the abbot's lodgings, a refectory and kitchen, a bathhouse or brewery, living quarters and storerooms, an infirmary, and stables, all surrounding a cloister with herb gardens and a well. One small cell held a stove and a bookshelf. Finds of sulfur, wax, colored stones, and other tools show the monks made ink and parchment and, we can assume, wrote books. Excavating the cemetery revealed the bones of the poor and the sick who sought hospice care. They suffered from syphilis, tuberculosis and other lung diseases, cleft palate, gum disease, broken bones, tapeworms, and unidentified infections; some had been treated medicinally with mercury. Steinunn's crew found lancets, scalpels, and surgical pins—more proof there were doctors on site.

In 2013, Steinunn began a three-year research project to survey all fourteen of Iceland's monastic sites. She and her team came to Helgafell three times in 2014, where she expected to find the same quadrangular structure as at Skrida. She looked in likely places—the semicircular path, just visible in the grass under certain lighting conditions, known for generations as the Abbot's Walk. She looked in unlikely places—the parking spot beside the farmhouse. She even looked under the cowbarn, she told me: Hjortur's sons were busy at the time reconfiguring it into a sheephouse. "They had dug into the floor and I could see ten-meter profiles"—thirty-three-foot-long swaths of the sheer trench walls—"and I could not see anything medieval there." Some distance from the main farm buildings on the south side of the hill, I pointed out, are an intriguing set of knolls. "It's a very nice ruin of a typical medieval farm," Steinunn explained. "Hjortur called it Solheimaholl, Little Hill of the Sun's Home," she said, adding, "There's a huge difference between a medieval farm and a monastery," as her work at other sites has shown. Perhaps the monastery at Helgafell is indeed hiding under the modern farmhouse. Perhaps it is under the church and the cemetery. Perhaps it is under the lake, whose borders have repeatedly shrunk and grown over the five hundred years since the monastery closed. We may never know. Three hundred fifty years of Helgafell's history have simply disappeared.

The only stories that remain are mocking ones from much later. In his book *An Oxonian in Iceland*, saga pilgrim Frederick Metcalfe writes of riding south from Stykkisholmur in 1860. "We skirt the low isolated precipice of Helgafell, a spot of the greatest sanctity in pagan Iceland," he writes, adding, "The little wooden church, now under its shadow, is but a poor apology for the monastery." He sweeps his eye across the landscape—wetlands cut by brooks fingering into small bays, wet hayfields, low-growing birch and willows, thin pasture, with bare sand and black knuckles of volcanic rock breaking through here and there—and his eye alights on a rock outcrop. "That eminence, yonder, is called Munkr-skard"—Monk's Ridge—"for it was from thence that, according to tradition, the expelled monks took a last look of their beloved sanctuary," he writes. When the Protestant Reformation came, they were evicted from their longtime home. Helgafell and the ninety-six farms it controlled passed into the ownership of the Danish king, then Iceland's overlord.

Metcalfe, an Anglican priest, is not sympathetic. Of the evicted Catholic monks, those writers of sagas, makers of beautiful manuscripts, and, perhaps as at Skrida, healers of the sick and comforters of the dying, Metcalfe writes, "Their heart, doubtless, was with their treasure buried in a hillside close by." A later Lutheran decided to dig for it, Metcalfe writes, "but when he had dug some depth, looking round he saw the church of Helgafell in flames, and off he ran with his companions to extinguish the fire"—only to find it was an illusion. "According to another account, the diggers delved out the strong-box, and fastened a rope to it. 'Now then pull, if God will,' said the first digger: 'Now then pull, God will or no,' said the second digger: at the same moment the rope broke, and they saw their house was in flames. When they came back from putting out the fire"—not an illusion, this time—"the hole was filled up; and since that time not a single peasant can be prevailed upon, for love or money, to excavate there afresh."

In 1184, when the monastery was moved from the island to Helgafell, the Church owned several other farms nearby. Why was Helgafell chosen for the monks' new cloister? Because of the hill's well-known holiness, I believe. Throughout Europe in the Middle Ages, the Christian Church systematically redefined pagan holy sites—hills, lakes, groves of trees, springs—renaming them after saints or Mary and rewriting their stories. By siting a monastery at Helgafell, the hill could remain holy, still a locus for pilgrimage and prayer, a landmark signifying shelter and stability.

Only the source of its holiness shifted. When the Protestant Reformation came, by contrast, the hill was stripped of all power. The stories told of the Holy Mountain changed key. Helgafell became a source of shadow: poor, isolated, the home of greedy blasphemers and frightening phantoms fighting over an imagined casket of coins. Its 350-year history as a Christian holy site was erased. The hill became just a hill, until romantics and nationalists in the nineteenth century rediscovered the sagas.

Walking Withershins

One night at Helgafell, my sleep was broken by banshee screams. Fully awake, I realized it was a child, dreaming a terrible dream. Her mother woke and shushed her, and the household settled back to sleep.

I was traveling that year with Jenny Tucker, an artist and herbalist from Pennsylvania. Through my rudimentary—and at times, I admit, rude—translating, over breakfast she and the girl's mother, Asta, discussed the child's night terrors, which were frequent. When I'd told them at Helgafell that Jenny was an herbalist, Asta and her sisters, like others of my Icelandic friends, began referring to her with a word that means witch. I thought they were joking. But Asta simply nodded when Jenny diagnosed the child's dreams as the efforts of an ancestor to speak with her. Translating this bit, I objected that I didn't believe in ghosts. Asta accepted that. She wondered aloud if the ghost might be the girl's grandmother.

Jenny made a potion of St. John's wort oil and Rescue Remedy and showed Asta where to rub it on the child's skin. (Jenny rubbed it on her own skin, too.) Then we went outside and Jenny gathered wildflowers to make a "blessing bundle"; placed under the girl's pillow, it would signal to the ghost that it should approach more gently.

That night we all slept soundly.

A thousand years before, another little girl at Helgafell dreamed a terrible dream. She dreamed a woman came to her, an angry old woman, cloaked and hooded. "Tell your grandmother it doesn't please me," the dream-woman said in *Laxdaela Saga*, "to have her thrashing about over top of me all night and letting drip such hot drops that I'm burned all over." The girl's grandmother was Gudrun Osvifursdottir, who, after seeing her four husbands and her lover to the grave, had become deeply religious, the saga says, naming her Iceland's first Christian nun. Gudrun prayed each night by candlelight in Helgafell's church. When the little girl related her dream, "Gudrun had them tear up the floorboards of the church where she liked to kneel and dig deep into the ground. They found bones under there; they were blue and evil-looking. They also found a little brooch, and a great sorcerer's staff. It seemed clear to everyone that this was the grave of some kind of witch. The bones were taken up and moved far away, to where few paths led."

No saga names the witch of Helgafell, though earlier in *Laxdaela Saga*, Gudrun's second husband was drowned in a squall called up by another witch, this one a man: He and his wife were stoned to death. One of their sons was trussed up, tied to a rock, and dropped in the bay to drown. The other son escaped for a time, but eventually was caught. A bag was pulled over his head so he couldn't curse his captors, as his brother had, but there was a rip in the bag. Through it, the witch "caught sight of the hillside across the valley, a beautiful grassy landscape, and it seemed as though a whirlwind struck it: The earth turned upside down. Never afterwards would grass grow there. It's now called Brenna," or Burnt Place.

Many places in Iceland could be called Burnt Place. Visiting in 1810, Sir George Mackenzie, a mineralogist from Scotland, writes, "The surface was covered with black cinders; and the various hollows enclosed by high cliffs and rugged peaks, destitute of every sign of vegetation, and rendered more gloomy by floating mist, and a perfect stillness, contributed to excite strong feelings of horror." Another noble English scientist, William Lord Watts, endeavoring to surmount an Icelandic mountain in 1876, describes "the abyss which opened at our feet, with its black pits and grim chasms all contributing to the general aggregate of steam, and loam, and stench, and horrid sound; while behind us stretched a wild waste of glen, desert, and mountain, a country moaning in ashes, and howling with desolation."

I'm reminded of J. R. R. Tolkien's depiction in *The Lord of the Rings* of the garden-loving hobbit Sam Gamgee arriving on the outskirts of Mordor, home of the Dark Lord: "The gasping pools were choked with ash and crawling muds, sickly white and grey, as if the mountains had vomited the filth of their entrails upon the lands about. High mounds of crushed and powdered rock, great cones of earth fire-blasted and poison-stained, stood like an obscene graveyard." It was "a land defiled, diseased beyond all healing—unless the Great Sea should enter in and wash it with oblivion. 'I feel sick,' said Sam."

Strangely, there are no similar descriptions of Iceland's bleak volcanic landscape in the sagas. We are told in *The Saga of Christianity* that "earth fire" erupted on a nearby farm while the Althing, the yearly gathering of Iceland's chieftains, was debating official acceptance of the new Christian faith, outlawing the public worship of the old gods, Odin and Thor, Freyja and Freyr.

"It is no wonder," people muttered about the eruption. "The gods are angry at such talk."

It was Snorri Godi, the wily chieftain of Helgafell, who quelled that rumor. Gesturing to the landscape around him, he asked, "And what were the gods angry about when they burned the place we're standing on now?" Only if you've visited Thingvellir, the assembly site, with a guide would you know that the black pits and chasms, the plain of clinker and cinders and ropy lava, were there before any people came to Iceland. The saga does not describe it.

There's a story in *The Book of Land-Taking* about a great flood caused (we know now) by an eruption under a glacier. Another tale tells of early settlers who were forced to move when "fire came up" and "burning lava flowed down." An eruption wiped out part of a farm I frequently visit on Iceland's west coast: "One night when he was old and blind," Haukur Sveinbjornsson, the farmer who worked the land, told me in 1996, "Sel-Thorir saw a huge man row up to the mouth of the River Kalda in a great iron boat. He walked over to the sheep pen and dug a hole at the gate. That night the eruption started. Lava came shooting out of the hole. Where the farm was then, the crater Eldborg stands now."

But that's about it. As Oren Falk of Cornell University notes, "The entire corpus of Family Sagas, thirteen thick volumes'-worth in the standard modern editions, seems to know nothing of lava and ash plumes." These are the sagas, like *Laxdaela*, that read like historical novels; Falk does not count *The Saga of Christianity*, which is a religious chronicle, or *The Book of Land-Taking*, which is a history. The Family Sagas are the ones, writes Falk, that are "rightly celebrated for their gritty realism and insightful portrayals of human character," yet they "show little insight when it comes to portrayals of the natural world."

If Iceland's landscape is shorted in the sagas, so is Iceland's weather—and as any Iceland traveler knows, you bet your life on the weather report. True, in the sagas there are storms and fog and rain and snow and a few splendid sunny days, but according to climatologist Astrid Ogilvie and anthropologist Gisli Palsson, only "some few of these may reflect reality. More frequently, weather descriptions seem to be used as a literary device; for example, as a metaphor, or to create a mood." Or they're examples of witchcraft. Seventy-eight people in these sagas are named witches; thirty-nine are men, thirty-nine are women. They "are not necessarily noted as sinister in any way," note Ogilvie and Palsson. Often, they "are not accorded any kind of moral judgment."

One of my favorites is Svan. In *Njal's Saga*, we read, "Svan picked up a goatskin and swung it around his head, calling out:

> Come fog!
> Come phantoms
> And wonders of all kinds
> To fool those who follow you."

And a man on the run, hidden in the rush of fog, was safe—for a time, at least.

Once, on a four-day hike in the Hornstrandir, a part of Iceland that was farmed for hundreds of years but now is abandoned to campsites and summer cabins, I saw the fog come in that fast, as if a witch had swung a goatskin over the sky. We had set up our tent over a little knoll, out of sight of other hikers. I was relaxing in the lush green grass, the sun warm on my shoulders, watching the dance of kittiwakes wheeling over the blue, blue sea, waiting for the tea water to boil, when the sea fog rolled in, magnificently. A great, roiling, boiling, billowing gray mass lit to gold at its heart, hands and tentacles reaching out to fill every crack, pull everything in, blot everything out. It came rushing into the bay as if a door out at sea had been flung open wide. Within half an hour it filled the whole space, erasing equally the high peak across the bay and a cabin that was a short walk away. The piles of driftwood—whole, huge, salt-white, seaworm-riddled logs from Siberia—sitting on the beach disappeared. There was no grass, no kittiwakes, no sea, no sky. Fog spilled over the mountain behind me, blanking out the cairns and the cliffs, and the way back. It swept in and around me and transformed everything I could see. It writhed and spun like smoke in a wind. But I felt no wind.

Another of my favorite saga witches is Ljot, from *Vatnsdaela Saga*. Ljot's son Hrolleif had killed a man, and the dead man's three sons came looking for revenge. They hauled Hrolleif from his hiding place. Just then they spied old Ljot, and cried out, "What devil is that coming at us!" The old woman had "flipped her skirts up and was walking backwards, with her head sticking out between her legs," says the saga. "Her gaze was horrible, her eyes shooting side to side like a troll's." Quick, said one brother, "Kill Hrolleif now!" And they did. The witch unwound herself and stood up. She complimented the brothers on their luck. She "had meant to turn the whole landscape upside down"—Falk interprets her threat as an earthquake, but I think of an eruption—and to send them squealing away like pigs, crazy with fear, "and so things would have turned out, if you had not seen me before I saw you."

I recall walking the witch's way as a child, upside down and backward, head between my legs. I'd thought it the definition of the word *withershins*, so often found in descriptions of witchcraft. I was attending to the shins. The word really means walking wither to, or opposite to, the path of the sun, or as we'd say today, counterclockwise, which the witch Ljot was probably also doing, as moving in that direction is itself a magical act.

I don't notice when I'm walking withershins nowadays—who takes care to follow the path of the sun? Nor do I watch the world from between my shins—I'm no longer so flexible. The Scottish writer Nan Shepherd, though, thinks I should try. In *The Living Mountain*, written in the 1940s, she suggests that when the natural world ceases to astonish us, we need a change of perspective: "Face away from what you look at, and bend with straddled legs till you see your world upside down. How new it has become! From the close-by sprigs of heather to the most distant fold of the land, each detail stands erect in its own validity . . . Nothing has reference to me, the looker. This is how the earth must see itself."

On a beach in southern England, a modern-day shaman handed anthropologist Susan Greenwood a stone with a hole in it. "If you look through a holed stone—a witch's stone—you get a different perspective," the shaman said. I've done that, too, not knowing it was witchcraft. But the perspectival shift induced by holed stones seems to me not as extreme as that of the witch's walk. How the shaman found the holed stone, however, is another gentle magic I have practiced. As she told Greenwood, "They find you." It requires a certain state of consciousness in which you shift your awareness and "let the boundaries go." I do it not only on a pebbled beach, but when faced with a used book sale. I shift my awareness, run my unfocused eyes (and often my fingertips) across the stacks, and let the books I need find me. Among the books I've acquired this way are *Sea Spell and Moor Magic*, *Strange Tales from Many Lands*, and *Icelandic Folk and Fairy Tales*.

Witches, according to Jack Zipes in *The Irresistible Fairy Tale*, are "kin" to fairies and elves. All derive from "pagan goddesses in the Western world," he says. "That is, not only were the goddesses transformed into witches, they were also the precursors of the fairies and their kin." Research by folklorists has shown that "most people believed in witches, fairies, wizards, and magic up through the Renaissance." But in spite of the "hundreds, if not thousands, of different types of tales about witches and fairies" that have come down to us, "we cannot exactly define a witch, fairy, or fairy tale."

An Italian-English dictionary from 1598 defines *fata*, unhelpfully, as "a fairie, a witch, an enchantres, an elfe" and *strega* as "a witch, a sorceresse, a charmer, a hag, or fairie," while in his *Discouerie of Witchcraft*, written in 1584, the Elizabethan skeptic Reginald Scot "dismisses the idea of witches as 'old women which danse with the fairies.'"

We can be sure, though, of what witches, fairies, and their kin were not: compatible with Christian doctrine. "The 'great accomplishment' of Christianity," writes Zipes, "was its transformation of goddesses, sorceresses, and fairies into demonic and malevolent figures." Notice Zipes's use of gendered terms. Think of your everyday witch—perhaps the one in Disney's *Tangled*. "Obsessed with beauty and her own desires, the Disney witches are stereotypical products of the Western male gaze and mass-mediated manipulation of the images of women that date back to the Christian church's demonization of women. There are connections to be drawn," Zipes concludes. "All one has to do is read a bit of history."

Perhaps my friend Jenny Tucker is a witch after all, if that word means a woman wise in the old ways of knowledge bad-mouthed by centuries of Christian men. That does not mean she can cause volcanic eruptions or control the weather, but that she sees the world in a different way, more like the way the earth might see itself.

In *The Anthropology of Magic*, Greenwood acknowledges that she herself, though a working scientist, is a witch. "Studying the experience of magic calls for a different anthropological approach," she writes. She has "participated in many witchcraft rituals, trained as a high magician, and worked with shamans." Early on she met a witch in northern England whose preferred form of magic was storytelling. "She told me," writes Greenwood, "how her stories were spells that could change people's lives." The witch explained, "I don't have to say to people 'I'm working on your unconscious now' . . . If I've done my work right something will happen."

Sociologist Arthur Frank speaks of storytelling in a similar way. Without reference to witches or magic spells, he says, "Stories work *on* people, affecting what people are able to see as real, as possible, and as worth doing or best avoided." They "bring people together, and they keep them apart."

Stories create societies. They can be more important than food or family, anthropologist Daniel Smith found when he studied the Agta, who have lived as hunter-gatherers in the Philippines for over 35,000 years. Their camps are a three-day hike from what we like to call civilization, and the stories they tell—like "The Sun and the Moon" or "The Monkey and the Giant"—have recognizable morals. They "convey messages relevant to coordinating behavior in a foraging ecology," Smith writes. The Agta's stories stress the importance of getting along; doing your part; being generous, not greedy; valuing each other's differences; and seeing the other side. And they do it well: The better the storyteller, the higher the camp scored on the scientists' test of cooperation. And the Agta noticed, too. When asked who they would most like to live with, the Agta chose the person who told good stories twice as often as the next most popular person, the one who caught the most fish. Controlling for kinship, age, sex, and other variables did not change the outcome. The Agta know the value of stories.

Do we? We all tell stories. Humans always have. But we don't always take responsibility for the effects of our storytelling. "Our culture doesn't think storytelling is sacred," writes Ursula K. Le Guin, whose Earthsea series reinfuses witchcraft with morality. To her, writers "pursue a sacred call, although some would buck and rear at having their work labeled like this." Yet, she adds, "If you believe that words are acts, as I do, then one must hold writers responsible for what their words do."

Stories shape how you see the world. They determine not only how you think of witches—or elves—but how you think of such "real" things as hills and mountains. "When we look at a landscape," writes Robert Macfarlane in *Mountains of the Mind*, "we do not see what is there, but largely what we think is there . . . We *read* landscapes, in other words, we interpret their forms in the light of our own experience and memory, and that of our shared cultural memory . . . What we call a mountain is thus in fact a collaboration of the physical forms of the world with the imagination of humans—a mountain of the mind."

A story that cast a magic spell upon all mountains was Edmund Burke's *A Philosophical Enquiry into the Origin of Our Ideas of the Sublime and Beautiful*. Burke, from Ireland, published it in 1757, when he was twenty-eight. He was, writes Macfarlane, "interested in our psychic response to things—a rushing cataract, say, a dark vault or a cliff face—that seized, terrified, and yet also somehow pleased the mind by dint of being too big, too high, too fast, too obscured, too powerful, too *something*, to be properly comprehended." Instead, such things inspired "a heady blend of pleasure and terror. Beauty, by contrast, was inspired by the visually regular, the proportioned, the predictable." It's the frisson of fear that makes a volcano, a Burnt Place, a cliffside swathed in fog, sublime.

Burke's book, says Macfarlane, "provided a new lens through which wilderness could be viewed and appreciated." Macfarlane's own books do much the same for me. In *The Old Ways*, he mentions an archaeologist named Anne Campbell who was "close-mapping" a moor. Why that moor? "It is the most interesting place in the world to me," she told Macfarlane. "So I spend most of my time walking shieling tracks, paths, and the streams and the walls that used to divide up the land. Then I talk to people and try to fix their memories to those particular places." I once visited that part of Scotland, the western edge of the Isle of Lewis, but did not meet Campbell walking her moor. Still, a story Macfarlane tells, a little aside, gave me a new perspective on Iceland (the most interesting place in the world to me). Macfarlane writes, "When it wasn't too cold, and not so dry that the heather was sharp, Anne liked to walk barefoot on the moor. 'It takes about two weeks to get your feet toughened up so that it's no discomfort. And then it's bliss. You should try it when you're out there. Take those big boots of yours off!'"

I tried it. On the western tip of Iceland's Snaefellsnes peninsula sits the long-abandoned farm of Laugarbrekka, where Gudrid the Far-Traveler was born in about 982. I've written two books about Gudrid, sister-in-law to Leif Eiriksson, the Viking explorer credited with "discovering" the Americas some five hundred years before Columbus. Yet Gudrid spent more time in Vinland, as the Vikings called it, than Leif did. Gudrid is the real Viking explorer, and a recurring inspiration to me. In 2016, on a sunny Sunday in late July, I visited her monument at Laugarbrekka for the umpteenth time. I walked out to the *laug*, or bathing pool, which is no longer bathwater warm, took off my boots, rolled up my pants, and waded in, but the sharp stony bottom of the lake kept me from going far. Back on the bank, I dabbled my toes in the water and gazed at the glacier-capped volcano, Snaefellsjokull, its coruscations of lava catching the light, until it was time to go; then, remembering Campbell's bliss, decided to walk barefoot back to the car. It was lovely, like meeting the land for the very first time. The heath was springy and soft and comforting to my feet—though they had not been toughened up. Picking along, carefully placing each foot, I found ripe crowberries and almost ripe blueberries, some very blue but still tart. The grass was soft, too, but I found myself preferentially stepping on the berry bushes and fragrant creeping thyme, which tickled.

Barefoot, you cannot stride. "As a rigidly mechanical, straight-legged oscillation from the hips, with eyes gazing ahead rather than downcast, the stride only works with booted feet," writes anthropologist Tim Ingold. Only in boots can we conquer the world. But for most of history, humans did not stride. They "picked their way with bare, sandaled, or moccasined feet," Ingold says. Picking their way, they picked up knowledge about the world.

Nineteenth-century Darwinists noticed that barefoot tribes could do things with their feet: climb trees, row boats, pick up a spear, hold cloth while sewing it. They assumed such savages retained ape-like toes. Ingold blames not evolution, but the boot. Stiff leather, worn from childhood, crippled the foot. Instead of being able to grasp (in all its meanings) the ground, the booted foot became a "stepping machine." The word for boot in Icelandic, strangely enough, is literally "stepping machine": *stigvél*. Grasping with the hands, using tools, was considered civilized; grasping with the foot, being grounded, was savage. The modern human, writes Ingold, "is every inch a scientist on top, but a machine down below."

Where have our stories and our stepping machines brought us? To the brink. In 2013, British writer Ben Rawlence moved from

NANCY MARIE BROWN

London to a cottage in Wales. "It felt like another world," he writes: "The view from the window was of sheep rather than the top deck of red London buses." He was surprised to find a "constellation" of writers and artists out in "the middle of nowhere." Surprised, too, to find his perspective on the real world soon changed. "Away from the city, climate change as a totalizing political and cultural concern is hard to avoid," he writes. As one member of his new book club asked, "How can anyone, now, justify writing a book that is not, in some way, about our relationship to this planet?" Moving to Wales was for Rawlence like looking through a holed stone, peering at the landscape upside down, between his knees, taking his boots off and becoming grounded. What he'd grasped in the middle of nowhere was the idea of the Anthropocene.

This Epoch of Humans, the current geological age, began in 1945 with the testing of the first atomic bomb—or so the working group of the International Commission on Stratigraphy proposed in 2016, when it recommended the name be codified. Others date the Human Age to the invention of fire, or agriculture, or the steam engine, or plastic. Each leaves its mark in layers, or strata, of rock. In the late 1700s, scientists began naming these strata, sectioning Earth's autobiography into volumes (eons), chapters (eras), paragraphs (periods), and sentences (epochs or ages). The commission, founded in 1961, approves the names and start dates, each marking a planet-wide change. Thus, Earth's first eon was marked by volcanic eruptions, its second by ocean formation, its third by one-celled organisms excreting oxygen, its fourth—ours, starting 540 million years ago—by the rise of animal life. Our eon is further divided into three eras, twelve periods, and thirty-three

80

epochs, not counting the current epoch, the Anthropocene. To a nonscientist, perhaps only one period, midway through the eon, leaps out: the Jurassic. We know stories (mostly false) about the Jurassic. We live in the Quaternary Period of the Cenozoic Era. The Quaternary Period began with the Pleistocene, or most new, Epoch (aka the Ice Age), which ended 11,700 years ago. At that point the Holocene, or wholly new, Epoch began.

Until 1999, we lived in the Holocene. That year, at a Holocene-focused conference, Paul Crutzen, who won the Nobel Prize in Chemistry in 1995 for his work on the ozone hole, "suddenly thought this was wrong. The world has changed too much," he said. He proposed a new epoch: the Anthropocene. In 2000, he and biologist Eugene Stoermer, who had been using the term since the 1980s, jointly published "The Anthropocene" in the *Global Change Newsletter* of the International Geosphere-Biosphere Programme of the International Council for Science. In 2014, the word *Anthropocene* entered the *Oxford English Dictionary* (along with *selfie*, appropriately enough).

While the International Commission on Stratigraphy withheld its final approval, the concept spread. We are facing "the end of nature," as Bill McKibben wrote in 1989. Nowhere on Earth remains free from human influence. We have changed the chemical makeup of the atmosphere, the oceans, and the polar ice. According to Macfarlane, whose lyrical descriptions of nature so move me, "the notion of a world beyond us has become difficult to sustain." We need, he says, "fresh vocabularies and narratives that might account for the kinds of relation and responsibility in which we find ourselves entangled." But writing about Anthropocene art in *The Guardian* in 2016, he finds it to be "obsessed with loss and disappearance"; its "ur-text" is Cormac McCarthy's apocalyptic novel *The Road*. Readers and viewers of such art will respond to its layers of loss, Macfarlane fears, with "stuplimity"—a term coined in 2000 by cultural theorist Sianne Ngai in opposition to sublimity. If the sublime brings us "a heady blend of pleasure and terror," the stuplime blends astonishment and boredom, "such that we overload on anxiety to the point of outrage-outage," Macfarlane writes. "Art and literature might, at their best, shock us out of the stuplime," he pleads. He thinks, he hopes, that by upsetting our notions of nature and culture "the Anthropocene has administered—and will administer—a massive jolt to the imagination."

THREE

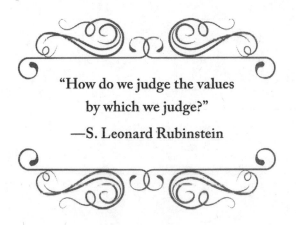

"How do we judge the values
by which we judge?"

—S. Leonard Rubinstein

Eyjafjallajokull

Windows

One August evening in 2015, I walked eight miles through a lava field to peek into the windows of an abandoned farmhouse I'd rented for the summer nineteen years before. The trail was a well-worn lifeline of mine, in anthropologist Tim Ingold's terms, well-knotted with stories. In 1998, my husband published a book about the old place at the trail's northern terminus, *Summer at Little Lava: A Season at the Edge of the World*, and though that subtitle had always struck me as hyperbolic, the old house was indeed defined by edges. It sat on the edge of the lava field, on the edge of the sea, on the edge of tidal flats that linked it to the edge of civilization, if civilization was defined as a drivable road, electric lights, indoor plumbing, and the phone at the neighboring farm of Great Lava. I described the house at Little Lava, too, in my 2001 book *A Good Horse Has No Color: Searching Iceland for the Perfect Horse*. Little Lava was for me "a singular place of retreat" with "the amenities of a tent." A concrete box, it was left unfinished when the family, diminished by World War II, decamped to the city. Their old turf house, left empty, soon sagged and slumped and crumpled before finally subsiding into a hillock in the yard of the concrete box. Drafty, with a leaky, asbestos roof, the house at Little Lava had one virtue: windows. As I wrote about the summer we lived there,

I could hear the horses before I saw them, their hoof-beats the high slap of cupped hands clapping, beating the punctuated four-beat rhythm of the *tölt*, the breed's distinctive running-walk gait. From our summerhouse, I watched them through binoculars. Pinpricks on the silvery wet sand, they shimmered like a vision out of the Icelandic sagas . . .

Briefly the horses took shape as they cut across the tide flats—necks arced high, manes rippling, long tails floating behind. Their short legs curved and struck, curved and struck. I would watch them until they disappeared beyond the black headland and wonder who their riders were, where they went on their rapid journey.

I wanted to go with them.

Icelandic folktales warn of the gray horse that comes out of the water, submits briefly to bridle and saddle, and at dusk carries its rider into the sea. For me, it was the watcher who was carried away.

We'd had no horses that summer. We'd traveled shank's mare everywhere, our everyday hike always along or across or in some way intersecting the trail I took through the lava field that August evening in 2015.

The trail dated to the tenth century. It was well hidden, grown over by dwarf birch and blueberry, when I discovered—or recovered—it in 1992. I'd been camping at Little Lava with Petur, whose brother was my mathematician friend at Penn State, and his friend, Anna, whose mother had been born at Little Lava. One bright July morning we took off, cross country, careless of the ankle-twisting volcanic terrain—they were in their twenties still; I, thirty-three—scrabbling over lava ridges and scrambling through gaps and gorges, crossing ropy lava (like well-tarred hawsers coiled on ships' decks), slipping on scoria, kicking up pumice dust, to reach the jagged rim of Eldborg, the perfect spatter-ring crater of the volcano the giant in the great iron boat had ignited when he dug a hole at the gate of the sheep pen.

In my journal entry for that day, I wrote, "Wind so strong my lips flapped if I walked with my mouth open."

A sea eagle flew over us, white tail flaring in the sun, cackling like a hen—and "all nature was silent while the eagle flew," as the Icelandic saying goes. We crouched, kept still, hoping to lure him closer, to see his wicked yellow beak. In June 2000, that same eagle or its mate would swoop down at me, repeatedly, force me trembling, hunched on the ground, hard up against a lava ridge for safety—I'd come too close to its nest.

Petur flushed two ptarmigan, half in their winter-white plumage, from a birch thicket. The sides of Eldborg were half green-clad. From a distance, I'd thought the greenery was grass. It turned out to be scrubby trees, six to ten feet tall—tall enough to crawl under, to rest in the shade. There I found purple wood geraniums, buttercups, dandelions, and brown mushrooms with round caps the size of tea saucers.

At the base of the crater, we came upon a hard-beaten path. We followed it to the farm of Snorrastadir, walked past the stables, past the parking spot for tour buses, past the new house, cow barn, old house, without stopping (Anna was related, but they weren't then on speaking terms), down the road to the river's mouth, and back through the pastures and wetlands until we reached the sand flats at the seaward edge of the lava field. Anna had heard of a path home to Little Lava. We spread out to search.

It was "narrow as a sheeptrack in places," I wrote in my journal at midnight, when we arrived home, "but elsewhere were wide bridges, red lava rocks piled up in a gorge and smoothed to a level surface five feet wide. The cairns were old and rubbly, moss-grown. I found the path right off from the sand flats, but Petur and Anna didn't believe me. I myself wasn't sure. And they went off other ways until Petur saw me moving along so fast he knew I must be on a trail."

Nineteen years later I didn't stride out so smartly. My feet are partly crippled, with bunions and bent toes, though I've eschewed high heels my whole life. Stiff leather boots were evil enough. Still, I remember that evening's hike as a walk of joy. At the midpoint on the path I flung my arms out and turned a circle and saw—nothing new under the sun. No one knew I was there, or would find me if I failed to return. No one but the eagle and the fox. I was ecstatic. (And no, I carried no mobile phone.) The air expanded all around me.

It was sunny and warm, if windy. I'd left Snorrastadir about six P.M., with no real plan but to picnic on the trail. I at least wanted to locate the trailhead. I hiked the river road down to the beach, crossed two marshy headlands, and there it was, well-marked with a stake adorned with colorful rubber fishing-net floats, a common find among the detritus that pollutes Iceland's shores. The path was grown shut in places, like the year I first found it. The birches rustled, their pungent twigs snapped, as I pressed through a forest of thigh-high trees. The boulders turned to trolls behind my back. I stopped at the big cairn halfway to Little Lava to rest and eat; a sea eagle circled, checking me out. From there I could spot a new summer house beside the abandoned farm; I decided I must take a look.

"It's a beautiful little house," I wrote in my journal the next morning, "but it broke my heart to see it so close to Little Lava. New fences and six horses. A tractor, a horse trailer, a boat. I did not peek into their windows but I did look into those at Little Lava. It's been used. The bed frame Petur built us is still there. Water container, bunsen burner. The table is in the main room now, with chairs and benches. The storeroom is still a mess. Our old treasures still sit on the window sills—shells, stones, feathers, bones—or maybe they're new treasures. Three green glass fishing floats."

I took the new road home—bulldozed through the lava to reach the new summer house and also to bring geothermal hot water back to Snorrastadir farm, which has a guesthouse, where I was staying, and five summer cottages, each with a hot tub. The walk home took me two hours. "Beautiful views and good riding surface," I wrote, "but not the same!" Exhausted, I reached my room at eleven and went right to bed. I spent the next day "being a writer." I wrote: "Great view of the mountains out my window, Eldborg just off to the side. But can't keep the window open—it's blowing in sand onto my keyboard. Spent all day watching the clouds come in over the mountains. Strong wind drumming on the windows. Read *Stillness* by Pico Iyer."

The Art of Stillness is subtitled *Adventures in Going Nowhere*. "In an age of distraction," Iyer writes, "nothing can feel more luxurious than paying attention." Eydis Einarsdottir, the daughter of an Icelandic friend of mine, provided the book's photographs, all shot in Iceland. "They are not an attempt to capture the perfect image, but to capture the feeling I experience as I witness the things in front of me," Eydis writes. "I get lost in such a beautiful way that it's hard to describe; it's as though I find a piece of me that I had lost without really knowing that I lost it."

I know what she means. The first time I came to Iceland, I felt I had found a piece of me that, if not quite lost, had long been suppressed, a piece formed early in my childhood by the books read to me, chief among them J. R. R. Tolkien's *The Hobbit*.

In her own exploration of her childhood love of escapist fiction, *The Magician's Book: A Skeptic's Adventures in Narnia*, Laura Miller writes, "Anyone who has done much reading aloud to children knows that long passages of environmental description can be risky. Even adults reading novels meant for adults tend to skim over scene-setting paragraphs devoted to geology or weather patterns. (At least, I do . . .)" She preferred the works of C. S. Lewis to those of Tolkien for that reason. "I had trouble, I think, with

The Hobbit's longish passages of description. I couldn't visualize any of these places."

I didn't have that trouble. Neither did my son: I read him *The Hobbit* four times and *The Lord of the Rings* (1,008 pages of very small type) three times before he was eight, before we took him to live at Little Lava for three months, where the geology and weather patterns are as fantastic as anything Tolkien thought up, where the imagination is set free and the mind urged to pay attention.

To me it felt like coming home. As Tom Shippey points out in *Tolkien: Author of the Century*, "It appears that people have to be educated *out* of a taste for Tolkien rather than into it . . . Tolkien would have replied that he was satisfying a taste—the taste for fairy-tale—which is natural to us, which goes back as far as we have written records of any sort, to the Old Testament and Homer's *Odyssey*, and which is found in all human societies. If our arbiters of taste insist that this taste should be suppressed, then it is they who are flying from reality."

Vladimir Nabokov might agree. Before reading Ilan Stavans's *Quixote: The Novel and the World*, I would not have imagined citing Tolkien (escapist fantasy) and Nabokov (literary realism) in paired paragraphs. But Stavans quotes Nabokov as saying, "*Don Quixote* is a fairy tale, so is *Bleak House*, so is *Dead Souls. Madame Bovary* and *Anna Karenin* are supreme fairy tales. But without these fairy tales the world would not be real." Comments Stavans (and I agree), "I like Nabokov's last point. Despite his aversion to *El Quijote*, he is sure the world would 'not be real' without it because in the end, fairy tales such as the one Cervantes gave us show that life isn't what the eye can see but what our imagination makes with the raw material that surrounds us."

Booksellers file Nabokov under literature, Tolkien under fantasy. Both of those genres are new—quite new, compared to the *Odyssey* or the Old Testament. *Literature* did not replace *poetry* as the umbrella term for creative writing until the late eighteenth century. Realism was not favored until 1750—sixty-three years after Newton defined gravity in the *Principia*—when the lexicographer Samuel Johnson noted that "the works of fiction, with which the present generation seems most particularly delighted, are such as exhibit life in its true state, diversified only by accidents that daily happen in the world, and influenced by passions and qualities which are really to be found in conversing with mankind."

The "fairy way of writing," in the poet John Dryden's phrase, had been the norm before 1750. Find me a story from the Western world before the Reformation began in 1517 that makes no reference to the supernatural—including saints, angels, devils, and divine miracles. I can't think of one. To the Protestant reformers, these Catholic "superstitions" were as insubstantial as fairies. To Shakespeare, the Reformation was a gift: He added fairies to *A Midsummer Night's Dream* in 1595, and witches to *Macbeth* in 1606, without concern the Church would complain about mixing pagan magic with Christian faith. But there were deeper effects. The Protestants destroyed "an entire structure of belief that underlay both Catholic and pagan magic: the belief that words could 'work upon the world,'" notes literary critic Kevin Pask. "Language began to lose its incantatory power: the Eucharist's 'hoc est corpus meum' became mere 'hocus pocus.'"

One theater critic in 1698 thought things had gone too far. Dryden's *King Arthur* was lumping together all too much, complained Jeremy Collier. "Why are truth and fiction, heathenism and Christianity, the most serious and the most trifling things blended together, and thrown into one form of diversion? Why is all this done unless it be to ridicule the whole, and make one as incredible as the other?"

"It is difficult for a modern reader to take Collier's attack very seriously," Pask notes. Yet critics of fantasy still sidestep questions of religious belief. As I've asked before: If Icelanders are crazy to talk to elves, are Christians likewise crazy to talk to God? In "On Fairy-stories" Tolkien, a devout Catholic, wrote, "The Gospels contain a fairy-story, or a story of a larger kind which embraces all the essence of fairy-stories." Reprinting the essay in 2014, Tolkien's editors felt it necessary to point out that "In calling the Gospels of the New Testament, the story of Christ, the most successful fairy-story because it is the one that has been accepted as true Tolkien is not making light of the Gospels, but revealing the underlying gravity and essential truth of fairy-stories." The questions no one will answer are, once again: What immaterial beings are we allowed to believe in, and who is allowed to do the believing?

"The fairy way of writing" is the earliest attempt to define the fantasy genre. Readers with "cold fancies," wrote Joseph Addison in 1712, "object to this kind of poetry that it has not probability enough to affect the imagination. But to this it may be answered that we are sure in general there are many intellectual beings in the world besides ourselves." (If Addison were Icelandic, I'd think he was referring to elves.)

Edmund Burke, who defined mountains as sublime, had a very cold fancy. Writing in 1757, he found the fairy way of writing appropriate only to "unpolished" and "uncultivated" people. Homer, in writing about the one-eyed Cyclops, Burke said, was demonstrating his "weak" mind. The same influential book that cast a magic spell on mountains cast a curse on tales of elves and dragons. Well into the twentieth century, fantasy was considered suitable reading matter only for those with similarly weak minds: women, children, and the lower classes. Real men read realistic fiction, if they read fiction at all.

C. S. Lewis suffered from Burke's disdain in 1952. Snipped the lauded author of *The Chronicles of Narnia*, "Now the modern critical world uses 'adult' as a term of approval." Such critics, he charged, "cannot be adult themselves. To be concerned about being grown up, to admire the grown up because it is grown up, to blush at the suspicion of being childish; these things are the marks of childhood and adolescence . . . When I became a man I put away childish things, including the fear of childishness and the desire to be very grown up." If losing something you loved as a child was a virtue, he mocked, "Why should not *senile* be equally a term of approval? Why are we not to be congratulated on losing our teeth and hair?"

Lewis would be pleased to learn that his friend Tolkien has brought about the end of Burkean literature. Writes Pask, "Tolkien's vast readership suggests that fantasy might outlive or transform the increasingly brittle literary system organized around the novel, realist or experimental." Since the publication of *The Lord of the Rings* in 1954–1955, "literature" has diminished and gone into—not the West, like Tolkien's elf queen Galadriel—but "the academy," notes Pask. It no longer resides at the heart of culture. "What's left outside the academy is dominated by 'genre' fiction, including fantasy. Tolkien has thrived."

Macfarlane, in *Mountains of the Mind*, admires not only Burke, for his concept of the sublime, but Tolkien, too. He even manages to combine them in a paragraph about Edmund Mallory and Mount Everest: "He doesn't want to see Everest 'sharply defined,' he wants it to retain its mystery, to remain a conspiracy of imagination and geology, a half-imagined, half-real hill. This is the Sublime at work inside Mallory, stimulating his appetite for intimation, for haze, for mystery, convincing him that what is half-seen is seen more intensely. Mallory is attracted by what J. R. R. Tolkien would later call glamour—'that shimmer of suggestion that never becomes clear sight, but always hints at something deeper further on.'"

Tolkien himself laid out his ideas most clearly in "On Fairy-stories." Tolkien had been asked to give a speech to commemorate the work of Andrew Lang, famous for his twelve colored fairy books, beginning with *The Blue Fairy Book* in 1889 and ending with *The Lilac Fairy Book* in 1910. Tolkien was a professor of medieval literature at Oxford, not an expert on fairy tales. He had published his own fairy tale, *The Hobbit*, and was at work on *The Lord of the Rings*, but it was not going well: He was a hundred pages in, the hobbits had reached the inn called The Prancing Pony, and Tolkien "had no more notion than they had of what had become of Gandalf"—their wizard guide—"or who Strider was"—the king in hiding who would claim his throne by the book's end—and, he wrote, "I had begun to despair of surviving to find out."

"On Fairy-stories" helped him find his way through Middle-earth. Speaking in 1939 to an audience of folklorists, Tolkien sounded unsure of himself. When he revised the lecture for publication in 1965, write his editors, Tolkien was "a different man . . . He was now the author of one of the most popular pieces of fiction in the English-speaking world." His thoughts on art, however, had not changed. He took exception to Lang saying his colored fairy books represented "the young age of man true to his early loves, and have his unblunted edge of belief, a fresh appetite for marvels." Commented Tolkien, "I suspect that *belief* and *appetite for marvels* are here regarded as identical or as closely related. They are radically different." When talking about fairy stories, Tolkien continued, you cannot use "*belief* in its ordinary sense: belief that a thing exists or can happen." Nor is *the willing suspension of disbelief,* a phrase coined by Samuel Taylor Coleridge in 1817, "a good description of what happens" when we read or hear a fairy story. "What really happens," said Tolkien, "is that the story-maker . . . makes a Secondary World which your mind can enter." You believe it "while you are, as it were, inside. The moment disbelief arises, the spell is broken; the magic, or rather art, has failed."

The ability to create—and believe in—such stories is what makes us human. "To ask what is the origin of stories," said Tolkien, "is to ask what is the origin of language and of the mind." That a story contains images "of things not in the primary world (if that indeed is possible) is a virtue not a vice," Tolkien continued. Fantasy is not "a lower but a higher form of Art"; it is "the most nearly pure form, and so (when achieved) the most potent."

Fantasy has, above all, the advantage of "arresting strangeness." The wonders of this world fade when "we say we know them," Tolkien wrote. They become "like the things which once attracted us by their glitter, or their colour, or their shape, and we laid hands on them, and then locked them in our hoard, acquired them, and acquiring ceased to look at them."

Fantasy allows us to see the world's wonders again, to "look at green again, and be startled anew (but not blinded) by blue," Tolkien wrote. It lets us "clean our windows; so that the things seen clearly may be freed from the drab blur of triteness or familiarity—from possessiveness."

Seeing Is Believing

The winter of 1168 was the Winter of Marvels, says the otherwise prosaic *Saga of Gudmund Arason the Priest*, "for many wondrous things occurred. That winter, two suns were seen in the sky at once. A host of elves and other marvelous people rode together through Skagafjord; they were seen by Ari Bjarnarson. At the farm of Hegranes, a pig jumped out of the pigsty one night, burst through the door of the house, and jumped into one of the beds. A woman and child were sleeping there, and the pig attacked the child and bit it to death, then ran out again back to the sty, leaving the dead child behind."

This saga was written soon after the death of its subject, the Icelandic priest and bishop Gudmund the Good, in 1237. It was scavenged by another author, who wove bits and pieces of it into the long, historical *Sturlunga Saga*, which details the feuds leading to Iceland's loss of independence in 1262. Modern scholars dissected

Sturlunga Saga to reconstruct the tale of Gudmund's youth. Why all of them preserved this account of the Winter of Marvels, with its two suns, host of elves, and infant-eating pig, is beyond me. Nothing more about elves appears.

Iceland's medieval bishops' sagas are not generally marvelous, but miraculous—and most of their miracles run to the ordinary. Bishop Gudmund, for instance, called up a sailing wind, calmed a flood, and saw to it that springs never ran dry. True, there was that time he was blessing a bird cliff—a sheer rockface down which brave foragers dangled on horsehair ropes to collect seabirds' eggs—when a voice rose out of the rocks: "Even the wicked need some place to live." The bishop passed over that spot in silence.

After 1550, the bishops of Iceland were Lutheran. Late in the century, Bishop Oddur Einarsson wrote a geographical treatise on his home island and included a description of its elves. They "live in the hills close to men," he wrote, and are not dangerous unless harmed. They are "endowed with bodies of incredible subtlety, since they are even thought to enter into mountains and hills. They are invisible to us unless they wish to appear . . . yet the properties of certain men's eyes are such that the presence of no spirit can ever escape their sight."

The idea that some people can see elves while most of us cannot has a long history in Iceland. When Ragnhildur Jonsdottir wrote to the mayor on behalf of the elves of Galgahraun in 2013, she called herself *sjáandi*, a seer; she did not have to define the term. But what are these "properties" that allow seers like Ragnhildur to see elves? No one knows. Then again, seeing itself remains somewhat of a mystery.

"Seeing is something you do," geologist Mott Greene reminds us in *Natural Knowledge in Preclassical Antiquity*, "not something that happens to you."

It's not true that we cast an eye or lay an eye or fasten an eye upon someone; nor can we catch sight of them. Greene does not mean that kind of doing. No one truly has a piercing gaze or, despite the Renaissance poet Andrew Marvell's claims, a "sparkling glance that shoots desire." These metaphors are holdovers from a time when people thought light issued from the eye, not the other way around.

Alcmaeon of Croton came up with this extramission theory in 450 BCE after being hit on the head and seeing stars. "The eye obviously has fire within it," he concluded, "for when one is struck this fire flashes out." This fire, Plato explained, flows from the eyes and alights on a target, allowing us to see it. Euclid stated the concept mathematically: "Rectilinear rays proceeding from the eye diverge infinitely; those things are seen upon which the visual rays fall and those things are not seen upon which the visual rays do not fall." Ptolemy quibbled that the light rays issuing from the eye formed a cone.

Equally famous Greeks—Democritus, Epicurus, Lucretius, and Aristotle—favored various intromission theories: Something came into the eye to trigger sight. Lucretius, in "On the Nature of Things," described that something as a "simulacrum" and compared it to the shed skin of a snake. "Particles are continually streaming off from the surface of bodies," explained Epicurus.

Around the year 1040, a Muslim scientist in Egypt, Ibn al-Haythem (known in the West as Alhazen), expanded upon the

Greeks' ideas of eyesight. His *Book of Optics* proved the intromission theory true: Something (though not snakeskin) did come into the eye and trigger sight. Translated into Latin at the beginning of the thirteenth century, Alhazen's *Optics* led to Johannes Kepler's 1611 theory of the retinal image, and thus to the modern science of vision.

Yet extramission lingers: "Witches may kill by their looks," claimed George Mackenzie in *Laws and Customs of Scotland* in 1674. A 1962 survey of 379 new mothers in a Beirut hospital found that 81 percent, whether Christian or Muslim, believed "the 'evil eye' affected their infant's health," psychologist Charles Gross reports, while "most people believe they can feel someone staring at them." (Count me among most people.)

It's curious, as sophisticated and scientific as we are these days, that we still can't fathom our own senses. Consider, as anthropologist Tim Ingold does, how we imagine our heads. "The ears are imagined as holes that let the sound in," he writes, "whereas the eyes are likened to screens that let no light through. Inside the head, then, it is noisy but dark. As sound penetrates the inner sanctum of being, mingling with the soul, it merges with hearing. But light is shut out. It is left to vision to reconstruct, on the inside, a picture of what the world 'out there' might be like."

Ingold seems to be saying we should let the sunshine in. Neuroscientist Chris Frith might reply that we need to rethink our ears. "The brain creates the world," he writes in *Making Up the Mind*. "From the very limited and imperfect signals provided by our senses," from our experiences and our expectations, from what we've been taught and what we've read, the brain creates "a prediction of what ought to be out there in the world," a prediction "constantly tested by action." Experiments with brain scanners back him up. "You could say that our perceptions are fantasies that coincide with reality. Furthermore, if no sensory signals are available, then our brain fills in the missing information." Concludes Frith, "The surprise is that our brain ever gets things right."

How do we see? At the back of each eyeball is the retina, a layer of light-sensitive cells. At the center of each retina is a cluster of closely packed, color-sensitive cones. Surrounding the cones are the rods; these cells are spaced farther apart and detect only light and shadow. Thus, says Frith, "the edge of our view of the world is blurred and has no color." The world doesn't seem blurred or colorless because we shift our eyes constantly, bringing each inch of the scene occasionally into our direct line of sight; our brain makes this patchwork make sense. This making sense is what Greene meant when he said "seeing is something you do." This making sense is an active process. "But even when we think we have looked at everything in the scene," warns Frith, "we are still deluding ourselves."

In 2017, psychologist Miguel Eckstein and his colleagues created a series of computer images of common scenes—a bathroom, a city street—and flashed them for twenty seconds on a screen. Find the toothbrush, they asked viewers; find the parking meter. In some pictures, the toothbrush was on the floor, and in some it was on the sink—but four times its usual size, and was thus rendered invisible to many viewers. A parking meter the size of a phone pole? Likewise invisible. Scale, the researchers learned, matters. Sweeping a scene, our brains rapidly discount well-known objects that are the wrong size. "This strategy allows humans to reduce false positives when making fast decisions." Once the viewer realizes size doesn't matter, though, that previously invisible huge toothbrush snaps into focus—which shows the problem is not our eyes but our expectations. We see what we have been taught to see and fail to see what doesn't fit.

The concept of change blindness, discovered in 1997, reveals more about seeing—and not-seeing. Take two photos of an intricate scene; the second has something missing. In Frith's version, it's the engine of the plane. He sits you down in front of a screen and shows you the two photos repeatedly—"but critically with a uniform gray screen in between." You see no difference until he draws your attention to the missing engine—there, that bright white cylinder right in the center. "You rapidly perceive the gist of the scene," he notes: It's a plane on a runway. "But you do not actually have all the details in your mind." You are blind to the change. "In real life," Frith writes, "our peripheral vision, though blurred, is very sensitive to change." It's the uniform gray screen in between the two images in Frith's test that confuses us. From intricate photo to flat gray is a huge change. When the what's-wrong-with-this-picture example comes up, your eye doesn't know where to look.

Ordinarily, your sight would zoom in on the change—on what's new. Novelty, as Diane Ackerman writes in *An Alchemy of Mind*, "is riveting . . . Novelty ignites the senses. Learn something new (or someone new) and you discover an avalanche of details. But soon the brain switches to a kind of shorthand. Once the brain perceives something, it's primed to recognize it faster the next time, and even faster after that, until it needn't look at it carefully again." It's then, when it's become trite and known, that, as J. R. R. Tolkien says, we need to clean our windows. Or as Ackerman puts it: Pay attention. "We can't enchant the world, which makes its own magic; but we can enchant ourselves by paying deep attention," she says. "What we pay attention to helps define us."

Consider the slug, she says:

> Any novelty can distract an animal from whatever it's doing. Chewing and digesting stop. Instinctively it turns toward the culprit and becomes rigidly aware. It loses sight of everything else for about half a second in what's known as an attention blink. Even slugs do it. After a garden talk the other evening in which I confessed to liking many things about slugs (for example, their yen to mate at the end of slime gallows), a man shared a curious slug story of his own with me. He'd been doing construction work when a tractor overturned, trapping him under it. While he waited for help, he noticed a small movement nearby and, turning his head, saw a slug standing up like a tiny giraffe, raptly watching him.

The novel, the changed, the arrestingly strange—these are the keys not only to seeing, but to remembering. They are the tools the mythmakers used to teach us what not to forget. "What is old tends to be viewed as rather dull," write Elizabeth and Paul Barber in *When They Severed Earth from Sky*. "Have you noticed (as Thomas Mann did in *The Magic Mountain*) how much longer it seems to take to drive to a place you've never been than it does to get home later? All your senses are furiously busy registering all that new data on the outbound; it's much duller on the way home. So a 'good' storyteller will pepper a narrative with the new and vivid."

The myths that have made it down to us, from ancient cultures all over the world, were told by good storytellers. They are not only vivid, they are "preposterous," they are "gibberish," they are fun. Some encode information that has lasted ten thousand years—such as how to tell when the magic mountain will erupt, for instance. Why do we tend to read such myths as fiction, not science? Because "humanists typically don't study sciences," the Barbers say, "and so don't recognize the data."

How can scientific data be passed down, uncorrupted, for ten thousand years? Often it can't. "The conditions must be right for this to happen," the Barbers agree. The information must be vital. It must refer to something seen, such as the magic mountain on the horizon. And it must "be encoded in a highly memorable way." The "sillier and funnier" the story, the Barbers assert, the more memorable it will prove to be.

The vividness can mask the data. "Analogy pervades our thinking," note the Barbers. "'What was it like?' we ask." And over time the "like" gets lost. "Red liquid trails down a mountain 'like red hair,' 'like snaky locks,' 'like blood'; presently it *is* the red hair or snaky locks or blood of a giant." And when you see the mountain from farther away, as a dark head on the horizon with a glowing red spot? "Since ancient Mediterranean peoples thought vision occurred by light coming *out* of the eye, rather than into it, the volcano may be described as having a great eye."

Remember when Edmund Burke, who thought mountains sublime, accused Homer, writing about the Cyclops, of having a weak mind? Burke was blind to Homer's meaning. "When Odysseus resents the inhospitableness of a giant with one great eye, who eats some of Odysseus's men and then hurls huge rocks at him as he tries to escape," the Barbers write, "we might at least *suspect* that we are hearing an old story of a volcano."

Eyesight doesn't answer the question *What is this?* but instead *What is this like?* Moshe Bar of the Center for Biomedical Imaging at Harvard Medical School writes, "Our perception of the environment relies on memory as much as it does on incoming information." Seeing proceeds from analogy to associations to predictions, he says, which means that "at a given moment, we integrate information from multiple points in time. We are rarely in the 'now,' but rather combine past and present in anticipation of the future."

It matters who *we* are. In *The Geography of Thought*, psychologist Richard Nisbett tells how a student from China upended Nisbet's understanding of the mind. "The difference between you and me," said the student, "is that I think the world is a circle, and you think it's a line." Writes Nisbett, "I was skeptical but intrigued . . . I believed that all human groups perceive and reason in the same way," regardless of their culture or upbringing. He decided to investigate. After several years spent reading philosophy (Aristotle, Confucius) and running laboratory tests, Nisbet had to admit that his student was right. Culture mattered. "Cognitive scientists were wrong," he concluded. "Human cognition is not everywhere the same."

For thousands of years people in the West have thought differently from people in the East. They have seen—and responded to—a different world. Westerners, Nisbet found, slot objects into categories and find rules; their problem-solving relies on formal logic. Easterners see objects in context. Given a panda, a monkey, and a banana and asked *Which two go together?*, a Westerner will pair the panda and monkey (both animals), while an Easterner will pair the monkey with its food, the banana. Shown an animated video of an ocean scene, both the Westerner and the Easterner will remember the biggest fish. But only the Easterner will also recall the color of the water.

The Easterner's world is "more complex," Nisbet argues: For them, "understanding events always requires consideration of a host of factors that operate in relation to one another in no simple, deterministic way." They do not rely on formal logic. "In fact, the person who is too concerned with logic may be considered immature."

For thousands of years before the Protestant Reformation, people in the West thought more like people in the East. They saw a more complex world than most Westerners do today.

Take dragons. Examining the "practical uses" of dragon-slaying in Old Icelandic literature, folklorist Armann Jakobsson finds "the legend is not about something else; it is about us." Dragons answer the question *What is fear like?* The dragon, he concludes, "may be said to represent, even embody, terror." As soon as the hero overcomes his fear of it, the creature is destroyed. The hero's courage "is something that everyone in the audience can relate to," Armann notes. We have all known fear; we have all had to "rely on bravery," though our "relationship with it varied quite a bit."

Tim Ingold sees the same connection between dragons and fear. He retells a story from the sixth-century *Life of St. Benedict of Nursia* of a restless monk, cramped by his safe cloister, who wanted to see the world. "Then go," said St. Benedict. The monk gathered his bundle and strode through the gates to find a dragon blocking the road. Terrified, he cried out for help. His brother monks led him, trembling, back to safety, and "from that day on he never again went astray," the story goes. What is fear *like*? The dragon, Ingold writes, "was the palpable incarnation of what it meant to 'know' fear." The other monks saw no monster, only their brother's fear of facing the future alone. "The dragon existed as fear exists, not as an exterior threat but as an affliction instilled at the core of the sufferer's very being. As such, it was as real as his facial expression and the urgency in his voice."

What is reality? The "father of empiricism," philosopher Francis Bacon, made a fateful mistake, Ingold thinks, when he concluded the mind was a cracked mirror deformed by flaws, and "God forbid," as Bacon said, "that we should give out a dream of our imagination for a pattern of the world." Since 1620, writes Ingold, scientists "have colluded in the division between what Bacon called the 'world itself,' the reality of nature that can be discovered only through systematic scientific investigation, and the various imaginary worlds that people in different times and places have conjured up and which—in their ignorance of science and its methods—they have taken for reality."

The consequences of collusion are severe. With imagination "cut adrift," Ingold writes, "life itself appears diminished." It "no longer gives cause for wonder or astonishment." In school we are taught "to distrust the sensuous, to prize intellect over intuition, and to regard the imagination as an escape from real life rather than its impulse." Since 1620, writes Ingold, "to know is no longer to join *with* the world in performance but to be informed *by* what is already set down there."

The world is a closed book. In such a world, one offering only data, not advice, dragons—or elves—cannot exist. "Dragons, along with other beings that rear up or make their presence felt along the ways of the world, can be told but they cannot be categorized," Ingold says.

Yet, like fear, that does not make dragons—or elves—any less real.

Susan Greenwood, the anthropologist and practicing witch, sees not dragons or elves but spirits. "Seeing spirits as real can be disorientating for Westerners versed in scientific rationalism," she writes, "and the experience is often denied."

Scientists coined the term *animism* in the early twentieth century to describe the inspirited world of earlier cultures. Animists saw sickness and death, dreams and visions, as the work of spirits. They saw spirits in their fellow creatures, too, and even in inanimate objects, such as mountains and rocks. As human thought "evolved" over time, according to scientists in the early 1900s, these spirits became gods and, in the modern mind, were finally replaced by rational scientific explanations. "This evolutionary view is now outmoded," Greenwood writes. Animists are not primitive, childlike, or undeveloped thinkers. They simply see—and respond to—the world in a different way. How can modern anthropologists "develop our understanding of spirit without losing our scientific objectivity?" Greenwood asks. Her answer: "We have to step outside of the Western view of reality." We have to disavow Rene Descartes, who, in the seventeenth century separated "the thinking mind, which had a soul, from mechanistic, soulless matter" and left the world "despirited." We have to learn anew how to see.

Archaeologists Henri and Henriette Frankfort show us how. Once the world was not an It, they write in *The Intellectual Adventure of Ancient Man*, but a Thou. The difference is profound. You identify an It; you experience a Thou. You can relate an It to others like it; you can lump it into a species, pigeonhole it, apply universal laws to it. But Thou is unique. "'Thou' has the unprecedented, unparalleled, and unpredictable character of an individual, a presence known only in so far as it reveals itself. 'Thou,' moreover, is not merely contemplated or understood but is experienced emotionally." The world is "neither inanimate nor empty but redundant with life; and life has individuality." Each beast you meet, each plant you see, is as unique as each person—and so is every phenomenon: "the thunderclap, the sudden shadow, the eerie and unknown clearing in the wood, the stone" you stumble over.

Even the magic mountain on the horizon, adds geologist Mott Greene, has individuality. "Volcanoes are not like gas molecules—countably infinite in number and best treated by statistical aggregates and predictions. There are particular volcanoes." Each has a name. Each has a signature "expressed in the pattern and frequency of its eruptions, the kind of material it throws out, and even the chemical composition of that material." Knowing his volcanoes, treating each as an individual, has allowed Greene, like the Barbers, to find the science hiding in ancient myths.

Hesiod's *Theogony* is, he admits, rather boring. Most of it reads like the begats in the Bible. But "as the first document of Greek mythology, it is the beginning of the beginning of Western civilization." It is "an account of how order came to the cosmos," say other scholars, or "an account of the origins of political society and the ordered succession of kingship."

They are missing the point. The *Theogony* preserves a scientific report. It is an exact description of a natural phenomenon. "The principal elements are things felt—shaking and trembling, intense heat," notes Greene, "and things heard—terrible echoes, groans, thunderous cries, and a final deafening uproar. The visual aspect is limited to lightning, the immense flame shooting into the air, the boiling of the sea, and the arrival of windblown dust. The image of gigantic beings in contest"—the god Zeus fighting the giant Titans—"is the poet's inference from what he can hear, feel, and see of the effects of the conflict on the world around him."

What is it like? A volcanic eruption. "Nothing else happens on earth that could be described in this way," writes Greene. The poem gives enough detail that Greene, a geologist, can infer "the kind of eruption and the kind of volcano being described." Knowing roughly when and where "leaves but a single plausible candidate—the volcano at Thera (Santorini)." The scenic island we now see in the Aegean, sitting between Athens and Crete, is but a sliver of the circular rim of a volcanic caldera: the remains of an island that exploded in 1625 BCE. Scholars believe this eruption destroyed Minoan Crete. It provided the pillar of smoke and fire that guided the Jews out of Egypt and the tsunami that parted the Red Sea. It may be the original Atlantis. It was so impressive, so important, so visibly present in the Greek world—and the myths it engendered so vivid and fun—that its story survived nearly a millennium to make it into Hesiod's poem.

How, over the next two millennia, did we lose the poem's meaning? "It is so long since we came indoors and left the study of nature to specialists who speak to each other in languages only they understand," Greene says, "that we sometimes forget that the Greeks lived outdoors, in the natural world." And their natural world, like the world of modern-day Icelanders who see elf homes and churches in striking formations of lava rock, was an inspirited world. Its volcanoes were alive.

View from Hellnar.

Berserkjahraun lava field.

ABOVE: *On the path through Berserkjahraun.*
BELOW: *On the path to Little Lava.*

On the new Eldborg road.

View from the top of Eldborg. Photo by Charles Fergus.

ABOVE: *Helgafell, the Holy Mountain.*
BELOW: *The farm at Helgafell.*

ABOVE: *In the West Fjords.*
BELOW: *Bird mounds at Helgafell.*

On the beach at Helgafell.

ABOVE: *Lamb's grass at Helgafell.*
BELOW: *On a Snaefellsnes beach.*

On the path through Berserkjahraun.

Landscape at Hallkellsstadahlid.

The Volcano Show

I n 2010, I met a volcano. *What was it like?* Not a cyclops or a Titan; the Greek classics did not shape my worldview.

As art critic John Berger writes in *Ways of Seeing*, "The way we see things is affected by what we know or what we believe."

My volcano was a dragon. Not the fear-dragon of St. Benedict. To me it was the dragon J. R. R. Tolkien described when he "desired dragons with a profound desire," adding, "Of course, I in my timid body did not wish to have them in the neighborhood . . . But the world that contained even the imagination of them was richer and more beautiful, at whatever cost of peril." Tolkien's dragon—and mine—was sublime.

My volcano-dragon was clearly an individual—not an It. But not having yet read the Frankforts, I didn't address this dragon as Thou. I called it by name: Eyjafjallajokull, a non sequitur, since the word literally means "glacier on the mountains near the islands."

In Iceland, fire often resides under ice. The island has thirty active volcanic systems. It sits above a mantle plume, a never-ending gusher of magma, and straddles two tectonic plates, the North American and the Eurasian, which are drifting apart by eight-tenths of an inch a year. That's half as fast as your fingernails grow, but still, it's measurable. Since the Icelandic parliament was established in the year 930 in the rift valley of Thingvellir—where Snorri Godi, the wily chieftain of Helgafell, once stood while Christianity was being debated and quipped, "What were the gods angry about when they burned the place we're standing on now?"— the valley has widened by seventy-two feet. Ten percent of Iceland's landscape is lava.

I've stood on the Law Rock in Snorri's stead and studied the sheer bleak brilliance of the rift valley wall. I've climbed the crater Eldborg and lived in its lava field for a summer. I've collected volcanic ash and pumice, used sea-rounded basalt blocks as bookends. Once I walked on five-month-old ash that had landed on snow, insulating it so that even by July the snow hadn't melted. It was like walking on a waterbed.

But until 2010, I'd not seen a volcano erupt.

Around midnight on March 21, the day after the equinox, a section of mountaintop between two glaciers unzipped on Iceland's south coast. Lava oozed out. It overflowed a famous hiking trail and plummeted down a cliff toward a favorite campsite. The eruption was so luxuriously slow and contained that the press dubbed it a "tourist eruption." And the tourists came. When I arrived, ten days later, over the long Easter weekend, I joined fifteen thousand people—mostly Icelanders—who hiked, rode snowmobiles or jeeps, or took helicopters and small planes to witness the birth of a new hill. That's about 5 percent of Iceland's total population—the same percentage that say they've seen an elf.

"We only see what we look at," writes Berger in *Ways of Seeing*. "To look is an act of choice."

My friend Thordur Gretarsson and I drove as close as we could in his sedan. From there the volcano was a tiny black bulge on the horizon—you wouldn't notice it if not for the plume of smoke, like smoke from a chimney. Even a volcano is very small in Iceland's vast landscape.

The wind was icy. Bundled up in goose down, I barely stayed warm. My hand grew too numb to take notes. We stayed until dark, when the scene changed. *What is it like?* The flame was like a beacon, flaring and fading; the flares were like pulsing strobe lights set on slow. Sometimes a coil of steam jetted up pink in the glow. I walked across a stony field and up the berm onto a farm road that skirted the marsh, and down it toward a farmhouse, from where I could just barely make out lava pouring over the mountainside in a hot-pink curve. In my notebook I wrote: "Need to get closer!" We headed home, stopping for hot dogs at half-past midnight, and laughed ourselves silly when I misread a sign. We were punch-drunk on beauty.

Two days later, the lava still oozing, I took a high-wheeled bus to the cliff-bottom campsite: Thordur had booked me a bed in a hut and outfitted me with a sleeping bag and hiking poles—but it was the wrong hut. The other twelve tourists were headed to Basar, right beneath the volcano. My hut, Langidalur, was across the river. The bus driver said I'd have to wade. I asked a nice man who had shared his thermos of tea—had I misunderstood him? "Oh no, he was just kidding. Ask him again. Sit up front with him. He's a nice guy. Nothing to be afraid of." Straight across the braided river we drove, bucking up over boulders bigger than basketballs, our bus rocking wildly back and forth.

I checked in with the ranger. "Climb up the hill and you'll see the eruption," she said. She handed me a flashlight.

There was no one else on the path. The way up was made easy with steps and erosion barriers. I went about halfway, found a spot out of the wind, and watched the light show as it got dark. It was sublime. Like staring into a giant's fireplace—a god's forge, a dragon's maw—but a good ways off, with a valley in between us. I had it all to myself. Once, I gasped and said *Wow!* out loud and a ptarmigan roosting in a nearby copse croaked—*Krak!*—and flew off. The lava rose and fell and rose and fell and rose and fell and threw out sparks like a sparkler. I wrote in my notebook: "So I'm sitting alone on a mountain in Iceland, just seeing lights of cars, hikers, planes, and a glorious volcano throwing lava high into the air. Surreal."

But still not close enough.

Two days later I met Thordur and three other tourists in an enormous jeep. We drove for two hours over a glacier—part of the time driving blind in a blizzard, our driver guided by GPS. We reached the eruption site and parked in a long line of jeeps, half a mile away, as directed by the search-and-rescue squad, and joined the hundreds of people watching that night's volcano show.

We saw two black cauldron-shaped craters, each with gray-blue arms of just-born rock reaching out over the snow. The craters sighed and snored like a dragon's nostrils, *whoosh-shoosh, whoosh-shoosh, whoosh-shoosh*, *whoosh-shoosh*, and snorted red-orange fountains of flame. Stars fell down the sides of the new-made hills. Lava drops bounced and rolled like gold coins. Black ash peppered the snow. At the tips of the dragon's cooling limbs, the lava still moved, bulging and breaking, tinkling like broken glass, but more rhythmic and musical. As the sun set, the colors bloomed. A fat yellow tongue of living rock oozed over one crater's side. Orange eyes twinkled in the dark arms of rock. The lava fountains turned hot pink. I filled my camera's memory card. I filled my mind until my visual sense was stupefied. By the time we rolled off the glacier, well after midnight, I was stunned. "Wake up!" Thordur nudged me. "Northern Lights!" I cracked open an eye. Swirls of green light danced over the volcano. "Beautiful," I murmured, and fell asleep.

Eyjafjallajokull was the first eruption I attended in person, but my love affair with lava dates back to my first trip to Iceland in 1986, when I went to the Red Rock Cinema, marked by a large rock, painted red, on a side street in the old part of Reykjavik, to watch *The Volcano Show*. There I met the filmmaker Vilhjalmur Knudsen, who, like the family at Helgafell, instantly made me his friend.

Two years before, on September 4, Villi recounted while narrating his film, he picked up his studio phone and heard that a new crater near Lake Myvatn had opened in Iceland's north. He ticked the gear off the Volcano Panic List posted on his wall and drove to the Reykjavik airport, where a plane waited. Within hours he was stalking a horseshoe-shaped gash in an old lava field east of the lake, from which great plum- and pumpkin-colored balls were exploding, while pink magma oozed over the black barrows of earlier eruptions.

Watching the film, I felt I'd been jarred awake.

"It was the most beautiful crater I've ever seen," he recalled, screening the film for me again in 1990, when I interviewed him for *News from Iceland*. Villi is a big man, then red-haired and florid, with a hunched, bearish stance. His wide, round face, under a domed forehead, reveals very little emotion; he narrated the action of his films in English in a soft, strangely uninflected monotone. "I was three hundred meters away—even that didn't seem too safe, the stream was acting crazy. But then, as I was filming, I saw someone up there, even closer. It was Maurice Krafft, the French geologist and filmmaker. I was so very mad then. Because that meant I had to go up there, too. We ended up only five meters away."

On June 3, 1991, Krafft and his wife, Katia, were killed while filming at Mount Unzen in Japan. A pyroclastic flow—a fiery whirlwind—burst from the volcano and enveloped them.

The Volcano Show, screened at the Red Rock Cinema, began in 1947, when Mount Hekla in southern Iceland exploded. The mountain spewed ash twenty-eight thousand feet in the air, some of it sprinkling down as far away as Russia. Over thirteen months of activity, it added forty-six feet of lava to its summit. Osvaldur Knudsen, Villi's father and a professional house painter, filmed the eruption. Over the next few years he became more and more of a filmmaker and less and less of a house painter, until in 1954 he evicted the paint cans from their storage area behind his new house in Reykjavik and converted the old farm buildings on the property into a studio and screening room.

Osvaldur made films of nature—not exclusively of volcanoes— and country ways. "He had a very good sense of the feeling of a documentary," Villi told me. "He got on film a very important time in Icelandic history, when Iceland was changing from the old ways to the new."

Villi screened the classic *Country between the Sands* for me: Men to their knees in a water meadow, cutting hay with hand sickles. Women in long skirts on the banks, raking the cut hay to dry it. A long train of ponies, each animal dwarfed by a hay bundle, fetching it home to the farm. This was in 1960, the year after I was born, three years after Russia launched the first satellite, Sputnik—and Iceland was still in the Middle Ages.

Villi's parents separated in 1950, when he was five. An only child, he grew up in Copenhagen, where his mother was studying art. She remarried, to an artist Villi disliked, so on a whim one summer, while visiting his father in Iceland, he decided to stay. He was twelve years old.

He soon missed Copenhagen. There he had been at the top of his class; here he couldn't speak the language. One day, bored, he picked up a camera. His father was working on a documentary about artists, and he let Villi shoot the artists' brushes. Villi made his first film—an animated one—and soon began carrying the second camera for his father's films. He filmed his first eruption at nineteen, when Surtsey rose spectacularly out of the sea southwest of Iceland's Westman Islands in 1963. The Surtsey eruption lasted for nearly two years; it was the first time anyone had filmed the birth of an island, from the first fire exploding out of the sea to the tentative visits of birds and the tender vegetation that grew up around their droppings.

The Knudsens' films of Hekla, Surtsey, and the 1973 eruption that devastated a small town on Heimaey in the Westman Islands were prized by filmmakers for their technique, as their numerous foreign awards demonstrate, and by scientists as perhaps the first films to illustrate volcanic drama. Leading Icelandic geologists, particularly Sigurdur Thorarinsson—who invented tephrochronology, used by geologists and archaeologists to date layers of soil using volcanic ash—helped write the narrations, and the films were sold to university collections worldwide.

Father and son worked together until Osvaldur's death in 1975, though not always congenially: "We argued constantly about technique," Villi told me. "He held one camera and I held another, but he always had more lenses. One time at Hekla in 1970, I needed a certain lens to make a certain shot. To get it from him was almost impossible. It took me three hours to convince him."

He got out the lens to show me. It was enormous—eighteen inches long. With it, Villi could peer deep inside the lava face and see it shatter and crumble as it advanced.

"And then, for instance, he always wanted to pan the camera from right to left." Villi continued. "I said that's crazy. So on Heimaey in 1973, he finally ended up doing one movement for himself, right to left, and one for me, left to right, and we decided when we edited the film which looked best."

Best did not mean most beautiful. At one point, Villi took the filter his father liked to use off his lens. He wanted to make the scene bluer, colder, more like the way it made him feel inside.

As Berger writes in *Ways of Seeing*, "It is seeing which establishes our place in the surrounding world; we explain that world with words, but words can never undo the fact that we are surrounded by it. The relation between what we see and what we know is never settled. Each evening we *see* the sun set. We *know* that the earth is turning away from it."

The year Osvaldur died, the volcano beneath Lake Myvatn erupted for the first time. The coming of television in 1966 had erased the market for private screenings of documentaries, so Villi chose to focus on *The Volcano Show*. "All kinds of things interest me," he told me, "but life is so short you have to limit yourself. I would like to live in the woods in America, for instance." I lived in the woods in America at the time and worked at Penn State University, where Villi's wife had gone to school. We both knew a volcanologist there, Barry Voight, and for this reason I was treated as family (Villi refused to let me pay) whenever I visited the Red Rock Cinema. "It is very nice there," he said about Pennsylvania. He paused, his close-set green eyes looking evasively off into space, building suspense as a grin began forming in the middle of his unruly red beard. And then he laughed, softly, like letting off a little steam. "If it weren't for those bloody volcanoes!"

"Maybe it's imagination," he told me another time, "but when you've been doing this for a long time, the volcano becomes like a person. You get a feeling you know what they're up to. Everyone feels it in Iceland—a closeness, a link with nature somehow. When you're around a volcano, you don't get scared. You don't think like that."

Before I left the city to meet Eyjafjallajokull on Easter weekend of 2010, I visited Villi again at the Red Rock Cinema. I had hoped to fly with him over the eruption, but an invitation did not come.

"It's just some more volcano shots," he said. I had not seen him in several years and was struck by how very thin he was, his jeans and flannel shirt baggy and loose. His red hair had faded mostly to gray, his characteristic monotone seemed even more world-weary. The Volcano Panic List was still on the wall, yellowed and old-fashioned in its typewriter typeface, but he wasn't rushing to catch a plane.

"It's very straightforward," he said. "I went there on Wednesday and Friday. I'm planning to add footage to the show for the summer, just a little bit. It's not a complete film, not like the film of Lake Myvatn. Myvatn is the special one. Myvatn is the real thing. At Myvatn, the magma chamber was filling and emptying..." In 1993, a fire broke out in his studio one night and destroyed the almost-finished final copy of the Myvatn film. Villi's face and hands had been badly burned, fighting the blaze, and he spent several days in the hospital.

"Eyjafjallajokull—this little splash now," he said, "is not really interesting. You cannot endlessly film fantastic lava scenes. You cannot show that for half an hour or longer." He motioned toward a photo on the wall of lush, almost erotic pink lava. "I don't like that kind of picture," he said. "I hate time lapse. I hate pretty pictures of volcanoes. It's more complicated to take pictures that are not so beautiful but are more true. At Myvatn, I could slowly build up a relationship, like with a person. Myvatn is going to be a very complicated story, and it's very complicated making complicated things simple. It's the story of a magma chamber. You know the Greek story of Odysseus, of the sirens wanting to lure him closer? I was working on this theme with the composer of the soundtrack. Unfortunately, he died."

We sat side by side in the row of red and black chairs beside the cash register. Villi looked very tired, and I told him so. He nodded. "I was hoping this eruption would not happen now," he said softly. "I'm in the middle of all kinds of things. Something happened to me three years ago. I had a stroke. I'm very happy about it. It's been very interesting. It's an endless process. The brain is a very complicated thing. I stay up often many hours in the night to sense different things."

Shocked, I encouraged him to continue.

"My taste has changed. It's getting a little back to normal now, but I don't drink beer anymore. I don't like it. I remember when it was not possible to drink beer in Iceland." I remembered that, too. In an odd quirk, prohibition was lifted for spirits and wine in 1935, but not for beer until 1989. "When I went to London to get film developed, I went straight to a pub," Villi said. "I liked to sit there just reading a newspaper. Now it's too much noise. After this happened, it took me half a year to be able to spell 'London' again! It was very strange. I guess I have a certain library in my brain, and often in my mind I look at different words, simple words you didn't even think about that are now not simple any more. It's only five or six letters, but I have to look it up in the dictionary. Or even four letters. And at the same time, when I'm reading words, I sense them differently.

"*Jæja*, I have plenty of things to do, organizing, and learning how to read and write. In a way, I am learning Icelandic again, like I did when I was twelve."

One of Villi's friends, a man of his age, Henry Hansen, had come in, and the three of us decided to walk a block up the hill to the Hotel Holt for coffee. It's an old hotel that was once very elegant, with a famous art collection on the walls. Villi spoke to a woman at the main desk, then led us into a lounge off the lobby.

"That is my mother," he gestured toward a painting on the wall over a computer desk. It was a bright and cheerful composition in blues and yellows and greens, a realistic scene of three sturdy girls handling triangular slabs of fish—*The Saltfish Ladies*, the title read in a brochure I picked up later from the hotel desk. The artist was Gunnlaugur Blondal, the painting from 1935. Two of the women wore headscarves. Villi's mother, in the middle, went bareheaded, her flame-red hair billowing out. All three looked very serious, hard at work. No smiles.

"And over there," Villi turned to the far wall, "is my grandfather." A moody painting in blues and grays of a gray-bearded man in a white shirt and vest slumped to eat from a traditional Icelandic lidded bowl, an *askur*, the size of a saucepan that he held on his lap, the spoon comically delicate in his big hand, his wide-brimmed hat covering his eyes. *An Icelandic Farmer* by Finnur Jonsson, 1922–1923.

A waitress brought in a tiny ceramic tray with three espressos and a plate of bonbons.

Villi slumped into the soft leather sofa. The espresso cup was comically small in his hand.

In *Ways of Seeing*, Berger writes that the camera, especially the movie camera, changed the way Westerners saw the world. Two-dimensional art, before then, was timeless. It turned on the idea of perspective, which "centres everything on the eye of the beholder. It is like a beam from a lighthouse—only instead of light travelling outwards, appearances travel in. The conventions called those appearances *reality*. Perspective," Berger writes, "makes the single eye the centre of the visible world." Gazing at a painting, you become God. But to the camera lens there is no center. Each image is a moment, a glimpse. "The camera showed that the notion of time passing was inseparable from the experience of the visual (except in paintings)," Berger writes. "What you saw depended on where you were when." This new language of images, he writes, conferred power: "Within it we could begin to define our experiences more precisely in areas where words are inadequate."

"Why do you like volcanoes?" I asked Villi.

He put the tiny white cup back on the tray with a click and took a couple of bonbons. "People have often asked me that question, but I can never answer it," he said. He leaned back, as if settling in for a nap. "All the different smells, the gasses. Sometimes you have to run away."

"I remember the first time I came to see *The Volcano Show*," I said. "You were showing pictures taken from the air, and you told how you had scared the pilot by accidentally turning the plane's engine off. It terrified me."

"I did not really explain it well enough. It was so noisy, and I had to record sound, so I just turned it off."

"It was not an accident?"

"No."

"The first time I saw a live volcano," his friend Henry put in, "I was sitting in the pilot's seat."

At this, Villi smiled. "That was the worst flight I ever made."

"I thought I'd be scared," Henry continued, "but I wasn't. Next, I want to go in a helicopter. If I had the money, I'd do it tomorrow. No question. My logic is, in the lifetime we have, we are not supposed to see so much of nature. We are witnessing what nature does. I must experience this with my own eyes. That's something I would cherish. I'm doing this for my inner self. I don't think I'll see anything like this again before I pass away. This will be a cherished memory for me for a long time."

Villi closed his eyes.

"Aren't you sick of volcanoes?" I said teasingly, trying to wake him up.

"Aren't you sick of life?" he mumbled back.

"The memory gives you a warm feeling," Henry continued, as if there had been no interruption, "but also a feeling you're in a danger zone. I was depressed because I didn't have a job, and this eruption at Eyjafjallajokull woke me right up. Mother Nature was playing a role in my life."

"And it's just beginning," Villi said.

Send Cash, Not Ash

T he day after I visited the dragon by jeep tour, I called on my
friend Kristin Vogfjord. At Penn State, while earning a PhD
in geophysics, she had helped me write letters to Helgafell. Now
at the Icelandic Meteorological Office, she was developing an
early-warning system for volcanic eruptions, reading shockwaves
from earthquakes like a brain scan. She had mapped the lava pool
thirteen thousand feet beneath the glacier Eyjafjallajokull: It
spread in layered bands like the trunk and branches of an enormous
tree. Throughout February and March, she showed me, a flurry
of earthquakes rattled the region—a thousand shallow quakes a
week—which she interpreted as a lava branch growing toward the
surface. Still, when the crack opened on March 21, Kristin learned
of it first from her brother; he lived in the dragon's neighborhood.

The lava branch surfaced in a patch bare of ice: ergo the tourist
eruption of lovely fire fountains. When hot lava hits ice, on the

other hand, it quick-freezes and shatters into ash: tiny shards of glass are hurled high into the sky. Sucked into a jet engine, these shards melt and cause the engine to flame out and die—which explains why an ash plume is a no-fly-zone.

Imagining the dragon at Eyjafjallajokull, I wasn't dreaming of ash. I should have been. When Kristin learned we'd parked our jeep west of the crater, up on the glacial ice, to enjoy the volcano show in the dark, she was shocked. "Didn't you look at my maps? The lava pool was directly beneath your feet."

Ten days later, with a white-out keeping tourists away, the volcano forced a tube straight up from the lava pool. It split open a new mile-long crack beneath the glacier, melting enough ice to flood the valley below. Ash blasted five to six miles high, hit the jet stream, and headed east. Airports across Europe closed, all flights were canceled. Thousands of travelers were trapped for days. The airlines logged a billion dollars in losses, the *New York Times* reported. The *New York Post* called it "Hellfire: The Volcano That Shut Down the World." CNN wondered how the eruption might "change the world."

In the neighborhood, floods and mudslides wiped out roads and bridges, water pipes and electric lines. Ash coated every surface—cars, roofs, fields, sheep's backs. Back home in the United States, out of the neighborhood, I watched internet videos of black blizzards. Of day visibly turned to night. Of farmers in gas masks corralling frantic horses and trucking them away. Of others sealing the windows of their barns, pitching their cows mounds of hay, and then—walking away, evacuated, forced to abandon their beloved animals.

No one could help the other creatures, the wild ones that are categorized—ravens, greylag geese, black-backed gulls, arctic terns—but not individually named. "The birds have no shelter. They fly into the dark cloud, flap their wings like they have lost their bearings and then fall down and die," mourned the *Iceland Review* website. It was springtime; the breeding birds were migrating back. "Our reporters saw a flock of geese fly straight into the deadly ash. Farmers have told of the desperate sound coming from the birds battling death." Describing an eruption of Mount Hekla in 1341, the Icelandic annals note: "People headed for the mountain when it spouted and it sounded to them as if a big boulder were being tossed about inside the mountain. Birds appeared to them, flying in the fire, both small and large, with various noises; people thought they were souls." At one point in 2010, Eyjafjallajokull was ejecting 750 tons of ash per second. Said a policeman, "It is unlike anything else I have seen. I have never before experienced the darkness found in the middle of the night on a sunny day."

Volcanic ash can contain toxic levels of fluorine. In 2010, the ash, luckily, did not. In 1226, it most likely did, for *Sturlunga Saga* implies the eruption that year, remarkable for its "darkness at midday," killed a hundred cows owned by the wealthy chieftain Snorri Sturluson of Reykholt—a fortune at a time when most farms owned only five to fifty cows. Snorri was also a poet and a writer of sagas. His *Edda* and *Heimskringla* preserve a great deal of ancient Icelandic poetry: nearly a thousand verses by more than sixty poets. These poems are packed with mythological allusions; to explain them, Snorri packed his *Edda* with tales of Norse gods and giants.

For if such tales were "consigned to oblivion," Snorri writes, no one would understand the old poems. A whole literature would be lost.

Much of Norse mythology had already been lost. By Snorri's day, Iceland had been Christian for two hundred years. The old stories of the gods of Asgard—one-eyed Odin, the mighty Thor—had holes, some of which Snorri imaginatively patched. He also, at times, shifted the stories' emphases to reflect more of an Icelandic than a pan-Scandinavian world. A volcanic world. The Icelandic annals for the year 1184, six years after Snorri was born, reported "darkness across the south." In 1206, "the third eruption of Mount Hekla." In 1211, "Lava came up out of the sea." In 1222, "the fourth eruption of Mount Hekla." In 1226, "Lava in the sea off Reykjanes"—the headland curving south from today's Reykjavik—and "darkness at midday." Again in 1238, and then in 1240, the year before Snorri died: "Lava off Reykjanes." Seven eruptions in one lifetime: no surprise they colored his prose.

Take the Norse creation of the world. According to a poem Snorri quotes, *The Song of the Seer*, in the beginning there was "no sand, no sea, / no sighing wave; / no earth was seen, / no sky above, / no thing but a gap"—a great, yawning emptiness. "Nowhere was green," the wise woman continues, "until Bor's sons / bore up the earth / and made great / Midgard," our Middle-earth.

Wait—something's missing, you'll say if you've read Norse mythology. *What about the giant Surt, with his flaming sword? The rivers of fire that flowed until they turned hard as slag from an iron-maker's forge, then froze like ice?* That is Snorri's version and (I argue) Snorri's invention: The ice-rime grew, layer upon layer, he writes, till it bridged the mighty, magical gap. Where the ice met sparks of flame and still-flowing lava from Surt's home in the south, it thawed and dripped. Like an icicle, it formed the first frost giant—or if you translate a few words differently, the first rock giant, formed from lava and layers of ash, not ice. From this giant, Odin and his brothers fashioned the world: His flesh is the earth, his blood the sea, his bones and teeth are stones and scree. The giant's name, in one poem, is Aurgelmir. *Aur* means wet sand or gravel. A *gelmir* is the kind of boiling, churning, belching, shrieking mud pot we call a roarer. The world is made from a giant wet-gravel roarer: a volcanic eruption.

There's another eruption in Snorri's mythology, one so well hidden I spotted it only after Eyjafjallajokull erupted and I knew what to look for. One day, Snorri writes, the god Odin rode his eight-legged horse Sleipnir into Giantland, where the giant Hrungnir complimented him on his marvelous steed.

"There's none in Giantland to match him, I'll bet," Odin snootily replied.

Hrungnir took that badly. His horse had a much longer stride. He leaped into the saddle and raced off after Odin in such a "great giant fury," Snorri writes, that he passed the gates of the gods' city of Asgard before he knew it and reined to a halt before Odin's feast hall, Valhalla. Extemporizing, Odin (who was no fighter) invited him in for a drink.

The love goddess Freyja poured Hrungnir ale. He turned into a disagreeable drunk and soon began to boast. He was going to level Asgard—except for Odin's feast hall. He'd carry Valhalla back to Giantland as booty. He'd kill all the gods—except for beautiful Freyja and Sif of the Golden Hair, Thor's wife. They could be his bed-slaves. But first he'd drink up all the gods' good ale. He hollered for more.

The gods called out for the red-bearded thunder god, Thor. He entered Valhalla with his magic hammer raised. "Who let a giant into Asgard?"

"Odin did," Hrungnir answered, with a level stare. "I am his guest. And you'll win no honor by killing me unarmed."

Instead, he challenged Thor to a duel. Thor agreed. No one had ever had the temerity to challenge him to a duel. The giant galloped home to get ready.

To be his second, Hrungnir created a golem, a giant figure of mud animated by a mare's heart; it was nine leagues tall—an imposing twenty-seven miles high.

Thor's second was his servant boy, a little human boy named Thjalfi, whom he'd taken from his parents some years ago as payment for them breaking the leg of his magic goat (long story). Thjalfi ran ahead of Thor to the battleground. He ran right up to the giant—we see the monster through the boy's eyes: a towering figure of stone, with a heart of stone, a head of stone, a shield of stone. His weapon, too, was stone, a huge whetstone, or hone.

Little Thjalfi was unimpressed. "Quick! Stand on your shield!" he cried. "Don't you see? Thor is coming at you from underground!"

The boy lied.

The giant Hrungnir threw down his great stone shield and jumped on it. At that instant, Thor rushed down from the sky in a storm of thunder and lightning.

The golem, it's said, wet himself in terror. Little Thjalfi knocked him down, "and he fell with little glory."

Thor threw his mighty hammer. Hrungnir threw his whet-stone, and the two weapons collided in midair. The whetstone shattered, raining stones all around. One shard lodged in Thor's forehead, knocking him down with a thundering crash. But Thor's hammer smashed the giant's skull. Hrungnir, too, came crashing down—and landed with a leg across Thor's neck. The giant was dead. Thor was fine (barring a bad headache), but the mightiest god could not get up until his little three-year-old son (whose mother was a giant) arrived and lifted the huge limb.

A flurry of small earthquakes (the horses' galloping hooves). Immense power from a shield-shaped stony mountain. Loud crashes . . . stones raining from the sky . . . thunder and lightning—which in Iceland occur mostly during eruptions. But the detail that con-vinced me Snorri was describing a volcanic eruption was the giant's golem, the creature made of mud who trembled and wet himself and was defeated so handily by Thor's human servant boy.

The golem's name was Mokkur-kalfi. *Kálfi* is a calf, or, when applied to a person, a clumsy dunce with the wits of a calf. *Mökkur* means a dense cloud, the significance of which eluded me until I read the word over and over in news accounts of the ashfall from Eyjafjallajokull. In one night in 2010, four inches of gray-black ash fell on the farm of Seljavellir in south Iceland. A newspaper report shows people with bandannas over their faces, outlaw-like, shoveling it off the farmhouse so the roof would not collapse. The curator of a folk museum down the road reported eight inches, and more was still coming down. "The ash is so light and its particles so tiny that it seems from photos to behave in part like rain and in part like fog," wrote Icelandic crime writer Yrsa Sigurdardottir.

"It creeps through any crevice and as it piles up on the ground it seeps up moisture and becomes a bit like semi-hardened concrete." As in the myth, it was humans who had to deal with the fallen ash. It was a lot of hard work, with no glory, but as Snorri's tale explains, it was within human capabilities to clean it up. Even a diligent boy could do it.

Scholars who had not witnessed the laborious mucking up of ash-mud have interpreted the myth of Thor and Hrungnir as a thunderstorm in the mountains, an initiation ritual, a worker cultivating the soil, the creation of the cosmos, or proof that Snorri was aware of the Jewish tradition of the golem (though I used the word in retelling the myth, Snorri did not). Only a scientist, Jan Bergstrom, writing in the *Journal of the Geological Society of Sweden* in 1989, saw that Snorri was describing a volcanic eruption. What else should a fight between a rock giant and a thunder god look like?

The poem that Snorri wanted to explain by telling this myth was *Haustlöng* by the ninth-century poet Thjodolf of Hvin: "Earth's son drove to the iron-game and the moon's way resounded beneath him . . . The entire abode of hawks did flame . . . all the earth was lashed by hail . . . mountains quaked and cliffs burst; the sky flamed." Like many Old Icelandic poems, it's almost unintelligible if you don't already know the story, know that Earth's son is Thor, and that the iron-game is a duel, etc. Thjodolf, a Norwegian, could indeed be describing a thunderstorm—Norway has frightening thunderstorms. But in Iceland, rainstorms rarely include lightning; volcanic eruptions do. So Snorri added the two seconds to the duel, the boy and Mokkur-kalfi.

He also added his signature humor—a particularly adolescent brand of humor. Snorri wrote his *Edda* to impress the fourteen-year-old king of Norway. Young King Hakon presumably would have enjoyed how easily the human boy overcame the huge but cowardly monster. He would have laughed at the monster wetting himself upon sighting Thor. It would have charmed the teenaged king to think the mighty Thor needed the help of a boy.

Snorri's Icelandic audience had the additional pleasure of equating the mud monster with the messy aftermath of a eruption. For them, the myth turns a hazard of Icelandic life into a joke.

Icelanders joked about the 2010 eruption, too—not in terms of gods, giants, dragons, or even elves, but in terms of a more modern intangible force: money. The first airport to close when the ash plume hit the jetstream was Britain's Heathrow. "The word on the street," quipped an Icelandic paper, "is 'We said send cash, not ash!'"

The reference was to the Icesave debacle. In October 2006, Landsbanki, a private bank in Iceland, set up a branch in the United Kingdom called Icesave and offered online savings accounts earning up to 6 percent interest—much exceeding the rates of other banks. Iceland was high on banking. Spurred by the government's "modernization" program of the 1990s, Icelandic bankers took on more and more risk. In 2000, the assets of Iceland's banks equaled 96 percent of the country's gross domestic product; in 2006, it was 900 percent. Iceland's bankers became known as the New Vikings. They "purchased helicopters, Ferraris, department stores"—including a stake in Saks Fifth Avenue—"soccer clubs, and investment firms in Britain and elsewhere in Europe," writes Arthur Centonze in the *Journal of Financial Education*.

Two years later, when the international financial crisis hit, Icesave's three hundred thousand British savings accounts were worth more than 4 billion British pounds, about 704 billion Icelandic krona. It sounds like a lot, but it wasn't. Iceland's total foreign bank debt was 6.4 *trillion* Icelandic krona. "You have to understand," an official from the International Monetary Fund told Michael Lewis, reporting for *Vanity Fair*, "Iceland is no longer a country. It is a hedge fund."

The Icelandic government nationalized the banks. It assured Icelandic depositors that their savings were protected, but the announcement "did not appear to give the same assurance" to British depositors with the Icesave accounts. Britain claimed Iceland had "effectively defaulted." Activating its 2001 antiterrorism legislation, Britain froze Landsbanki's assets—"unintentionally," Centonze charitably writes, branding Iceland a terrorist state. It became "extremely difficult for Iceland to move foreign currency in and out of the country. Financial transactions and trade with Iceland came to a screeching halt." Calling the United Kingdom's action "a hostile measure," Iceland prepared to take legal action. To avert a crisis, Norway, Sweden, the Faroe Islands, Finland, and Poland offered Iceland loans. The International Monetary Fund stepped in. Though the full Icesave debt would not be paid off until 2016, by 2011 the Icelandic economy had returned to growth. Why? A dragon intervened: Eyjafjallajokull.

The tourist eruption ended when the lava hit ice. With the ash plume randomly canceling flights, tourists began canceling their plans. In three weeks, tourism declined by 30 percent. Icelandair and Iceland Express (later renamed WOW Air, and now Play) joined with the Icelandic government and—on the advice of UK ad agency Brooklyn Brothers—called upon the Icelandic people to "turn the cycle of negativity on its head" by deluging social media with "positivity." On June 3, schools, shops, and government offices were shut for Iceland Hour, during which President Olafur Ragnar Grimsson opened the Inspired by Iceland campaign live on television and the internet. By June 4, the Inspired by Iceland Facebook page had received forty-five thousand "likes" and 27 percent of Iceland's population had shared something positive with their friends overseas. Often they shared the first Inspired by Iceland video, a two-and-a-half minute clip of Icelanders in beautiful and exotic landscapes dancing to "Jungle Drum" by Emiliana Torrini who, in spite of her Italian-sounding name, is Icelandic. The video begins with a close-up of the singer standing in a moss-grown lava field, wearing a traditional Icelandic sweater, and whispering, "Hi! You're not going to believe where I am now. *(Sigh.)* Iceland! It's amazing, really! Have a look at this, yeah?"

Other famous people with ties to Iceland were taped answering how they were "inspired." For Yoko Ono, "North is wisdom, power." Eric Clapton came for the salmon fishing. Monty Python's Terry Jones explained, "It's a cultural place." Others named the food, many the music scene—especially after the Inspired by Iceland concert with Damien Rice was live-streamed in July. In ten weeks, the internet was awash in 22 million "stories of positivity." Rather than crashing, the August tourist numbers went up by 43 percent.

On YouTube there were hours of Icelandic concerts associated with the ad campaign. Videos of Icelanders sharing their "secret places." Interviews with a hundred happy tourists. A series in which "the people of Iceland invite you to" have pancakes with the president or sushi with the mayor, hunt geese, round up sheep, ride horses, swim in the sea, collect mussels, make mutton soup, milk a cow, hold a concert in the living room, or knit a sweater.

By 2015, tourism had increased by 264 percent. It accounted for 31 percent of Iceland's foreign exchange earnings, up from 18.8 percent in 2010, and surpassed both fishing and aluminum production as drivers of Iceland's economy. "Those are some staggering hot-startup-like growth rates," commented one industry website, "especially for a country." Inspired by Iceland wasn't the only driver: The airline price war and expansion of routes instigated by WOW Air in 2012 was another factor, as was the popularity of the HBO series *Game of Thrones*, which began filming "beyond the Wall" in Iceland in 2011.

Still, the ad campaign had succeeded beyond anyone's dreams. And unlike earlier campaigns, it did so without highlighting Iceland's elves. Looking through 374 videos, I found only three elf references. In his two-minute introduction, Iceland's president equated elves (rightly, I think) with art, saying, "Iceland is indeed a country where one can still witness the creation of the earth. Our nature has had a profound impact on our culture and our history, as we can see in the sagas, and in the stories of the elves, the Hidden People, and the trolls, and also in the very rich modern artistic scene."

A twelve-second Secret Places video from 2013 features a man named Aki standing in front of a large rock formation. He says, "This church is my secret. This is where the elves live." Then he stares at the camera. He is not smiling.

In 2015, the ad campaign featured "a human competitor to Google," the Ask Gudmundur Search Engine. Two of the hundreds of questions answered by Icelanders named Gudmundur were about elves. *Where do I go to dance with the elves?* Gudmundur of the North replies, "We don't know where to dance with them, but we do know where they live. They live in this rock right here." He indicates a lava formation beside a road and tells a story of mechanical difficulties while road building. The second question was, *Do elves exist?* In this video, Gudmundur of the West strides up to a diamond-shaped monolith, balanced on its point, and says, smiling, "Yes, I do believe in elves, and they live in large rocks and beautiful cliffs with nice views." He waves and strides away, saying, "So come to the West and visit the elves!"

FOUR

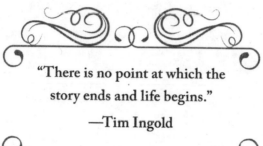

"There is no point at which the
story ends and life begins."

—Tim Ingold

Thingvellir

In the highlands near Surtshellir.

Eruption at Eyjafjallajokull.

ABOVE: *New lava at Eyjafjallajokull.*
BELOW: *The eruption at dusk.*

ABOVE: *View over new lava at Eyjafjallajokull.*
BELOW: *Evening view from the eruption site.*

View from Litla Hraun.

Waterfalls at Hraunfossar.

ABOVE: *Trekking horses in the highlands at Langavutn.*
BELOW: *Trekking horses in the highlands at Landmannalaugar.*

The glacier Snaefellsjokull.

Tidal flats below the glacier.

ABOVE: *The glacier Snaefellsjokull from the west.*
BELOW: *The glacier at sunset.*

View from Arnarstapi.

Evening view from Skogarnes.

Elf Stories

In May 2012, an Icelandic minister of parliament, Arni Johnsen, called upon Ragnhildur Jonsdottir to verify that elves lived in a large rock he believed had once saved his life in a car crash. The rock lay beside Iceland's Ring Road and was in the way of a highway widening project. According to Arni, as reported by *Iceland Review*, Ragnhildur found the rock to be the home of three generations of elves. "She said an elderly couple lives on the upper floor, but a young couple with three children [live] on the lower floor." With the elves' permission, Arni arranged for their home—all thirty tons of it—to be taken by ferry from southern Iceland seven miles across the strait to his home in the Westman Islands, where it would be placed on grass with the "window side" facing the sea.

Soon after the move, a foal was born in the shadow of the elf stone. It was named Alfur (Elf). Quizzing the horse's owner about the choice of name, the *Iceland Review* reporter did not ask, *Do you believe in elves?* Instead she asked, *Do you believe in elf stories?*

I believe in elf stories. I believe in the way they clean our inner windows. I believe in the way, as folklorist Terry Gunnell writes, they give "depth, history, personality, and mysticism" to a place. They tell us how to "behave in this landscape: what is right, what is wrong, *when* are they right or wrong, and *how* punishment is likely to descend on you."

One of my favorite elf stories is about the great auk, a flightless, black-and-white bird almost three feet tall, like a penguin. In fact, this auk is the original "penguin"; the better-known birds of that name in the Southern Hemisphere reminded explorers of the European penguin, a favorite mariners' food. Seamen sailing to Newfoundland in the 1600s took along little meat, relying instead on hunting great auks (though hunting is hardly a fair name for the practice of driving these placid birds through a funnel of sailcloth up the gangplank of a ship to be slaughtered). For centuries Icelanders ate great auks and their eggs; they stuffed pillows with their feathers, fine as eiderdown. A large colony bred on the steep-sided rocks called the Great Auk Skerries, twenty miles off Iceland's southwestern tip, in a channel notorious for crosscurrents. In 1808, British sailors anchored near the skerries and killed all the great auks they could find; a Faroese ship did the same in 1813. By 1821, the skerries were nearly bare of great auks; nine years later, during an undersea volcanic eruption, the rocks sank. The few birds left relocated to a more accessible island. There, the last two great auks were killed in 1844.

Shortly before 1862, when Jon Arnason published it in his collection of folktales, an old fisherman told this story: In the old days, men rowed out in open boats to hunt great auks and collect their feathers. But they never went to the farthest end of the rocks, for that is where the elves lived. One autumn day, a boat set out for the skerries as usual. It never came back.

Another version of the story begins a little differently. It sets the auk hunt in early summer and lets the boat successfully land, making no mention of elves. "Suddenly the sea began to get rough, so that the boat had to leave in a hurry. The egg-gatherers boarded the boat again with some difficulty, all but one. He was the last down from the rocks, for he had climbed the farthest." He was left behind. His mates meant to come back for him, but the weather worsened; they gave up hope.

The tales so far may be true. According to Hjalmar Bardarson's *Birds of Iceland*, a dozen men drowned at the Great Auk Skerries in 1628. Two boats on their way there were lost at sea in 1639. In 1732, auk hunters arriving after a long hiatus found two hovels, three cudgels, and "some weather-beaten human skeletons."

According to the old fisherman telling the tale in 1862, six months later one auk hunter from the missing boat reappeared, refusing to say where he'd been. The other storyteller leaves him stranded all year, until the next hunting trip: "When the egg-gatherers climbed up onto the rocks, they were amazed to see a man walking where no man was expected to be."

His friends rejoiced. No one asked questions. "Time now went by, and the news ceased to be talked about," until one fine Sunday a newborn baby was found at the church, tucked into a beautiful cradle, and covered with a cloth "of very precious stuff unknown to all." The pastor asked whose child it was. No one claimed it. The pastor took the auk hunter aside and asked if he didn't think the child deserved to be baptized and given a name. "Choose your words carefully," the pastor warned. But the hunter said no, the child was none of his responsibility. The pastor asked a third time. Again, no.

At that, a strange woman appeared, elegantly dressed, beautiful and stern. She snatched the coverlet off the cradle and tossed it to the pastor. "The church can have its fee," she said. "As for you," she told the auk hunter, "you shall become the most monstrous whale in the sea." She picked up the cradle and disappeared.

The auk hunter swelled to an enormous size, bursting out of his clothes except for his red cap. He began to bellow horribly. People tried to hold him, to bind him with rope, but he broke free. He ran toward the sea cliffs and jumped. Thereafter, for many years, a ship-sinking, man-eating red-headed whale patrolled the channel between Iceland's southwest coast and the Great Auk Skerries.

What is this elf story about? Extinction: Don't hunt to the far end of the skerries, but leave the auks (and elves) somewhere to live in peace. Don't transgress this taboo—or lie about your transgression—or what is given to you as a blessing (the auk's meat and eggs and feathers; the elf woman's love and her child) will be lost, you will be revealed as the monster you are, and your people will suffer for many years.

I've never gone egg gathering on a sea skerry or seen a great auk (except stuffed). When I sought out the Elf Lady's Cloth, a beautifully embroidered gold-colored fabric long used as an altar cloth and now in the National Museum of Iceland, I was disappointed to learn it was linked to a different elf story, the gift of a different elf woman. "The Redheaded Whale" is a tale I have read, not heard. It exists for me only in books.

It's often been the case as I've toured Iceland, though, that someone will tell me a folktale, or at least refer to one, on site.

Once there was a poor housemaid named Katla, who owned one treasure: a pair of shoes that let her run faster than anyone else. One autumn a shepherd who worked on the same farm stole Katla's shoes to help him round up the sheep. When she found out, Katla was so angry she strangled him and stuffed him headfirst into the big barrel of *skyr* (Icelandic yogurt) in the larder. As the winter progressed, and the level of *skyr* lowered, she grew more and more anxious. Soon her crime would be found out. When the tip of a toe broke through, Katla slipped on her magic shoes, ran up into the mountains, and dived into the volcano that now bears her name. When she gets angry, it erupts.

That story was told to me by Anna Maria Augustsdottir, who has a PhD in geosciences from Penn State. We were driving past Mount Katla, with Anna Maria's young children in the back seat of the car.

Thordur Gretarsson, who helped me meet the dragon, Eyja-fjallajokull, has worked as a real estate agent and studied law. He told me the story of the headland, Thordarhofdi, which shares his name. One winter night, a man named Thordur of Thrastastodum was walking to town to pick up supplies when he got lost in a snowfog. Suddenly he saw candlelight in a window. He rapped on the door and was welcomed in by a gentleman he'd never seen before. Well-dressed people filled a fine hall, dancing and singing, drinking and eating, and Thordur was invited to join the party. The next morning the gentleman filled Thordur's knapsack with flour and other supplies, adding treats for the children and a shawl for Thordur's wife. "Why are you being so kind?" Thordur asked. "Because you saved my son's life," the gentleman answered. Some years ago, when Thordur and a few other young men were waiting beside the headland for a boat, his friends decided to amuse themselves by pitching stones at a large rock. Thordur told them to stop—thereby saving the life of the invisible elf lad who'd been lounging there.

Though they told them well, it's clear both my friends had learned these tales from books, or from people who themselves had read the books of folktales first printed in the 1800s: The farmers in Anna Maria's story and the party-goers in Thordur's are antiques, their dress and habits those of nineteenth-century, or earlier, Icelanders.

In the 1800s, and long before, tales like these were told in many an Icelandic farmhouse as part of the *kvöldvaka*, literally "the time in the evening to stay awake." Like an Irish *ceilidh*, the entertainment at a *kvöldvaka* kept people alert as they worked on handicrafts during the long, dark winter evenings. As one elf story explains, "At Burstarfell it was the custom for people to lie down and take a nap in winter before the lamps were lit in the *baðstofa*" or main room. The farm was owned by the local sheriff, and it was his wife "who always decided how long they should sleep. She would light the lamps and wake the people herself for the evening work. One evening, however, she did not wake as usual, and the work-people got up and lit the lamps themselves. The sheriff would not have her woken. He said that she must be dreaming, and should be allowed to enjoy her dream. Late that night she awoke at last with a great sigh, and told her dream . . . "

A standard farmhouse of the time was a collection of small post-and-beam structures with peaked roofs and thick turf walls, linked in a maze or lined up like the teeth of a saw. From the outside, with its grassy walls, turf-grown roofs, and bright-painted wooden gable ends, the farmhouse looked like a hobbit hole. J. R. R. Tolkien, though he never visited Iceland, had read many travelers' descriptions of such farms. But whereas a hobbit hole "means comfort," in Tolkien's words, Ida Pfeiffer, touring in 1845, deemed the Icelander's houses "squalid and filthy": "On entering one of these cottages, the visitor is at a loss to determine which of the two is the more obnoxious—the suffocating smoke in the passage or the poisoned air of the dwelling-room, rendered almost insufferable by the crowding together of so many persons." Only the kitchen had a fire—and no chimney, just a smoke hole, often closed; in the smoky air, lamb joints and sausages were hung to cure. The *baðstofa*, where most people worked and ate and slept, was the room farthest from the drafty front door; it was warmed by body heat and lit by lamps that burned (foul-smelling) fish or seal oil.

A famous painting of an Icelandic *kvöldvaka* by the Danish artist August Schiott, from the early 1870s, shows a man tipping his book to catch the light of a single oil lamp, while the people around him in the shadows, standing or sitting, whittle, spin wool, and make rope. As entertainer, "the master of the house makes the beginning," reported Swedish theologian Uno Von Troil in 1772, "and the rest continue in their turns when he is tired. Some of them know these stories by heart, others have them in print, and those that have not, have them in writing." Books were prized—into the twentieth century, Icelanders were still writing out manuscripts in longhand, like medieval scribes, in order to own copies of a favorite book—but they were not necessary. The Icelandic historian Jonas

Jonasson in 1934 recalled, "It is incredible what a vast store of stories the people had, especially stories of outlaws and wonder-tales of kings and queens in their palaces and old men and old wives in their cottages. Then there were the stories about ghosts or fairyfolk, and of those there was an inexhaustible store." He added, "I knew one old man who was able to tell three stories a night all through the winter fishing season, 2 February to 12 May, and had still not reached the end of his repertoire."

The idea to collect such stories into books came from abroad, inspired by *Grimms' Fairy Tales*, which was first published in 1812. In 1845, an English scholar named George Stephens was studying Old Icelandic literature in Stockholm. Aware that much of Jacob Grimm's *German Mythology* of 1835 paraphrased the work of the thirteenth-century Icelandic writer Snorri Sturluson, Stephens (like Grimm himself) wondered what other ancient literary treasures Iceland might be hiding. He called upon the Royal Nordic Society of Antiquaries, twice, to commission an Icelandic *Grimms' Fairy Tales*. The society itself took no formal action, but among its members were Jon Sigurdsson, the leader of Iceland's independence movement, and Sveinbjorn Egilsson, rector of the Latin School in Reykjavik. These two recruited Jon Arnason, who along with teaching at the school, headed what would become the National Library of Iceland. In 1852, Jon and his colleague Magnus Grimsson published a small collection of forty-three stories, running to 140 pages. "These folktales are the poetic creation of the nation," they wrote in their introduction. "In them we see . . . the nation's longing for history."

Iceland in the 1850s was an impoverished colony of Denmark. The island had been settled about a thousand years earlier, at the height of the Viking Age, by "the chancers, the losers," the ones "who had nothing to lose," in the words of Agnar Helgason of Decode Genetics, who has traced the ancestry of modern Icelanders through their DNA. Their Y chromosomes, normally present only in male cells, show that modern Icelandic men are, genetically, about 75 percent Scandinavian and 25 percent Celtic. Most of the men who settled the island, therefore, came from Norway, Sweden, or Denmark. Most of Iceland's first women, however, came from the British Isles. According to their mitochondrial DNA (mtDNA), which is passed down only from the mother's side, modern Icelandic women are about 60 percent Celtic and 40 percent Scandinavian. We can imagine Viking men—outlaws, on the losing sides of battles—descending on Scotland and Ireland, wooing—or simply capturing—a bride, then sailing on to settle in Iceland, where land was plentiful and free for the taking.

When they arrived, in the late 800s, the island was unpeopled, except perhaps for a few walrus hunters, Irish hermits, and other transients: Icelandic society essentially started from scratch. As portrayed in *The Book of Land-Taking* and in the Family Sagas, its founders were idealists and individualists. "With laws shall our land be built," says the wise hero of *Njal's Saga*. The resulting Icelandic Commonwealth—Iceland's golden age—was kingless and law-driven, a land of consensus and negotiation, and it lasted nearly four hundred years. But between 1262 and 1264, wracked by decades of feuds, battles, and assassinations, Iceland's chieftains voted to become subjects of the king of Norway.

They did not consider themselves Norwegian: Iceland was to be a "tax land" of the king himself, who promised to send up to six trade ships a year—crucial for an island where timber for shipbuilding and repair was nonexistent. But the end of the thirteenth century in northern Europe also saw the rise of the Hansa League, a loose confederation of trading towns in what is now Germany. The Hansa merchants "seemed to do business just as they liked," according to historian Michael Pye. Having gained a monopoly, they refused to sell "winter essentials"—grain, flour, vegetables, and beer—to Norway until the Norwegian king gave them better terms. They blockaded the Norwegian ports until they got what they wanted. "Everything the Norwegians did after that seemed only to make them more dependent on the Hansa," Pye writes. The kings of Norway didn't always send the promised ships to Iceland—perhaps they couldn't. Icelanders got no grain, flour, vegetables, or beer, nor any iron, timber, cordage, or candle wax.

Then the weather worsened; Icelanders turned from farming to fishing to survive. Norway's royal line failed, and Iceland fell under the rule of first Sweden and then Denmark, for whose kings, writes historian Gunnar Karlsson, Iceland "was of little interest, and—for better or worse—this was in many ways characteristic of its history for centuries." Better, in that the Icelandic language survived; worse, in that the people suffered. In the 1400s, the Black Death killed a third of Iceland's population; in the early 1700s, smallpox killed a quarter; and in the late 1700s, a toxic volcanic eruption and the famine that followed killed a fifth. In 1800, there were about the same number of Icelanders—forty to fifty thousand—as there had been in 1200, at the peak of Iceland's golden age, when the sagas were first being written. It was this history the nation was longing for when the first efforts were made to collect folktales: those glory days in the Middle Ages when Icelanders treated kings as equals.

The first Icelandic book of folklore, however, received little notice, and Jon Arnason dropped the project until 1858, when a German scholar, Konrad Maurer, came to Iceland. Maurer, a professor at the University of Munich, specialized in the history of Scandinavian and German law; he edited the first German edition of an Icelandic saga and argued, at length, based on abstruse linguistical theories, that the sagas were not Norse or Old Norse, and certainly not Norwegian, but distinctly Icelandic. Maurer spent six months traveling about the island collecting folktales (which he would publish in German upon his return home) and impressed upon Jon the importance of doing the same in order to further Iceland's independence movement.

Jon, like the Brothers Grimm themselves, thought it more efficient to have the tales travel to him. He placed notices in two Icelandic journals calling for "antiquities." Letters from country pastors and other rural literati began to fill the librarian's desk. He sent the best of them to Copenhagen, to Gudbrandur Vigfusson, a learned Icelander best known today for the Cleasby-Vigfusson *Icelandic-English Dictionary*. Gudbrandur consulted with Jon Sigurdsson; the tales both men thought worthy were edited into the "correct" style and sent to Maurer, who prepared them to be printed in Leipzig in two volumes, totaling 1,300 pages, which came out in 1862 and 1864.

"It is no easy task working with materials like folktales and old wives' tales, ensuring that they do not become pretentious, or cliché-ridden blather," Gudbrandur wrote in his introduction. One must be "sensible" and "choose in such a way that the uncorrupted opinion of the nation appears, and not the exaggerated superstitions of certain individuals, or the jokes of idiots, or the disbelief of eccentrics."

The poetic creation of the nation . . . The uncorrupted opinion of the nation.

Like *Grimms' Fairy Tales* in Germany (then a scatter of principalities) and similar collections in Norway (then under Swedish control) and Scotland and Ireland (under English control), the folktale collections of Iceland were driven by the need to show that Iceland was indeed a nation, its culture rich and traditional and, most of all, unlike that of its overlords. And in the opinion of Iceland's leading nationalists of the time that culture was suitably expressed by "The Redheaded Whale," "Katla and the Magic Shoes," "Thordur of Thrastastodum," and "The Sheriff's Lady of Burstarfell," all of which appear in the 1862–1864 collection and were therefore not "exaggerated superstitions," "jokes," or the work of "eccentrics"—or should we say of crazy ladies and loony elf-seers?

"Nowhere does a nation bare its soul to the same extent as in its popular lore, its folktales," write May and Hallberg Hallmundsson in their 1987 collection, *Icelandic Folk and Fairy Tales.* "They contain the people's loftiest yearnings and deepest fears, their most ardent passions and hopes, their truest beliefs. They reveal their sense of honor, valor, and humor, their flights of imagination, their creative force—in short, the whole of their humanity as fashioned by the land in which they live." Which in Iceland's case, they add, "was never just an accumulation of inanimate matter—a pile of stones here, a patch of earth there—but a living entity by itself."

"Folklore is the Icelandic national character," explains writer and photographer Gudmundur Pall Olafsson in his 1995 coffee-table book, *Iceland the Enchanted*. In Icelandic folktales, he says, "there is a serious undertone of sincerity, trust, and the ceaseless quest for inner truth and of viewing the world from the three-dimensional perspective of reality and dreams and mysticism. Thinking about existence in these terms is healthy for us," he adds. "Folklore contains a mystery that develops and sharpens our consciousness and feelings for the living and the dead, and engenders a tolerant respect towards the world about us."

What did the sheriff's wife dream, when she overslept that evening at Burstarfell? She dreamed that a man led her outside to a great stone and, once they had walked around it three times, she saw it was a beautiful house. Inside was an elf woman in childbirth. Like the heroines of similar folktales found in Scotland, Ireland, England, Wales, France, throughout Scandinavia and into Eastern Europe, as well as in parts of Asia, including Japan, the sheriff's wife had been recruited as a midwife, or *ljós-móðir*, a word that has been called the most beautiful word in the Icelandic language: It means "mother of light." The sheriff's wife successfully brought the elf child into the light and, when she had bathed him, was asked to anoint his eyes with a certain ointment. Secretly, she touched her own eye, too. When she returned home and awoke, she was changed: "She could see all that went on, both on the earth and in it." The cliffs near the farm of Burstarfell were themselves a village—and the elf people there "were more prudent in their work, and more weatherwise, than others." When she did things their way, the farm at Burstarfell prospered.

Doors

Without my glasses on the other day I saw a headline that said Books, and I read Doors. I'm not sure I was wrong. Some books, wrote J. R. R. Tolkien, "open a door on Other Time, and if we pass through, though only for a moment, we stand outside our own time, outside Time itself, maybe."

The Book of Land-Taking opens such a door. Written in Iceland in the early 1100s, it's not a saga; it's a collection of notes: outlines, episodes, anecdotes. It names some 3,500 people and 1,500 farms, progressing clockwise around the country. It reads as fact—long genealogies, places still on the map—except when sorcerers, shape-shifters, and seers appear.

Their taste for fantasy hasn't tarnished the book's authors: Ari the Learned and Kolskegg the Wise are accounted as Iceland's first historians. Nor did the fantastic alarm the later scholars who copied *The Book of Land-Taking* and preserved it down to our time:

not Styrmir, whose copy from before his death in 1245 is now lost; not Sturla, whose manuscript made before 1284 was copied onto paper in the 1600s and then lost; not Haukur, whose 1306 manuscript only has fourteen out of thirty-eight leaves remaining; not the anonymous scribe who made a copy in the 1400s (two leaves remaining); not Bjorn, who used vellum manuscripts of Sturla's and Haukur's books to make his own before he died in 1655—it was copied onto paper before the original burned in 1728; not even Thordur, whose manuscript from before 1670 still survives in Iceland's national library. Each retained the fairy tales.

My favorite is the story of a horse race. In the mid-900s, a Viking ship carrying a cargo of livestock beached at Kolkuos, the conjunction of two river mouths in northern Iceland. As they were offloading, one horse escaped. A man called Thorir Dove-Nose bought the right to keep the mare, if he could catch her, and he did. He named her Fluga (Fly), for she was very fast.

Thorir Dove-Nose was a braggart, as well as beak-nosed, for a sorcerer named Orn soon got wind of Fly. Orn waylaid Thorir one summer night in the center of Iceland, on a black sand desert between the high glaciers, as Thorir was heading south to the Althing, the yearly meeting of Iceland's chieftains at Thingvellir.

Today Thingvellir is known to be a rift zone bridging two tectonic plates. To the Viking settlers it was a wide wooded valley with a fast-running river and a fish-filled lake, conveniently near the major routes through Iceland's uninhabitable highlands. Riding from north, south, east, and west, some on the road for two weeks or more, the chieftains brought sail cloth to roof turf-walled booths and settled in to legislate. The lawspeaker, Iceland's only government official, stood on a hilltop (the Law Rock) reciting the laws; the basalt rift wall rising behind him, like an acoustic shell, amplified his voice. The chieftains and their followers, on the slope below, agreed or raised legal challenges. Judges chosen by the chieftains settled lawsuits in four courts, one for each quarter of the country. Often the loser paid the winner a fine; more drastically the loser was outlawed, forced to flee to the highlands or sneak abroad. Surrounding these serious matters was a fair: Merchants peddled their wares. Horses were raced, fought, or traded. Ale was sold, stories told, wrestlers matched, marriages made, and duels fought on an islet in the Axe River. Everyone who could afford it attended the Althing.

But Thorir Dove-Nose's farm of Flugumyri (Fly Mire) was in Iceland's North Quarter. To reach Thingvellir, Thorir had to cross the full breadth of the island. The route he took is called Kjolur (the Keel). Centered like the keel of an upturned boat, the route rises from green and settled coastlines over high deserts of lava and snow and wind-sifted ash. It's impassable ten months of the year. Glaciers loom on either side, volcanoes snug under the ice. Kjolur crosses cold milky rivers roiling with till. It skirts hot bogs, where gushers, geysers, roarers, and screamers reside among sulfurous, bubbling pots of mud. Outlaws lurk in secret glens. The elf queen and her hunters sweep down from the hills. Rock trolls block high mountain passes. Kjolur is not a route to ride alone.

Thorir Dove-Nose did.

I did not. Chasing his story in 2009, I traveled with the Icelandic horse-trekking company *Íshestar* (Ice Horses). We numbered nineteen tourists, eight guides, and a herd of a hundred horses. We would be out six days and cover 140 miles.

The sorcerer Orn rode a gray stallion. He accosted Thorir near a place now called Dove-Nose's Racetrack—it's on the map; it's now an airstrip.

Orn scoffed at the braggart's fast mare.

"What do you bet?" asked Dove-Nose.

"Something worth winning."

"And if I lose?"

The sorcerer smiled.

They rode side by side to the level stretch of sand, marked off a course, and . . . *they're off!* Fluga flew. She galloped so fast the sorcerer's stallion was only halfway up the course when Fluga passed him, already heading back.

Orn, defeated, rode into the mountains and disappeared. (His name, incidentally, means Eagle.) Fluga was exhausted, so Thorir Dove-Nose set her free to graze in a grassy patch. (Like us, he had a string of horses along.) When he found her again on his return from the Althing, the gray stallion was with her. Eleven months later she bore a foal; from this line came the most famous Icelandic horse, a founding sire of the breed, Eidfaxi (Oath-Mane). A modern Icelandic horse magazine is named after him.

To travel that thousand-year-old track to the Althing and race, in my fancy, the sorcerer's horse, I bused north for four hours. The weather did not cooperate: low clouds, spitting rain, no spectacular views where I knew there should be. The mountains were cut off at their knees. The waterfalls were blurs and drips. Then the bus windows fogged up.

The bus dropped me near the farm of Flugumyri, at a communal corral where a hundred horses milled around. I milled around, too, with the other tourists, getting raingear, saddlebags, a saddle and bridle, and finally a horse. It was late by the time we set off. There was still some rain, a breeze, clouds, but the evening sun was trying to break through. We climbed a long gravel road to reach a rolling meadow of moss patched with soggy banks of snow. The herd of loose horses passed us and dwindled in the distance. We rode long into the night, the long summer night that never seems to darken. It was still bright at ten, though raining lightly, when we reached our lodgings, a sheep herders' hut. Hay had been trucked in; nothing grew here for our horses to eat. Our van, via a different route, had arrived long before, and the cook had sausages and potatoes ready. I ate, pulled my pack from the luggage pile, jockeyed for a bottom bunk, lined up for the john, and tried to sleep through the singing and silliness of the drinkers down the hall.

And up at seven—at least some people were, alarmed to find no electricity or hot water. I went back to bed. At nine the generator roared to life, and over a breakfast of cheese, bread, cold cuts, cucumbers, and a bowl of oatmeal, we discussed the day's ride. It would be a short one, only eighteen miles. We'd tack up at noon and take only one mount to cover the distance. We were invited to pick out a new horse (we were herding five per person), but I declined. I'd ridden in on a big gelding in the slate-gray color called blue dun. He was pushy and impatient and a wonderful ride. His name, Valur, meant either Chosen One or Hawk. Instead, I went for a walk.

It was mild and drizzling still, with enough gnats to annoy me, but not enough to warrant fiddling with my face net. I walked back the way we'd come. The landscape seemed barren and flat, but looking closely I could see some relief: ripples and dips and rills deep enough to disappear into, lying flat. Speckles of wild-flowers, white and pink, appeared among thin clumps of grass and the tangled knots of birch and silver-leaved willow trees—if the word *tree* can be applied to groundcover: Nothing here grew much above toe height. The riding track beside the gravel road was worn narrow and deep, the hoof-churned earth red and peaty. Swans called. Meadow pipits chittered. The generator cut out.

In the sudden stillness, from past the corral came the low *thrum* of a tractor. I turned to stare. Beyond the struggling machine, in the direction we would be riding, a long bog of mire and black sand barred us from a scattering of lakes—silver lines interrupted by blue blots of islands. A thin strip of blue on the horizon marked the high mountains I knew from the map—I had gone over it at breakfast with Hjalti, the leader of our riding tour. A blink of snow showed a glacier beyond. I was glad I had not brought a camera on the ride. I had intended to see the highlands through Thorir Dove-Nose's eyes, through medieval, unmediated lenses. But now I knew, here in the center of Iceland, a camera was simply useless. No frame could contain such vastness. Even eyes could not fathom the sky's great dome. It dizzied me to stand in the road and look up and turn a slow circle. I felt I could stand forever under this endless gray sky, and at the same time I was terrified. Like looking off a cliff and wishing to fly.

I walked to the corral, where the oldest of our guides leaned on the fence. Eyjolfur was a wiry, tough character at seventy, with extravagant eyebrows and a bulbous nose. In his basso voice,

Icelandic was all but indecipherable. He tried again, and this time I made it out. He was outlining our route, taming the landscape by giving it names. Hofsjokull was the ice cap straight ahead, he said. *Hof* means a high hill, or a temple; *jökull*, a glacier. I could only distinguish it from the clouds by its color: where ice glowed yellowish, clouds were more blue. The Burfjoll were the largest of the dark ticks in the distance. A *búr* was a squat covered bowl to store food in; *fjöll* were mountains. We'd ride past them. Krakur, the Crag, a solitary peak, made a good landmark to aim for. West of the mountains lay another ice cap, Langjokull, the Long Glacier. It was hidden now, but we'd ride between it and Hofsjokull. We'd overnight at its mouth.

I asked about the tractor. The farmer, he explained, fattened sheep out here in what once had been wasteland. He earned a tax rebate from the soil conservation service if he spread fertilizer. It's very new, Eyjolfur agreed, an experiment, to fertilize the highlands. A feeble effort, I thought. So much land surrounded us, so little of it green.

Four hours later, all human efforts seemed equally feeble. Riding Valur, I had marveled at the free-running herd strung out in front of us, single-file, a hundred horses silhouetted against the sand—gray, black, chestnut, dun, pinto, palomino, roan, bay, their lively legs blurring to wheels as they raced along, a line of moving color against a completely still landscape of barren ground, silver lakes, ageless mountains, the icy dome of Hofsjokull cutting the clouds ahead, the endless gray sky. Nothing changed all day but that pattern painted by the running herd. Nothing moved except ourselves. No sheep, no tractors or jeeps or ATVs went past—all of which had met us on the first day of our ride, as the road and the riding track crisscrossed.

But we were not alone.

This night's lodgings were sparer than the last—fewer rooms, each with more beds. I was tardy untacking and had to bunk in the dining hall. Lounging there, jotting notes, I felt eyes on my neck. I turned to see Hofsjökull outside the windows, stretching across three of them and around the corner like an intelligence looming between earth and sky, gleaming yellow-white unlike anything real—brilliant, misshapen, awake, a rising moon in wintertime, its edges blurred and shifting. It seemed to breathe. It drew me outside in spite of sore muscles.

I walked dead away from it, across the tussocky field to the gravel banks of the glacial river. The day was warm, now that the clouds had lifted. I took off my boots to wade—the water was not icy in the shallows, over black sand. It made me want to strip and bathe, but I was not quite alone. Other riders were about; one man perched on a rock right around the corner. I had never bathed naked in a glacial river before. I had never done—never thought to do—anything remotely like that on all my many trips to Iceland. I waded on, looking for a secret spot. Wind sang in my ears. A golden plover called *bí-bí, bí-bí*. The roar of the river was louder than either wind or bird, but somehow so constant as to mimic silence. A shadow rushed across the sun. I shivered and looked up. Unknowingly, I had turned a circle: The glacier was right in my face. Wings of black cloud rising behind the ice warned me the fine weather wouldn't last—but how long did I have? There was no scale here: I could not guess how far or high that icecap was. I walked barefoot across warm black sand braided with turf, soft and spongy and squishy with goose droppings. I decided to ignore their provenance. They felt nice between my toes. I picked up a goose feather.

A series of jagged peaks beside the glacier puzzled me: They were covered top to toe with snow, while the mountains in line with them were wholly snowless and blue.

Aha. I was seeing only the tips of high snow-capped peaks, their bases hidden beneath the horizon's curve. The glacier was half-hidden as well.

The black clouds flew closer. I picked up three rough rounded black rocks to remember the river by and let fly my goose feather as a gift in return. I quickened my pace, and was startled to see sheep tracks, way out here in the wild. The river now ran a greenish-gray, milky with silt, its swirling current deadly fast. The sand petered out. I hauled myself up the high grassy bank, startling geese and goslings, and saw nothing at all around me but river, mountains, ice, and sky—no hut, no horses, no signs of human life. As if I'd stepped through a door into another world, a door into Other Time.

Children see doors in the landscape. In *Landmarks*, Robert Macfarlane describes the result when two adults, an artist and a teacher, followed a pack of thirty first graders around a 170-acre English park for ten weeks one winter. "The hollows of its trees were routes to other planets, its subterrane flowed with streams of silver, and its woods were threaded through with filaments of magical force. Within it the children could shape-shift into bird, leaf, fish, or water. Each day brought different weather, and each weather different worlds."

Alice's door was a rabbit hole. Lucy's was a wooden wardrobe filled with old fur coats. International folklore contains countless tales in which a child or adult slips through an imaginary door and passes hours, days, or years in another world. Naturalists—grown men—occasionally imagine doors. "Between every two pines is a door leading to a new life," wrote John Muir in the 1890s. In the 1920s Stephen Graham mused, "As you sit on the hillside, or lie prone under the trees of the forest, or sprawl wet-legged by a mountain stream, the great door, that does not look like a door, opens."

Muir's door, and Graham's, are conscious metaphors. Since the Protestant Reformation in the 1500s, and increasingly so since the Enlightenment two centuries later, seeing doors in the landscape has been frowned upon as delusional. Magic has been banished from the world. As philosopher Egil Asprem writes, by the early twentieth century people's "attitudes towards the world had changed: they did not anymore expect to encounter genuinely capricious forces in nature, thinking instead that everything could in principle be explained." Philosopher Max Weber in 1917 termed this attitude *disenchantment*; to him it seemed the goal of modern Western culture. For Weber, explains historian Richard Jenkins, "in a disenchanted world everything becomes understandable and tameable, even if not, for the moment, understood and tamed."

Wonder was banished along with magic. Soon, Weber predicted, "there will be no more mysteries," with the result, Jenkins points out, that "religious and magical understandings of the world become at best charming, at worst ignorant and backward." Or in the words of historian Michael Saler, "states of enchantment might be delightful, but they were also delusory and regressive, at best suitable for children and other irrational beings, such as women, the working classes, and non-Western peoples."

Saler sees this prejudice even in our affection for stories. Enlightened thinkers "feared that the delights of the imagination would incite dangerous desires." Reading should be confined to utilitarian instruction. When Samuel Taylor Coleridge wrote, in 1817, that we enjoy fiction through the "willing suspension of disbelief," he "reflected this repressive attitude," Saler notes. "The default outlook is one of disbelief, which can only be circumvented temporarily through a conscious act of will. This is a labor-intensive way to relax with a good book, which the early Victorians intended it to be." Novelists use that phrase, *the willing suspension of disbelief*, casually today; I will never be able to look at it the same way again. Why should *disbelief* be our default? Why should we deride our sense of wonder? Why do we allow our world to be disenchanted? Do we simply fear looking silly?

Some philosophers have spoken up for enchantment—or, increasingly, for the *reenchantment* of the world. "A sense of wonder," writes Saler, was central to Ludwig Wittgenstein's outlook on life. In 1948, he wrote that "life's infinite variations are essential to our life." His philosophy, Saler explains, "awakens us to awe, possibility, difference, and a humble acceptance of the provisional nature of our understanding." In his 2007 book *A Secular Age*, philosopher Charles Taylor concurs; he suggests that people without any sense of wonder "lead 'flattened' rather than full lives."

But Macfarlane finds disenchantment to be widespread. Disbelief remains our default. "Our language for nature," he writes, "is now such that the things around us do not talk back to us in ways that they might." Our world is flat. "We have become experts in analysing what nature can do *for* us, but lack a language to evoke what it can do *to* us. The former is important; the latter is vital."

Facing that door to Other Time in Iceland's center, I backed away. The great glacier was half-cloaked in cloud. The wind had a bite of ice in it. Boots back on, I marched up a slight rise and spied the hut, not far off. My surge of relief surprised me. Before I reached shelter, the glacier was gone, swallowed up entirely. Rain swept in, stinging. The river, too, disappeared.

But the hut was warm and redolent with the smell of frying fish, courtesy of one of the guides, who was a fishing-boat captain in real life. He worked this ride as vacation, I learned when the tourists and guides introduced themselves to one another later that night, after some alcoholic punch and a round of rowdy singing. We were eight Icelanders, eight Germans, four Dutch, two French, two Austrians, one Brit, one American, and one Dane; three music teachers (it didn't show in the singing), one biology teacher, a vicar, a mental health worker, a hairdresser, a dentist, a quality-control expert, some who gave no occupation, two horse farmers, the fisherman, an actress, a retiree, several students, and me, a writer. The Icelanders were struck by the number of times I'd visited their country: That trip, in 2009, was number fourteen. Hjalti came over and quizzed me, in Icelandic, patiently reframing his questions until, with my limited grasp of the language, I finally understood, but still some were hard to answer: *Why do you come here so often?* I kept Icelandic horses at home, so it wasn't just the riding. How to explain that, in Iceland, I was a different person? At home, I was a master of words and grammar. Here, I spoke like a child. I was spoken *to* as a child. They told me stories.

I love the sagas, I said, *all the old stories.*

Hjalti nodded, satisfied, but I knew it wasn't a complete answer. In 1992, I attended a lecture at the International Medieval Congress in Kalamazoo, Michigan. In Iceland, Gillian Overing noted, the center is the margin. Geography is inside out. People settle on the temperate edges of the island, while its interior is a glacial desert, cold, inhospitable, and not even crossable most of the year. "What kind of self," she mused, "might these places reflect?" What kind of self has wilderness at its heart?

The House of the Steward

In the late 1990s, folklorist Valdimar Hafstein interviewed two Icelandic women, Regina Hallgrimsdottir and Erla Stefansdottir, who, like my friend Ragnhildur Jonsdottir, see and talk to elves. When he asked them to describe their elf friends, the women agreed the elves were old-fashioned. Regina laughed at the idea of an elf woman wearing jeans. Erla said watching the Hidden Folk was "like looking back in time." Valdimar interprets their answers scientifically. "On the psychological level," he writes, elf stories "express not only a mild nostalgia, but also guilt and anxiety about change."

Terry Gunnell finds the problem to be not nostalgia but genre: Modern elf stories are tainted by our reliance on books. "Had the legends never been published, perhaps the *huldufólk* would have attained cell phones, cars, and internet connections by now," he writes.

And some elf stories have transitioned into the modern world. When Ragnhildur and I paid a visit to Gunnell in his book-crammed office at the University of Iceland in 2016, he gave me the draft of a paper he was writing on Icelandic *álagablettir*—cursed or enchanted spots. These spots can be rocks—like the elf rocks road workers must be wary of—but often they are hills, mounds, tussocks, knolls, depressions, small islands, or an area of grass "that is not allowed to be harvested, or disturbed in any way," Gunnell writes, no matter how tempting it may be to people in need of fodder for their livestock. Enchanted spots are found on farms all over Iceland. Stories about them, Gunnell writes, "are among the most common legends still told in the countryside in Iceland," though they are rarely written down "because they are so short, so similar and only really relevant to those living and working on the farms in question." They are also "updating themselves all the time."

In 2001, for example, folklorist Bjarni Hardarson traveled through the southern county of Arnessysla (population twelve thousand) in an effort to record all its living legends. He found sixty stories of enchanted spots. In the oral history archives of the Arni Magnusson Institute in Reykjavik, there are eight hundred examples collected from all over Iceland in the 1950s and 1960s. In the earlier examples, sheep or cows might die if the enchanted spot were disturbed. In the twenty-first century stories, heavy machinery is wrecked—again, the farmers' most valuable possessions.

At a farm called Blesastadir, for example, Bjarni learned of an enchantment on Graenholl (Green Knoll). The grass on this small hill must never be cut, for it is the home of the Hidden Folk. The farmwife, Ingibjorg, told Bjarni that the taboo had always been respected, even though her husband dismissed such ideas as mere superstition. Their daughter, Hildur, said the family "respected the knoll, as it was a kind of sacred space." Only once in their time had there been serious talk of flattening the knoll, Bjarni writes. "A bulldozer was got in to carry this out. It was standing by the stable door when those living on the farm went to sleep, the idea being that work would begin the next day. That night, the bulldozer caught fire, and all ideas of flattening the hillock were abandoned."

Some enchanted spots may be graves, others may hide archaeological treasures. When archaeologists Jesse Byock and Davide Zori excavated Kirkjuholl (Church Hill) and Hulduholl (Hill of the Hidden Folk) in western Iceland in 2013, they found a Viking Age church under the first and a pagan burial under the second. Still other enchanted spots are simply natural places that in some way "stand apart from their surroundings," like Helgafell, the Holy Mountain that marks my friends' farm. Stories have protected these spots for hundreds of years—better, Gunnell adds, than any official government order could. Speaking to Ragnhildur and me, Gunnell noted that there are similar places in Ireland, where many of Iceland's first settlers came from. "Coming to Iceland, it was natural to have places you keep safe and do not touch, to have places on your farms that you kept wild for the spirits there." He sees the stories about them as "little keys into the past and the way people sensed the land around them." If the stories make us feel anxious or guilty about the way we are treating the land, he implies, that may be a good thing.

"We act as though we know more than previous generations," he says, "and we actually know less. They weren't stupid peasants. When the farmer goes out to urinate every morning, he is checking the direction of the wind, downloading information into his computer—his body. It's scientific for his time. He needs to decide whether he can safely go fishing that day. His family and his crew are depending on him."

If the horses turn their tails to the wind in good weather, says a collection of Icelandic folkways, you can expect a storm from that direction. If smoke lies low to the ground, or you hear the rumble of stones falling in the mountains in calm weather, then rain is on its way—a heavy rain, if the ewes are urinating more than usual in their pen. (People feel the need to urinate more, too, when the barometric pressure rises.) If, on the other hand, the sheep are restless and butting heads, expect high winds. If ptarmigan come down from the hills and flock against the house, fear the worst.

For the farmer, Gunnell says, "the countryside is a book. But the writing in this book is fading," he warns, "as people move away and forget the stories." When Konrad Maurer traveled through Iceland collecting folktales in the 1800s, almost 90 percent of the people lived on farms. Today, of Iceland's 365,000 people, two-thirds live in Reykjavik or its suburbs. Less than 2 percent—around 7,000 people—live on farms.

Before the writing fades to white, however, Gunnell and his colleagues will have recreated much of Iceland's storybook as a geographically mapped computer database. The Sagnagrunnur (Story Database) website contains some ten thousand stories from various printed volumes, and students are in the field collecting more. Each folktale gets a dot on the map. You can plot, as Feargus O'Sullivan did for the CityLab blog in 2016, all of the elf stories that take place in Iceland's uninhabited highlands. "Zoom into any corner of the map and you will find an incredibly dense scattering of sightings, stories, and legends about the hidden people," O'Sullivan notes. The elves, he says, "come across as embodiments of the landscape itself." To him, the "overwhelming impression to be gained from the tales listed on the map is of people trying to live in harmony, or at least come to terms with difficult natural surroundings."

It's a point Gunnell and other scholars have made repeatedly. When the first settlers came to Iceland in the ninth century, they faced the unknown. The island had no stories; it was the last of Europe's countries to be occupied. Historians Peter Foote and David Wilson note that the newcomers, finding the island empty of people, "were not so rash as to assume that it was empty of spirits, encroachment upon whom needed care and ceremony." But if they were savvy about nature spirits, they were less so about Iceland's fragile, subarctic nature itself. They thought of the forest as something a farmer must fight. A field in Norway, where many of the settlers came from, quickly reverts to woodland if not constantly grazed or plowed. The same is not true in Iceland.

When the settlers came, says *The Book of Land-Taking*, the island was forested "from the mountains to the sea." This forest they destroyed, cutting the useful timber for their houses and boats, collecting firewood, making charcoal for cooking and blacksmithing, turning their pigs and goats out into the brush to feed. Scientists estimate that in the late 800s forests blanketed at least 25 percent of

Iceland. Now they cover 1 percent, and about 60 percent of Iceland's topsoil has blown out to sea. "Man has made a desert of much of Iceland," concluded one research team. "Much of that 'landscape of ruins' so much appreciated by the visitor is, like the wild places of much of the rest of Europe, largely an inadvertent creation of human misuse." Dozens of Viking Age farm ruins "now stranded in gravel deserts," notes another study, "bear witness to the complete destruction of the environment in some parts of the country."

Much of the damage was done by the twelfth century, when Icelanders began writing down their histories, sagas, and myths. These texts omit, as I've noted, what most draws the modern eye in Iceland: that landscape of ruins, so stark and bleak and elementally black and white, born of fire and ice. But they do refer, offhand, to charcoal burning, to horses and cattle grazing where they oughtn't, to seed being sown and poor hay harvests, to hunger and desperate foul-weather fishing trips, to the joy of discovering a beached whale and filling the larder with meat. And they do refer to nature spirits—to what we now call Hidden Folk or elves.

Most of these texts are anonymous, but we can assume their writers were church-educated—there were no other schools. Elves, to them, were evil—or at least relics of long ago, before people knew better. Like us, these medieval writers laugh at loony elf-seers. These lines, for example, were inserted into a fifth-century sermon in a fourteenth-century Icelandic manuscript: "Some women are so foolish and blind as to their needs that they take food and carry it out into the open and put it under rocks, consecrate it to land-spirits and eat it afterwards, so as to make the spirits look with favour on them, and to make their households more prosperous."

Yet the clearest depiction of an elf from this time is sympathetic, even though it appears in two sagas about Iceland's conversion to Christianity. Driving the Ring Road north, along the edge of Hunavatn you'll pass a pretty picnic spot with a monument to one of Iceland's first missionaries, Thorvald the Far-Traveler. The monument is set before a large stone standing all on its own in the middle of a grassy field, a vaguely pyramidal stone, tall as a house, weathered gray, and speckled with black, green, and silver spots of lichen. Large cracks run deep into its interior.

According to these two sagas, Thorvald saw the light when he lived abroad; he was baptized and brought a Saxon bishop home with him in 977. The two of them traveled about Iceland spreading the gospel, but "most people made little response to their words," says *The Saga of Christianity*. Even Thorvald's father, Kodran, was "slow to respond." He and his kinsmen, he said, had always put their faith in the elf who lived in that magnificent large stone over there. He said the elf was the farm's steward.

"He is very helpful," Kodran explains in "The Story of Thorvald the Far-Traveler." "He tells me of many things that have not yet taken place. He protects my livestock, and he reminds me of things I ought to do, as well as warning me of things to beware of."

"Christ is stronger than the steward in the stone," Thorvald said. If the bishop proved it, would his father convert? After much persuasion, Kodran told his son that he would.

For three cold winter nights, the bishop chanted psalms while pouring buckets of holy water over the stone. If you know anything about ancient stone-working techniques—or even if you just know physics—you can guess what will happen when the water fills tiny cracks in the stone, freezes, and expands. Kodran, however, could not guess. Iceland has no stone-working tradition.

The first night, the elf—called a "false prophet" by the saga writer—came to Kodran in a dream. He looked sad, and he trembled with fear. "Ill have you done to invite those men here," he said. "They are pouring boiling water over my house, torturing my children with burning drops that trickle in through the roof. And though it doesn't hurt me so much, it's terrible to hear the screams of my little ones as they are burned!"

The second night, the "fiend," as the saga then termed him, came again. Usually he was bright and cheerful and beautifully dressed. Now he wore a ragged old fisherman's cloak and was frowning. He spoke in a shaky voice, "These men are trying to rob us both of good and useful things. They want to chase me from my family home and to deprive you of my loving care and foresight. Be a man and stand up to them," he pleaded. "Drive them away, or we will both lose much."

A third time the "evil spirit" appeared. His expression was mournful, his voice wailing and whining. The bishop, he complained, "has destroyed my house. He has poured boiling water over me and ruined my clothes, ripping them and making everything unusable. My family and I will never recover from the burns he has inflicted, and now he tries to cast us out into the wilderness. You and I must break off our friendship and never again live side by side. Who will look after your farm as faithfully as I have?" His last words to his friend were, "You call yourself a righteous and trustworthy man, but you have returned evil for good."

The next morning, the stone cracked in several places, and the elf came no more. Kodran and his wife and all their household were baptized—except for one son, who sided with the faithful elf. Did the medieval author of this story realize how much he was undermining his Christian message? It's hard to applaud the torturing of little children or to refute the elf's charge that Kodran had returned evil for good. It's hard not to agree that both man and elf would lose much if their long friendship were severed. What did Kodran choose? Strength over usefulness, power over loyalty, the universal over the local, conformity over individuality, the new over the old.

Recall, too, that the story was written down at least two hundred years after the events occurred (if they occurred). Through generations of retellings, and in spite of the saga author's Christian upbringing, whispers remain of an ancient pact between men and elves, of a time when the land and its guardian spirits were respected, and when such an approach—that magnificent large stones should be revered as elf homes, not bulldozed or buried—brought people happiness and a sense of community with the land.

Other sagas treat elves with similar hidden respect. Just before Iceland became Christian, says one, an old elf-seer announced that "many a mound is opening and every creature, great and small, is packing its bags and preparing to move on." Explains Sian Gronlie, one translator of *The Saga of Christianity*, "Such stories convey something of the radical change to the landscape brought by Christianity—not only the pulling down of heathen temples and the building of Christian churches, but more significantly the desanctification of the natural world." Think of that term, *desanctification.* With the coming of Christianity, Iceland was no longer holy earth. It was to be used, not revered, while holiness was confined within walls.

This desanctification is both an accident of Christianity and its root. Christianity's concept of time is linear—from creation to apocalypse—and not circular, from spring to winter to spring again. Christianity is also "the most anthropocentric religion the world has seen," writes historian Lynn Townsend White Jr., in a much-quoted essay on ecology published in *Science* in 1967. (I found it quoted as an epigraph for Annie Proulx's 2016 novel *Barkskins*; it deserves to be quoted even more widely.) "Christianity, in absolute contrast to ancient paganism and Asia's religions," writes White, "not only established a dualism of man and nature but also insisted that it is God's will that man exploit nature for his proper ends." (Proulx's *Barkskins* is a multigenerational saga of such exploitation; it's not a cheerful read.)

"What people do about their ecology," notes White, "depends on what they think about themselves in relation to things around them." And Western Christians (the Eastern Orthodox Church took a different path) think of themselves first as "superior to nature, contemptuous of it, willing to use it for our slightest whim."

Science and technology are part of the problem. White singles out the moldboard plow, invented in the 600s. This plow had two knife edges. One cut the furrow. The second sliced under the turf, which the moldboard then tossed aside, roots up. "The friction of this plow with the soil," writes White, "was so great that it normally required not two but eight oxen." No single farm family could afford eight oxen. With this new plowing technology, "distribution of land was based no longer on the needs of a family but, rather, on the capacity of a power machine to till the earth. Man's relation to the soil was profoundly changed. Formerly man had been part of nature; now he was the exploiter of nature."

By the year 1000, Arabic mathematics and astronomy were entering the West, changing the way Christian thinkers viewed God's creation. "In the early Church, and always in the Greek East," writes White, "nature was conceived primarily as a symbolic system through which God speaks to men: the ant is a sermon to sluggards; rising flames are the symbol of the soul's aspiration. The view of nature was essentially artistic rather than scientific." Between 1000 and 1300, when a rush of scientific translations from Arabic to Latin hit Europe, this natural theology changed: Instead of "decoding . . . the physical symbols of God's communication with man," educated Christians worked to "understand God's mind by discovering how his creation operates."

By White's day—and ours—many Western scientists had rejected the idea of God. But they did not reject the Christian concepts of linear time or of the superiority of humans to farm fields, flames, or ants. And they have, emphatically, not rejected the Christian interpretation of dragons, elves, or other nature spirits. Writes White: "In Antiquity every tree, every spring, every stream, every hill had its own *genius loci*, its guardian spirit. These spirits were accessible to men, but were very unlike men; centaurs, fauns, and mermaids show their ambivalence. Before one cut a tree, mined a mountain, or dammed a brook, it was important to placate the spirit in charge of that particular situation, and to keep it placated. By destroying pagan animism, Christianity made it possible to exploit nature in a mood of indifference to the feelings of natural objects."

Saints, some say, replaced these guardian spirits; if so, their tenure lasted only until the Protestant Reformation in the mid-1500s. But White thinks the equation of saints with nature spirits is false. Saints are human and respond in understandably human ways. They are not *in* the shrine or holy well dedicated to their names; they are in heaven. Saints are not natural—not a part of nature—at all.

For our current ecological crisis, White wrote in 1967, "Christianity bears a huge burden of guilt. What we do about ecology depends on our ideas of the man-nature relationship. More science and more technology are not going to get us out of the present ecologic crisis until we find a new religion, or rethink our old one."

Icelanders, with their amalgamation of Christian and pagan views, might show us the way. When Iceland became Christian in the year 1000, the shift from an artistic view of nature to a scientific one was just beginning to affect European culture; it did not greatly skew the Icelanders' outlook. Having no major crops but hay, Iceland never adopted the moldboard plow and its eight-oxen team; Icelanders' relationship with the soil did not change much until tractors and bulldozers were introduced in the twentieth century. In the Middle Ages, a few Arabic science books were translated into Icelandic, but most of Iceland's educated thinkers were producing not science or technology, but sagas and poems. During the Enlightenment, Iceland suffered from famine, piracy, smallpox, and catastrophic volcanic eruptions; its thinkers focused on preserving the sagas. The Industrial Revolution did not arrive on the island until 1902, when the first fishing boat was motorized.

In 1918, when Iceland was declared an independent nation in a personal union with the Danish king, a new coat of arms was required. From the sixteenth century until 1903, Iceland's symbol had been a dried codfish. From 1903 to 1919, it was a silver falcon. The design chosen in 1919 references a tale told by the medieval writer Snorri Sturluson of four magical beings that once protected Iceland from attack. In the early 990s, the story goes, the king of Denmark decided to chastise the Icelanders for making up rude poems about him. The king sent a wizard, in the shape of a whale, to spy on the country for him and find its weaknesses. In the east of Iceland, the wizard-whale was chased off by a dragon, in the north by an enormous bird, in the west by a monstrous bull, and in the south by a giant. The wizard told the king that Iceland was too well protected to attack.

On Iceland's coat of arms, a red and white cross on a blue field is surrounded by a dragon, an eagle, a bull, and a (stately, white-bearded) giant. These four protecting spirits are so suspiciously similar to the symbols of the four Evangelists—Matthew (a man), Mark (a lion), Luke (an ox), and John (an eagle)—that no one can say if they pre-date Christianity. But they do not fight alone; each is accompanied by an army of lesser nature spirits that Snorri calls *landvættir*. As he writes, when the wizard-whale approached Iceland, "He saw that all the mountains and hills were full of land-spirits, some big and some small." Some take the shape of humans, some of serpents, some of birds, and some are shapeless. In fact, the first law passed in the country, according to *The Book of Land-Taking*, acknowledged these same spirits of the land: The gruesome carved figureheads on Viking ships, those dragon heads with gaping mouths, had to be lifted off the ships' prows before the Vikings came within sight of land, so as not to upset the land spirits.

And in spite of Christian missionaries cracking open their homes and sending them packing for a thousand years, Iceland's land spirits have endured. In 1964, the American poet W. H. Auden revisited Iceland. In Reykjavik he met the young scholar Paul Beekman Taylor, with whom he would later translate poems about Norse gods and giants from the medieval collection known as the *Poetic Edda*. Auden and Taylor discussed the "mythic truth" of Old Icelandic literature, which was neither fiction nor history. "One does not believe a saga or *Edda* character," said Taylor, "but finds him true."

"That is what distinguishes the *Edda*s and the sagas from European literature," Auden said in a lecture a few days later. "The Icelanders' world of story does not differentiate a primary secular world of tenuous social survival from a manufactured secure world of art. I heard an example of this yesterday. It appears that a number of inexplicable accidents occurred recently in a quarry near Akureyri where there was drilling for hot water. One evening, the foreman on the site dreamt of a visit by rock elves, whose leader said that they were upset because they hadn't had time to find new homes. The foreman advised the town council, and the work was suspended for a few days, after which everything went on without incident. So, you see, the Icelanders still live on a terrain which holds the essential elements of story their pagan ancestors wove into myth. They live in a world in which 'mythic reality' is indistinguishable from any other reality." In 1964, wrote Taylor years later, Auden rediscovered "an Iceland in which poetry was practiced as a craft that forges mythical treasure items in and for the public good."

A few years later, Icelandic poet Sveinbjorn Beinteinsson and some friends mined Norse mythology and Icelandic folklore to create the modern animistic religion of Asatru. They visited Iceland's minister of justice and ecclesiastical affairs in late 1972 to register the new religion (earning it a cut of the national religion tax), but the minister brushed them off. He made vague references to "the necessary paperwork." They found him insincere. "Clearly Thor the Thunder God thought so too," reported the Icelandic newspaper *Vísir*, "for as the minister stood up to show them the door, a mighty thunderbolt fell from the sky, causing damage in the middle of Reykjavik not far from the government offices."

Thunder and lightning are rare in Iceland, usually occurring only in conjunction with volcanic eruptions. No one Michael Strmiska spoke with about this incident "insisted in somber tones that it be understood as a miracle," he writes in *Nova Religio: The Journal of Alternative and Emergent Religions*, "but many took a mischievous delight in the possibility. This mixture of reverence and humor is a distinctive characteristic of the Asatru religious attitude, winking at the sacred more often than worshipping it, but with an extremely affectionate and knowing wink, like that shared between friends or lovers."

In May 1973, Asatru was officially recognized. It is now the fastest-growing religion in Iceland. Asatru is, says a recent handbook, "a way of thinking and connecting with the natural world."

A Kind Troll

In 2017, Ragnhildur Jonsdottir moved thirty-five miles from town to the steep shores of Whale Fjord. That June, over tea and rhubarb pie, we sat with our husbands in her glassed-in porch, watching the neighbor's horse herd roam and graze and Ragnhildur's cats stalk along the tin roof of her studio/gallery space and chicken coop; we tried to ignore the bright blue-painted stacks and blocks of the cement plant and aluminum smelter across the fjord. Tired from a midnight horseback ride, I didn't ask for an elf walk, though this property—renamed Elf Garden—was the site of the first public elf walk Ragnhildur ever gave, a spur-of-the-moment idea at the opening of an art exhibit in 2009. Instead, we shared stories.

One was the story of this house. The farmers who lived next door at Kidafell had converted the old barn and stable into an exhibit space and lecture hall; they rented out rooms in the house to tourists. When they decided to sell it, they put the property on the market and received a fair offer. That night the farmwife, Begga, dreamed of Ragnhildur, though they had not kept in close touch after Ragnhildur's exhibit. She dreamed of her for several nights. Finally, she had to call and tell her that they were selling the house. She thought the dreams meant they should sell it to Ragnhildur and not accept the good offer they had already received. She did not know that Ragnhildur was looking for a house out of town and had just had an offer on a property refused. Ragnhildur and her husband walked through the Whale Fjord house and it felt so much like home they bought it. They moved in shortly afterward.

"On the ridge behind the house," Ragnhildur said, reprising a tale she had told on her elf walk in 2009, "there lives a *skessa*." The word is usually translated as troll woman, though its definition is problematic. Begga was out herding sheep one autumn and the ridge was very icy. Chasing a stray, she found herself stuck—she could go neither up nor down the mountain for fear of slipping on the ice and falling. While she stood there, confused and scared, she felt a large hand lift her up a few feet to a secure place, from which she could scramble to safety. Ragnhildur learned about the incident from the *skessa*. Feeling her presence in the mountain, Ragnhildur asked her if she was a kind troll or an evil troll, and the troll woman said she should ask Begga about the sheep roundup. Begga was surprised. She had not told anyone a troll woman had helped her.

"Kind troll" seemed to me an oxymoron. In the stories I knew, trolls were evil and ugly and stupid. They could be tricked, but never trusted. Large, benevolent mountain beings should be called giants—like the one on Iceland's coat of arms. That instinct of mine, to distinguish evil troll from kindly giant and insist that only one or the other can be translated to *skessa*, is a modern fault. It dates from the eighteenth-century system of taxonomy devised by Swedish botanist Carl Linnaeus, in which the living creatures of the world are sorted into imaginary boxes called species.

Scientists still quibble over the exact meaning of *species*. The lumpers like fewer large boxes; the splitters like many small ones. But a common meaning is that members of a species can mate and produce fertile young. That definition fails when faced with Icelandic folklore. Writing about the monstrous women in some sagas, scholar Sandra Straubhaar notes that "Trolls (*tröll*), giants (*jötnar*), and fabulous monsters (*finngálkn*) constitute variable categories among themselves; and any of them *might* be human enough to breed with." The same is true of elves.

Worse, *troll* and *elf* are interchangeable. In Old Norse texts, *álfr* means, not "an elf," but something broader. The word is used, says folklorist Armann Jakobsson, "for every paranormal figure that is clearly superior to humans—somewhat like a modern anthropologist might use the term 'god' (or 'deity') to mean 'a god' rather than 'God.'" Dwarfs and trolls are called elves in these texts—and so are some humans. There are no clear categorical divisions. "What stands out is the fluidity of the concepts."

Their association with good and evil is nearly as fluid. The first troll we meet in an Old Norse text is a poet. She appears in a forest, late at night, and challenges Bragi the Old to a poetry contest, which he (having been allowed to travel on) claims to have won. "There is no indication that she was larger (or smaller) than Bragi, and no indication that she was old or young, beautiful or hideous," writes John Lindow in *Trolls: An Unnatural History*. She is dangerous, but not necessarily evil: Having established the rules of their word-duel, she abides by them. She is "mysterious, inexplicable, and unknowable." She is the Other.

The earliest Norse elves are just as inexplicable. An episode in Snorri Sturluson's *Heimskringla* sounds like a modern elf story—except that Snorri calls the creature a dwarf. On a large estate in Estonia stood a rock the size of a house. One evening, after sunset, when he was very drunk, King Sveigdir saw a doorway open in the rock. A dwarf invited him in to meet the god Odin. King Sveigdir entered, and was never seen again. Snorri's source is a poem by Thjodolf of Hvin, dated to the ninth century; it contains the oldest use of the word *dwarf* (*dvergr*) in any Germanic language.

All that's clear about the elves is that they were once worshipped. Riding through Sweden in 1017, an Icelandic poet stepped into a farmhouse and asked for a place to stay. Realizing he was Christian, the farmwife turned him out. Sighvat, the poet, recounts the story in verse:

"No farther can you enter,
You wretch!" said the woman,
"Here we are heathens
And I fear the wrath of Odin."
She shoved me out like a wolf,
That arrogant termagant,
Said she was holding sacrifice
To elves there in her house.

Folklorist Jacqueline Simpson concludes that "we see that the word 'elf' existed in heathen Iceland, and we can deduce that it referred to something of importance, but beyond that we can only guess at the meaning or meanings it contained."

Terry Gunnell guesses that the word is a synonym for Vanir, the clan of Norse gods who fought with, and were subsumed by, the Aesir gods led by Odin. Thus, when the poem called *The Song of the Seer* asks, "What of the Aesir, what of the elves?" the seer may really be asking, "What of these gods, what of those?" *Vanir* is related to words for friend, pleasure, and desire. The Vanir gods include Njord, the god of the sea, and his children, Freyr and Freyja (whose names mean Lord and Lady), the god and goddess of rain and sun, wealth and prosperity, love and peace. Heimdall, called the White God, is also one of the Vanir. He stands guard at the rainbow bridge connecting the worlds of gods and men. His senses are so sharp he can hear the grass grow, says one text; another says Heimdall, like the other Vanir, can see into the future; a third calls him the "son of nine mothers," perhaps meaning the nine types of waves in the sea.

Gunnell concludes "we should be highly wary about ever referring to the earlier manifestations of *álfar* as 'elves,' unless we use the term in the Tolkienian sense of the word whereby they represent a form of godlike entity associated with the land." In *The Lord of the Rings*, we and the hobbits first meet the elves in a forest after sunset: "They passed slowly, and the hobbits could see the starlight glimmering on their hair and in their eyes. They bore no lights, yet as they walked a shimmer, like the light of the moon above the rim of the hills before it rises, seemed to fall about their feet." Later, an elf lord appears as "a white figure that shone and did not grow dim like the others," while the elf queen Galadriel, creator and protector of the forest of Lothlorien, is "beautiful beyond enduring, terrible and worshipful," and seems to have caught the evening star in the ring on her finger.

J. R. R. Tolkien, a philologist, knew that the root of Old Norse *álfr* and Anglo-Saxon *aelf* is an Indo-European word for white. *Aelf* appears in several Old English names, a few of which—like Alfred (Elf-Wisdom) or Elwin (Elf-Friend)—are still common. Beautiful women, even Biblical women like Sarah, the wife of Abraham, or Judith, who beheaded Holofernes, are described in Old English as *aelfsciene*. The second part of the word means shining or skin or, perhaps, illusion; *scinncraeft* is magic or sorcery. As linguist Noel Williams concludes, "It seems reasonable to suggest that Anglo-Saxons were aware of a group of supernatural beings having a shining appearance. Whether this group was evil or not before the advent of Christianity cannot be determined."

By 1230, there was no question that they were evil. In that year William of Auvergne, the bishop of Paris, wrote *De Universo* (*On the Universe*), wherein he systematically laid out the method for equating devils to elves (the native English term) and fairies (from Anglo-Norman French, the language of England after the Norman Conquest in 1066). By 1400, people who professed to see elves or fairies were branded, in an English sermon, as "faithless and worse than pagans, and four times a year they are cursed by the Lord and his holy church." The only supernatural beings it was safe to see were saints and angels—and even they were suspect. During her trial for heresy in 1431, Joan of Arc was accused of having seen not saints and angels, but elves or fairies under the well-known Fairy Tree or Tree of the Ladies near her home. Her visions were deemed "false and diabolical," and Joan was burned at the stake (though in later years her reputation was cleared and she herself was declared a saint).

When he analyzed 2,064 instances of the word *fairy*, spelled in various ways, in 468 English texts written before 1829, Williams found that before 1400 the word rarely referred to a being. The enchantress in the King Arthur tales, Morgan le Fay, for example, might better be translated as Morgan the Strange than Morgan the Fairy. Yet etymologists have routinely derived *fairy* from words that refer to supernatural females, such as the Latin *nympha* and the Arabic *peri*. The accepted etymology now traces the word to the classical Latin *fatum*, or "thing said," from which we get *fate*. Some early readers, whose Latin grammar was faulty, mistook the plural form, *fata*, to be a feminine singular noun meaning goddess. On its way through Old French to Anglo-Norman to English, *fata* lost a consonant and became *fée* or *fay*. Spelled *fey*, the word still means fated to die. The English *fairy* originally meant enchantment, or a place under enchantment: *Fée-erie* was the home of the *fées*. In *The Canterbury Tales*, Chaucer's Wife of Bath tells a story of King Arthur's court. In those days, she begins, England was "full of *fayerye*"—meaning enchantment. "The elf queen with her jolly company danced full often in many a green meadow." English elves became fairies after 1400, Williams suggests, simply because it's easier to rhyme on the sound "ee."

Chaucer also hints at how elves became devils and elf-seers became heretics fit for burning at the stake. According to the

Wife of Bath, no one sees elves anymore because of the crowds of monks and friars who travel the countryside "thick as dust motes in a sunbeam" blessing "halls, chambers, kitchens, bowers, cities, forts, castles, towers." It was a question of social control.

Already by Chaucer's day, in the late 1300s, the encounter with the elf queen was a cliché. A long-lived favorite first mentioned in the 1200s, and codified by Sir Walter Scott in the late 1700s, was the tale of Thomas the Rhymer. Having fallen asleep under a hawthorn tree, Thomas woke to see a beautiful lady riding toward him on a white horse. He greeted her—and that was his mistake, for having addressed the elf queen he was then in her power. They made love, says one version, seven times. She then took him (willingly) up on her white horse and off to her castle, swearing him to silence. After three (or seven, accounts vary) days, she returned him to his tree, where he learned that three (or seven) years had passed. As her parting gift she made him a poet and a prophet. Such fairy tales, writes Carolyne Larrington in *The Land of the Green Man*, "offer ways of thinking" about sex ("What would men and women be like if their sexual desires were uninhibited by the Church?"), about the passage of time ("Is it worth living for ever, if you lose contact with everyone you have ever known and loved?"), and about virtuosity (Whence come eloquence and inspiration? How does an ordinary daydreamer grow into a prophet and a poet?).

Needless to say, such thinking was not encouraged by the Church. Virtuosity was "the property of Satan," explains John Lindow. Thomas needed to be put in his place: Ordinary people should remain ordinary. The passage of time, on the other hand, was "the property of the Christian Church": The rituals of baptism, marriage, and burial ordered human life. Elves who could stop time or reverse it were a threat. Uncontrolled sex? That was not "the 'human' way of doing things," Lindow notes. Only animals and elves showed no restraint. For these reasons the Church spent centuries systematically suppressing fairy lore, writes Richard Firth Green in *Elf Queens and Holy Friars*. "The official record is the story of an ever-increasing demonization of fairies and infernalization of fairyland throughout the course of the Middle Ages," he writes, "culminating in the terrible witch hunts of the early modern period." For hundreds of years, believing in elves could get you killed.

How, then, did this belief evolve from perilous to ridiculous? How did elf-seers go from being cursed four times a year—even burned at the stake—to being labeled "loony"?

I blame the artists—and their patrons. What image comes to mind when I say "elf" or "fairy"? Do you see Santa's toymakers? The Keebler Elves? The Tooth Fairy? Tinkerbell? Or (like me) Galadriel, as so beautifully acted by Cate Blanchett? The storytellers who described elves and fairies over the centuries shaped the beings the words evoke. In English, the most powerful of these artists—before Tolkien, at least—was William Shakespeare. He did more than just bring elves to the stage when the Protestant Reformation gave him license to do so: He shrank them. In the famous scene from *Romeo and Juliet*, Mercutio says he dreamed of a fairy, Queen Mab, "In shape no bigger than an agate-stone," the gemstone in the ring on a rich man's finger. This fairy queen, rather than riding a shining white horse, comes in a chariot made from half a hazelnut shell and the gauzy bits of grasshoppers' wings, with spider's silk for the reins and traces. Her coachman is a gnat. "She gallops night by night / Through lovers' brains, and then they dream of love," or else she spends her time tangling girls' long hair into "elf-locks," or what my mother called rats' nests. Where once elves were godlike, now they're insectlike. Where once the elf queen had turned Thomas into a sex toy, now how would that work? The elf queen can sit on his fingertip.

In "On Fairy-stories," Tolkien quotes the definition of *fairies* in the *Oxford English Dictionary*, "supernatural beings of diminutive size," and takes issue with each adjective. "Supernatural," he says, can hardly be applied to fairies "unless *super* is taken merely as a superlative prefix." For fairies embody nature. As for "diminutive," Tolkien speculates that English fairies shrank when the world shrank. He writes, "I suspect that this flower-and-butterfly minuteness was also a product of 'rationalization,' which transformed the glamour of Elfland into mere finesse, and invisibility into a fragility that could hide in a cowslip or shrink behind a blade of grass. It seems to become fashionable soon after the great voyages had begun to make the world seem too narrow to hold both men and elves; when the magic land of Hy Breasail in the West had become the mere Brazils." In 1595, when Shakespeare wrote *Romeo and Juliet*, the Portuguese colony of Brazil was nearly a hundred years old.

Iceland's elves did not shrink when the world shrank, but did so several centuries later—or at least some of them shrank. In the polls from 1978, 1995, and 1998, which found some 48 to 70 percent of Icelanders believed in elves (or at least acknowledged the possibility of their existence), *elf* was not defined. Terry Gunnell's 2007 poll distinguished between flower fairies and house fairies, still without describing them. Elf-seer Erla Stefansdottir is one who saw flower fairies. As a child of six, she told anthropologists Gisli Palsson and Hugh Raffles shortly before her death in 2015, "I noticed that my girlfriends only saw the flower fairies in August. They were butterflies. I confused flower fairies with butterflies." While her friends saw them only in season, Gisli explained, translating for Raffles, Erla saw butterflylike creatures throughout the year. She also saw auras and energies, Hidden Folk like small humans, and very tall mountain elves, she told another interviewer. A reporter for the *Chicago Tribune*, who attended the Reykjavik Elf School in 2017, learned that there are "thirteen different kinds of elves, five kinds of *huldufólk* (hidden people), and any number of gnomes, dwarfs, and trolls" in Iceland. The elves "range in size from two to forty-seven inches in height," he was told. The Hidden Folk are "closer to human size." My friend Ragnhildur Jonsdottir has posted photos on Facebook of elves—they look like rainbow-hued lens effects to me—and her books include pictures of small people in old-fashioned clothes and funny hats. According to the Elf School report, "There are no pointy hats." Ragnhildur disagrees.

Armann Jakobsson calls this mix of visions the "New Age elf": "He reflects the uneasy relationship we have with nature, even to the point of tending to be regarded as slightly smaller than and inferior to us. Our role is to rediscover him and protect him, in very much the same way as our role is to protect an earth that is nowadays seen as in our power."

Iceland's elves have always been shapeshifters. The word is a bottle, the concept a liquid. Throughout history and across cultures, elves can only be seen when they wish to be seen, and they can take on whatever shape they like. Or perhaps what's true about mountains is also true about elves: We see what we've been trained to see, what our education allows us to see. In parts of Iceland, that still includes the Hidden Folk.

In 2008, Gunnell's student Juliana Magnusdottir heard this story from a sixty-five-year-old woman: Before she moved to her farm she dreamed of the place, the woman said. She was standing in the yard beside a large stone, which seemed to her to be a fine house itself. A woman lived in the stone, "an ordinary looking woman, except that I knew in my dream she was not of this world." Juliana's informant (she doesn't name her) spoke to the dream woman, "I was somehow so incredibly curious—and she said something like this to me: 'So long as you put your trust in me, you needn't worry about a thing.' And what is so strange is that I've often thought of this woman since. Often when I've thought, 'Well, we don't have two coins to rub together, how are we going to manage that?' something has come up that takes care of the matter." It was so strange, she added, that she asked the old farmer who used to live on the property if he knew of any Hidden Folk living nearby. No, he said, he didn't think so. Then he remembered the time his father began to build a little storage hut beside the big stone in the yard. He planned to make three wooden walls and use the stone as the fourth. He had started building but then he had a dream. He never finished the hut.

"Yes, isn't there a woman living in the stone?"

"Oh, I don't know anything about that," said the old man. "I've never heard about that."

FIVE

"There is a magic at work
there in the words."

—Ursula K. Le Guin

Snaefellsjokull

Wonder

I n the 1200s, the Icelandic Commonwealth self-destructed. The Icelanders' loss of independence is chronicled in *Sturlunga Saga*, a saga I long tried to ignore. Written by eyewitnesses, it has none of the narrative flair of *Njal's Saga*, the best of the Icelandic sagas—though it may be, in part, the same writer's work. The *Sturlunga* heroes are all fatally flawed. There are few you can root for, and if you do, they'll die, ignominiously, surrounded and stoned—not bravely with a bloodied sword—as Iceland fractures into feuding camps. It's altogether too real.

Such realism makes the few incursions of the supernatural all the more remarkable. I've already mentioned the "Winter of Marvels," when "a host of elves" rode through Skagafjord. In *The Troll Inside You*, Armann Jakobsson discusses another winter episode from *Sturlunga Saga*. In this story, a party of seventeen men ransacked two farmhouses and executed a man in each—spies, they said. They were heading home over the mountains when "they saw a great troll. It swung away," as if to avoid them. Some of the men, the saga says, "were startled," but Asbjorn, their leader "scolded them for it." Insisting they should ride on, Asbjorn spurred his horse into an ice-choked river and drowned, dragged under by his heavy cloak. He had dismissed the obvious: The ford was impassable. The natural world was not under his control. The troll, Armann writes, "is danger, death, and the vastness extending beyond the human grasp of the world. No small role has the troll." And yet it does nothing threatening. It's never even described. "Possibly it is too distant, a black shape in the night," Armann writes. "How then do they know it is a troll? One suspects their own feelings told them so. They are afraid, that is how they know." Like the dragon of fear that appeared to the wayward monk in St. Benedict's tale, the troll is a cultural artifact: It's how medieval Icelanders explained a certain nebulous feeling. What Armann calls "troll space" is not to be found in the landscape, but in our interactions with it. Troll space is "real," he says, but not "independent of human consciousness." These men and their troll are "inextricably intertwined."

Neuroscientists investigating mystical experiences—trips into troll space, but also orthodox religious practices—tend to agree with Armann, to a point. "Are they just illusions, delusions," muses Andrew Newberg in a 2015 interview, or are people "getting glimpses of something that is a far more profound perspective on the entire universe than typically experienced? The short answer is: We do not know."

Newberg is a founder of neurotheology, the study of "the different areas and functions of the brain and how they help us or restrict us in terms of engaging the spiritual side of ourselves." He and Eugene d'Aquili have scanned the brains of Buddhists meditating, Sikhs chanting, and Catholics, Jews, and Muslims praying, among others. In one experiment, they measured changes in the levels of serotonin and dopamine, neurotransmitters that govern anxiety and pleasure, after a seven-day spiritual retreat. In another, they detected changes in the brain's thalamus region, regarded by some as the seat of consciousness, after an eight-week course of meditation.

In a 1998 article subtitled "Why God Won't Go Away," they suggest that two of the brain's "operators"—their term for networks of neurons—are responsible for all religious experiences. The "causal operator" perceives causality: It traces a result back to its first cause; if it can't find one, it invents one. "We are proposing that gods, powers, spirits, or in general what we have come to call personalized power sources" (one of these terms doubtless applies to trolls) are "automatically generated by the causal operator." That is, given an unexplained phenomenon—a dark blot of fear in a snowy landscape—Asbjorn's brain plugged in a cause: troll. You can deal with a troll. You can ignore it, run from it, bargain with it. The causal operator gives us a sense of having control over the natural world (even when, as Asbjorn learned, we don't).

The second neural network, the "holistic operator," perceives wholeness in the midst of diversity. Rhythm awakens it, as does meditation, incense, flickering lights, fasting, prayer, and other ritual actions. It senses beauty, love, awe, and exaltation; it provides "a sense of insight into the world of the mysterious"; or it tips into trance, ultimately producing the state in which "the difference between self and other is obliterated. There is no sense of the passing of time, and all that remains is a perfect timeless undif-ferentiated consciousness" with no fear of death. D'Aquili and Newberg call that state Absolute Unitary Being. Depending on your point of view, it's the perfect union with God, it's Nirvana, it's the abyss, it's "a feeling of oneness with the universe."

Is, then, troll space—and God space—really all in your head? "Many find it deeply disturbing," d'Aquili and Newberg note, "that the experience of God, the sense of the absolute, the sense of mystery and beauty in the universe, the most profoundly moving experiences of which humans are capable, might be reducible to neural tuning, to specific patterns of neural blips on an oscillo-scope." But that's an overly pessimistic reading of their work, they say. Remember, "our experience of baseline reality (e.g., chairs, tables, love, hate) . . . can also be reduced to neural blips and fluxes of brain chemistry."

Does that make love, or the chair I'm sitting on, less real? How, I ask again, do we decide if something is "real"?

Interviewing people who claimed to have reached oneness with the universe, d'Aquili and Newberg found it was "virtually impos-sible to negate that experience, no matter what level of education or sophistication" the people had. "Neuropsychology," they conclude, "can give no answer to the question of which state is more real, baseline reality or hyperlucid unitary consciousness often experi-enced as God. We are reduced to saying that each is real in its own way and for its own adaptive ends." By adaptive they mean that our sense of each reality evolved to help humans survive.

Faced with the chaos of sensations that is our world, the brain "produces, at the very least, two basic versions," d'Aquili and

Newberg write. In one there are chairs and tables. In the other there are trolls, or God. Both seem "real." And both are guesswork, models of what is outside our skulls.

"One model may then be better than another, but all must actively be built upon ambiguous sensory data," writes anthropologist Stewart Guthrie in "A Cognitive Theory of Religion," adding, "The world is perpetually difficult and perpetually open-ended. When anthropologists (curiously) do not realize this, they are misled into arcane explanations of why otherwise reasonable people have specifically 'religious' beliefs"—or, as in the case of the medieval Icelanders, a belief in large, ugly, humanoid trolls. "They ignore the fact that all beliefs are similar in being attempts to resolve ambiguity."

Your choice of troll or God or both or neither is cultural: It depends on what you've read, what you've been taught, the stories you've been told. In 2014, a team of Danish cognitive scientists at Aarhus University's MINDlab recruited eight people who claimed to have had contact with spirits, seven who practiced New Age meditation, and eight with no mystical beliefs. Their average age was forty-one. One by one they were given a tour of the Aarhus Hospital's neurology wing. Then they were taken to the EEG laboratory and asked to sign a consent form testifying that they had no history of anxiety disorders, psychosis, or schizophrenia. They were given "highly suggestive" instructions on the test they were about to take. They were seated in a comfortable chair, blindfolded, and their ears were plugged. The "God helmet," a snowboard helmet fitted with a magnetic coil, was placed over their heads. The helmet was a sham, its electromagnetic field random and weaker than that of a wristwatch. The subjects' fingers were placed on a button, which they were told to press when they sensed a presence in the room. Then they were left, in the quiet, in the dark, alone, for an hour. Eleven of the twenty-three sensed another presence in the room.

"I clearly sensed that I was making contact with the other side," reported one subject, a self-proclaimed "spiritist." "I sensed a masculine energy . . . You know, when you walk past a person, it feels like there is a wind of sorts. That was how it felt."

"Our data clearly supports the potential for studying mystical experiences in a controlled environment," the researchers conclude. "We find, however, that successful elicitation of mystical experiences is particularly dependent upon the cultural background of the participants. Participants who believed in spirits reported stronger and more frequent experiences of sensed presence than the other two groups." The experiment also, strangely, "seems to depend on a high degree of belief in the wonders of modern science," the researchers note. "It appears that the participants' trust in the neural effects of wearing the electromagnetic helmet is important for eliciting unusual experiences."

We believe in spirits, we believe in science, we believe in elves, we believe in gravity, we believe in God, we believe in dark matter. We believe it's long past time to wrestle with that shapeshifting verb *to believe*. Does anyone really know what it means? Or is *belief*, like *elf*, simply a convenient vessel to pour our thoughts into?

Anthropologists, like himself, writes Rodney Needham, "appear to take it for granted that 'belief' is a word of as little ambiguity as 'spear' or 'cow'" when they write about the beliefs of this culture or that. Yet *belief* is kaleidoscopic. It translates a "bewildering variety" of foreign terms. Its root means to love or desire. Translators of the Bible used it to translate *trust* or *obey*. It means to follow a religion, to accept a statement as true, or to hold an opinion. You can say, "I believe I'll have fish for dinner" as easily as "I believe in elves."

Philosopher David Hume in 1739 defined belief as "something felt by the mind, which distinguishes the ideas of the judgment from the fictions of the imagination." Stuart Hampshire in 1959 defined a man's beliefs as "the generally unchanging background to his active thought," those things he "never had occasion to question" or to state. Jonathan Lanman, writing in 2008, defines belief as "the state of a cognitive system holding information (not necessarily in the propositional or explicit form) as true in the generation of further thought and behavior." Using this definition, Lanman asserts, we can "pursue a cross-cultural science of belief," as everyone has such beliefs. "All have cognitive systems that represent the world in some way and act according to what they believe to be true about that world."

Your beliefs define you. As fuzzy, illogical, or unquestioned as they may be, they control how you see the world and how you act in response. As Needham concludes, "An assertion of belief is a report about the person who makes it, and not intrinsically or primarily about objective matters of truth or fact." Belief, says Needham, is "ultimately a reference to an inner state." More, that inner state seems to be emotional. Yet we cannot say, in English at least, that someone is "believing" or "belief-full," Needham muses.

Philosopher Jesse Prinz thinks the emotion involved is wonder. It's wonder that produces both religion and science, as well as art: The three institutions "that are most central to our humanity," he says, are "united in wonder." They are not in conflict. They are not either/or. Each of the three feeds "the appetite that wonder excites in us," says Prinz. Each allows us "to transcend our animality by transporting us to hidden worlds." It's wonder, he argues, that makes us human.

"Wonder is sometimes said to be a childish emotion," Prinz writes, "one that we grow out of. But that is surely wrong. As adults, we might experience it when gaping at grand vistas." We wonder at volcanic eruptions, at a sudden sea fog. We wonder "when we discover extraordinary facts," he says, adding, "I was enthralled to learn that, when arranged in a line, the neurons in a human brain would stretch the 700 miles from London to Berlin." Adam Smith, the inventor of capitalism, wondered about wonder in 1795, Prinz notes. "He wrote that wonder arises 'when something quite new and singular is presented . . . [and] memory cannot, from all its stores, cast up any image that nearly resembles this strange appearance.'"

What is it like? the brain asks. *Like nothing I've ever seen before.*

Wonder is *sensory*: "We stare and widen our eyes," writes Prinz. Wonder is *cognitive*: "Such things are perplexing because we cannot rely on past experience to comprehend them . . . We gasp and say 'Wow!'" And then there is "a dimension that can be described as *spiritual*," Prinz says; what Smith termed "that swelling of the heart." Wonder, concludes Prinz, awakens us. "We don't just take the world for granted, we're struck by it."

Or we are not. Some people do not gape at grand vistas. I once had a boyfriend ask me to explain why I found a sunset beautiful. (I did not marry him.) For just as the Danish "God helmet" study found an openness to mystical experience to be cultural, emotions depend on culture, too. You will not sense wonder if you're never exposed to it.

Scientists used to think emotions were hardwired, that deep inside you was your lizard brain, covered by your mammalian brain, covered—and controlled—by your logical, human brain. That view of brain structure, says psychologist Lisa Feldman Barrett, is bogus. "Brains did not evolve in layers. Brains are like companies—they reorganize as they grow in size." There's no emotional "inner beast" tamed by logic. There's no archetypal battle between reason and passion. "We must discard the idea of the brain as a battlefield."

When Barrett's team at Northeastern University analyzed over two hundred studies of fear, sadness, anger, disgust, and happiness published between 1990 and 2011, they found that no emotion could be pegged to any one brain region. Neither did the more than twenty-two thousand people tested evince consistent physical responses. "The so-called fingerprints of emotion, like a grimace and elevated blood pressure for anger," are mere stereotypes. "Instances of a single emotion, such as fear, are handled by different brain patterns at different times, both in the same individual and in different people," Barrett explains. "This diversity isn't random. It's tied to the situation you're in." For Barrett, emotions are not triggered, they're constructed. Emotions are not obstacles, but tools, "ways to influence and regulate one another's nervous systems." And the more tools you own, the more effective you'll be.

Consider the brain's task. It is constantly bombarded with sensations from inside and outside the body: heart rate, temperature, breathing, sights, smells, sounds, that pain in your gut, the slippery feel of the rain on your skin. To keep you alive and well, your brain must interpret all these sensations, and it can't wait for a stimulus before it responds—it must be ready. It must have predictions in place to cover all options. Otherwise, says Barrett, you'd "never catch a baseball." You'd go through life "constantly surprised."

"How does your brain make sensations meaningful?" Barrett asks. "By categorizing them. This means using past experience, organized as concepts, to explain what caused the sensations and what to do about them." Without concepts, Barrett says, "you are experientially blind." The reverse is also true: The more concepts your brain understands, the better it can make sense of the world.

Among those concepts are emotions. The brains of "emotion experts," Barrett says, "can automatically construct emotional experiences with fine differences, like astonished, amazed, startled, dumbfounded, and shocked. For a person who exhibits more moderate emotional granularity, all of these words might belong to the same concept, 'surprised.' And for someone who exhibits low emotional granularity, these words might all correspond to feeling worked up." How do you become an emotion expert? "One approach is to learn new emotion words," Barrett says. "The words you hear affect how your brain is wired."

Here's a word: *ecstasy*. Not the drug, and not "being really happy." As defined by Jules Evans of the Centre for the History of the Emotions in London, *ecstasy* is "a moment when you stand outside your ordinary self, and feel a connection to something bigger than you. Such moments can be euphoric, but also terrifying." Since the eighteenth-century Enlightenment, it's been taboo to talk about ecstasy in the Western world. "If you suggest you're connected with the spirit world, you're likely to be considered ignorant, eccentric, or unwell," Evans notes. But 84 percent of the people he surveyed in 2016 admitted to having had an ecstatic experience; 75 percent agreed it was taboo to talk about it.

Philip Pullman, author of the fantasy trilogy His Dark Materials, is one who broke the taboo. He writes about a day in London in 1969 when, walking down Charing Cross Road, his "consciousness was temporarily altered, so that I was able to see things that are normally beyond the range of ordinary perception." He realized that "everything was connected by similarities and correspondences and echoes," that the universe was "alive, conscious, and full of purpose." His books, in which dark matter (Dust) is sentient, he says, are "an attempt to bear witness to the truth of that statement."

In *The Art of Losing Control*, Evans writes about his own quest for ecstasy. "The journey beyond the self is not safe or predictable," he warns. "On the other hand, staying in the self also has its risks—boredom, staleness, sterility, despair. Ultimately, there's something in us that calls to us, that pulls us out the door."

There's another way people have experienced ecstasy, though most of them wouldn't recommend it. In 1996, the neuroanatomist Jill Bolte Taylor had a stroke. The left hemisphere of her brain was incapacitated by a golf-ball-sized blood clot. It took her eight years to fully recover. In 2006, she published a book about her experience. In 2010, I sent a copy of *My Stroke of Insight* to my friend Vilhjalmur Knudsen, the volcano filmmaker who'd had a stroke.

"I'm very happy about it," Villi had told me, as he detailed his loss of a taste for beer, his inability to spell "London." Reading Taylor, I began to understand what he meant. She writes:

> The harder I tried to concentrate, the more fleeting my ideas seemed to be. Instead of finding answers and information, I met a growing sense of peace . . . As the language centers in my left hemisphere grew increasingly silent and I became detached from the memories of my life, I was comforted by an expanding sense of grace. In this void of higher cognition and details pertaining to my normal life, my consciousness soared into an all-knowingness, a "being at one" with the universe, if you will. In a compelling sort of way, it felt like the good road home and I liked it.

She felt "ethereal," like "a genie liberated from its bottle." She no longer ended "where my skin met air." She wondered how she would ever "be able to squeeze the enormousness of my spirit back inside this tiny cellular matrix" of her body. She wondered if she even wanted to.

She did recover and, being a brain scientist, studied her own recovery. When only the right hemisphere of her brain was functioning, she realized, she perceived people as "concentrated packages of energy." Some she felt brought her energy; some took it away. In addition to having to relearn to read and write, she had to be taught what color was: "I could not see color until I was told that color was a tool I could use" to put together a child's puzzle.

The same was true for seeing in 3D. Most importantly, she learned "how much choice I actually have about what goes on between my ears." She learned, "I may not be in total control of what happens to my life, but I certainly am in charge of how I choose to perceive my experience." She learned to "strengthen my neurocircuits of innocence and inner joy." She learned to "explore the world again with childlike curiosity."

There's much we don't know about the brain. But we know it categorizes. We know it uses concepts and words, finds causes, and crafts stories. We know it constantly simulates the world and makes multiple predictions of what we will sense and see—and what we should do in response. We know that it's wired for emotion, for wonder, for ecstasy, but that Western culture disdains and derides this side of the brain. We're taught to control our emotions, to give up wonder in childhood, to stifle our mystical experiences—or at least not to talk about them. Otherwise we'll be thought "ignorant, eccentric, or unwell." We'll be laughed at as loony elf-seers. But without words, without the concepts they describe, you are "experientially blind." Wonders may be all around, but you will not see them.

A Soul Clad in Air

On the westernmost tip of a peninsula that reaches out into the Atlantic some seventy miles north of Reykjavik sits an iconic snowy mountain like a pyramid with a divot in its peak, a shallow cone with horns. Its name, Snaefellsjokull, means Snow Mountain's Glacier. After my first time in Iceland I called it "the glacier," as Icelanders do, though it is actually a volcano crowned with ice. Once I watched it from a city balcony, a silhouette of blue against a sunset sky that dimmed from lemon to cantaloupe to salmon over the course of a long summer evening. In America, when we told our new friends, the three Icelandic graduate students studying at Penn State, that we wanted to go there, they approved. The economist said New Agers ranked the glacier the second most holy mountain in the world, after a peak in the Himalayas. The mother of the seismologist, who was visiting, added, "I know what they mean. I have never felt it like I felt it there." She did not define *it*.

Thordur Gretarsson, with whom I visited the volcano dragon, was a student when we met on that first trip in 1986. Hearing of our planned visit to the glacier, he told me the saga of its guardian spirit, Bard. It begins, as many Icelandic sagas do, when Bard must leave Norway after killing someone. He sailed to Iceland with his wife and nine daughters and established a farm beneath the glacier, near a hot spring-fed pool. His half brother settled on the neighboring farm, with his two young sons. One late winter day, when the children from both farms were playing on the beach, they dared each other to walk out onto the sea ice, farther and farther from shore, until the land disappeared in the cold sea fog. Helga, Bard's oldest daughter, won the dare and was the farthest out when the ice began to break up. The floe on which she stood sailed away west. Bard went berserk when he heard Helga was gone. He stormed into his half brother's house, picked up one boy in each hand, and carried them up onto the mountain. The elder boy, who was twelve, he threw into a deep crevasse. The younger he tossed over a cliff. Soon, filled with remorse, Bard himself disappeared. "People think he went into the glacier," the saga says, reappearing now and then as a typically embodied Icelandic ghost. While "he was more like a troll in looks and strength than like a regular human man," he was not an evil troll but a *bjargvættur*, a guardian spirit of the land. People trapped on the ice cap might suddenly find themselves rescued by a large ugly man in a hooded cloak, with a walrus-hide rope wrapped around his waist and a forked staff with two long iron prongs in his hand. People began to pray to him, to call out to him in need, the saga says.

"It's a magic mountain," Thordur agreed. "It's better, nicer in a way, to believe it than not. It's hard here in Iceland to find someone who believes in God," he added, "but everyone believes in ghosts. Especially when it's dark."

My husband and I took the bus out to Olafsvik, a small fishing village on the north side of the Snaefellsnes peninsula, and set up our supposedly Himalaya-proof tent. The wind blew it inside out. We packed up and checked in to the Hotel Nes. After a cold supper, we tried to hike up to the glacier, but the clouds came in, bringing rain in stinging horizontal sheets. We cried uncle. The backs of our legs got soaked as we hurried for the hotel. Out the window, we watched seagulls getting blown backward, rocking, pumping, going nowhere.

I never tried to climb the magic mountain again, but each of my succeeding trips to Iceland was made or marred by catching sight of it or failing to. As soon as my plane landed and I was on the airport shuttle, I'd crane my neck west to where the glacier might appear out of the sea. My journals are rich with sightings, or the wish for them:

Two horns on top like eyes on a skate, the glacier all white.

Went horseback riding for over four hours; the glacier kept itself hidden.

Last night around 9:00 we saw the top horns of the glacier appear above the clouds, impossibly high for a mountain and completely cut off from the land below.

The glacier came out after dinner, crisp against a rose-orange sky, one horn now dark, without snow.

Disa took me for a horseback ride. There were six to seven of us. Once I looked over and she and Juliane, both on white horses, were framed by the glacier and the shimmering silvery sands: a postcard.

The glacier was splendid at the end of the ness. The coves were full of birds . . . Tiny hoofprints of foals on the sand. Yellow sand, black rocks, green grass, blue ocean, white mountain in the distance.

We arrived in Reykjavik in time to see the glacier cut against a hot-pink sky—otherworldly.

No glacier, the clouds are too thick and low.

No glacier, but some other mountains came and went.

No glacier yet.

The glacier kept staring at us, beautiful and mysterious, with a creamy color on the ice.

A big group of sixty horses and eight to ten riders racing in a long line beneath the glacier, an image that just burns into your eyes.

Walking on the beach last night I felt the glacier drawing me on. The way back was so hard.

The first landscape painting from Iceland is a watercolor of Snaefellsjokull from the mid-1750s, I learned from my friend Haraldur Sigurdsson, the retired professor who runs the Volcano Museum in Stykkisholmur. The glacier is not only an "icon in art," he writes in *Snaefellsjokull: Art, Science and History of an Icelandic Volcano*, but "a mountain of many mysteries as well. Its relatively isolated location, far outside the main volcanic zones of Iceland, is a geologic puzzle." Speaking as a scientist, he admits, "We do not exactly know why it is there." It is "rather special and anomalous." It "creates a real paradox for geologists," as "it does not follow the simple paradigm of plate tectonics."

In 2013, I began leading tours to Iceland. One year, as we wandered by Bard's pool, Gabe Dunsmith, a twenty-three-year-old writer in our group, reminded me of the magical-realist novel *Christianity at Glacier*, published by Iceland's Nobel laureate Halldor Laxness in 1968. When I returned home, I reread it and was amused (or abashed) to find my obsession with Snaefellsjokull so well explained, my feeling that the mountain was sentient, that it was watching me, even when I could not see it, so beautifully expressed. "The glacier is never like an ordinary mountain," Laxness's narrator observes. "The sun shines on the glacier; it has once again moved closer. It was tantalizing this morning as it was tearing off the last shreds of fog; by midday it had come quite close, and yet one wanted it to come even closer." And the passage Gabe quoted: "It is often said of people with second sight that their soul leaves the body. That doesn't happen to the glacier. But the next time one looks at it, the body has left the glacier, and nothing remains except the soul clad in air."

A few weeks later I read Philip Marsden's *Rising Ground: A Search for the Spirit of Place*, about his move to an old farmhouse in England's West Country. "I'd been driving a good deal around Cornwall, sourcing and collecting materials for the house," Marsden writes. "Cresting a ridge or coming round the back of a hill, I played the game of trying to predict whether and where Rough Tor would be in view. When it was—however partial, however distant—its presence appeared to fill the entire view; and when it wasn't, there was a sense of unease, of expectation."

Unease or expectation—I feel it, too: anticipation, disappointment, fulfillment, emptiness, delight, despair—except that what blocks my view of the glacier is usually insubstantial mist.

The well-traveled Marsden reassures me, too, that the feeling of being drawn toward a magic mountain is universal. "I remembered the same feeling in Yerevan," he writes, "where the snow-capped presence of Mount Ararat dominates the city, so much so that when it was hidden behind a block, I found myself walking faster to see it again. I could feel it at my shoulder when it was behind me." And he cites others who share the feeling: "'I have cultivated in myself a sixth sense,' wrote Osip Mandelstam in the 1930s, 'an "Ararat" sense: the sense of attraction to a mountain.'"

That sixth sense is felt in Japan, too. In *Walking the Kiso Road*, William Scott Wilson speaks of Mount Ontake, "one of the holiest mountains in Japan": Though "it is only distantly visible from a few points along the Kiso Road, it dominates the spiritual landscape and is in some way there in the consciousness of everyone living in the post towns along this ancient route."

In just this way the glacier dominates the spiritual landscape of southwestern Iceland, looming across the bay from the city of Reykjavik, where two-thirds of Icelanders live, its presence growing stronger the closer you come. The Lutheran priest Arni Thorarinsson, whose parish in the early 1900s surrounded the glacier, spoke of the mountain's "enormous and strong magical radiation." Before his death in 1948 he remarked to an interviewer, "Do me the favor, dear, of stopping one day at Einarslon"—a nearby farm, once owned in part by the artist Johannes Kjarval, that "master of minute and exquisite gradations of gray" who painted the lava cliffs at Galgahraun in the rain. Einarslon, continued the priest, "is like in a supernatural world, the radiation from the Glacier is unreal, takes hold of the senses and puts your mind in an uproar."

As my friend's mother told me in 1986, *I have never felt it like I felt it there.*

Thirty years later, my childhood friend Ginger McCleskey and I spent several days under the glacier. She arrived a bit shaken after having encountered a ghost. The incident happened in the library of a guesthouse in southern Iceland that had once been a school. It was our second night traveling together, and I had a cold. Ginger stayed up late, posting photos of waterfalls to Facebook, warm in the knowledge that some other traveler sitting behind her in the lounge was also still working. She heard rustling, page-turning. Then she turned and found herself alone. As she told the story the next morning—to me and again to the young woman at the reception desk—she had felt her invisible friend follow her upstairs. She felt the ghost bounce on her bed, once, twice, three times, as if asking her to wake up and play. She was certain it was a child, a little boy. The third time she awoke, she told him to go away and not bother her again, and he did.

"Are there ghosts at this hotel?" she asked the receptionist.

The woman shook her head. She'd never seen one. But then she tilted her head to one side and added that sometimes she'd felt or heard things she didn't understand.

Dressing in many layers to walk through a lava field at the inland end of the Snaefellsnes peninsula on a drizzly day, the glacier invisible somewhere to our west, Ginger turned to me and joked, "We have the icy fingers of fog going on out there now."

"You might see the elves in this weather," I replied, in the same teasing vein.

She looked at me askance. "Let's just say I wasn't a believer, and now I think anything's possible."

Preparing for our trip, I'd purchased a little book called *The Magic of Snaefellsjokull* by Runa Gudrun Bergmann, who for many years ran the Hotel Hellnar, where we stayed when we reached the peninsula's tip. I read the book to Ginger aloud. One story concerned an elf rock called Einbui; the name means Hermit, or, literally, One Who Lives Alone. We'd passed the rock on a well-tramped trail from Hellnar to the next village, clusters of tourists in front and behind us. A tall lava stack, standing alone in a grassy dale, Einbui was not as photogenic as the black sea cliffs or the coruscated shoulder of the volcano, swathed in light clouds. To me it seemed like other tall solitary Icelandic rocks—a probable sun-struck troll. Yet, according to Runa, it was larger inside than out and housed a whole community of elves.

In April 2000, Runa writes, she was contacted by Norbert Maier, an Austrian harp player who wanted to play for the elves. Runa walked out to Einbui and asked her friends there for permission. "They were ecstatic and felt honored that their existence was being recognized in this way," she writes. The harpist set up his instrument beside the rock. Fifteen humans gathered round. Writes Runa:

> Once he started playing, it was as if the energy magically shifted and a large group of hidden people emerged and started dancing in a circle around us . . . When he stopped playing, the harp continued to play on its own for a few more minutes. In spite of the fact that there was a slight breeze, it was not the wind that was playing the harp, because the strings moved as if someone was pulling them. Afterwards Norbert told us that he had, on several occasions, played outdoors, but this had never occurred before. He also told us that during the entire time he played at Einbui, he felt there was someone standing beside him, playing the harp with him.

Ginger looked up from her iPad, where she'd been posting lava pictures to her Facebook album. "*That* I'll believe," she said, "after that dang ghost came and sat on my bed so many times the other night."

There's a lot in Runa's book we skipped over. Ginger lives in the San Francisco Bay Area, a hotbed of New Age thought, and

Runa's talk of an "energy vortex" and "ley lines" left her (and me) cold. It wasn't a vocabulary we were comfortable with. We did not follow her meaning, for instance, when Runa wrote that "In 1987, during the Harmonic Convergence, there was a major energy shift on Earth, and according to Erla there was also a shift in the Earth's Chakra system, and the heart Chakra, which had previously been in Tibet, was moved to Snaefellsjokull."

Erla, here, is Erla Stefansdottir, who said that seeing elves was like looking back in time; by profession she was a piano teacher. When anthropologist Gisli Palsson interviewed her in 2015, he asked how she sensed the places of power or energy.

"I cannot tell you that," said Erla. "I just see them. How can one explain? How do you see? I have never been able to [explain it]. It's just something I can both see and feel."

Runa begins her book with a similar statement: "As long as I can remember, I have heard talk about the mystique and the energy around Snaefellsjokull . . . If you had any doubt about the energy of the mystique, people would generally respond by saying that there was just something inexplicable about the area around the Glacier, and that one would just have to experience it to understand it." And she ends with: "Some may feel that parts of this book are a bit unfathomable. Perhaps you are not used to thinking and understanding the world the way I do, but I wanted to share this anyway. It's also good to remember that in an Icelandic thesaurus, another word for *unfathomable* is *spiritual.*"

At midnight, when the clouds lifted from the top of the glacier and its swirls and crests of ice began to turn lavender-pink, Ginger and I threw on our sweaters, jumped in the car, and drove as close to the mountain as we could go. As we stood out in the icy air, trying (and failing) to capture the splendor of the glacier in our photographs, we understood better what Runa was trying to say.

"No story is a lie, for a tale is a bridge that leads to the truth." Cognitive scientist Barbara Dancygier cites this line from *The Arabian Nights* in her book *The Language of Stories*, adding, "Perhaps 'the truth' is an exaggeration, but I found the quotation appropriate to this project, because it highlights the fact that whatever understanding a reader might acquire, it is not contained 'in' the story, but can only be arrived at through the interaction with it."

A story is not a box into which meaning is packed. A story—a book—is a path.

A Sense of Place

W riting from Reykjavik in 1871, William Morris, the writer
and Arts and Crafts designer, tried to convey to his wife
his first sight of Iceland from shipboard. He gave up. "It is no use
trying to describe it, but it was quite up to my utmost expectations
as to strangeness: It is just like nothing else in the world." Quoting
this letter in *The Idea of North*, Peter Davidson comments, "Like
other northern travellers before him, he was looking almost for
an otherworld."

And he seems to have found it. As did another traveler in
Davidson's book, Mariusz Wilk, who writes of life on islands
in the White Sea, "Reality in the North is thinner than anywhere
else, like a wool sweater worn out at the elbows, and the other
world shines through it."

Nan Shepherd, writing of the multiplying and merging blue
peaks and isles she saw in northern Scotland, in a poem from 1950,

says, "I have fallen through time and found the enchanted world."
Yet for her the geographical key was not northernness, but being
"on the edge of Europe" as "on the edge of being."

Edges resonate in the works of the artists Jane Ledwell spoke
about at a 2002 conference on Prince Edward Island: ambiguous
edges between sea and shore, self and other, present and past. The
role of the artist, Ledwell says, "is to show us the literal edge, and to
fear it, but not to fear the immersion of self, not to fear the blending
or melding of one identity with another, not to fear the possibility of
expansion of being through a relationship." An edge, says Ledwell,
"is a place of uncertainty and instability." It's where "things happen
that could not happen anywhere else."

Islands like Iceland are defined by their edges. Islands are
parcels of land—in a nineteenth-century Scottish definition they
must be big enough to "support at least one sheep"—surrounded
by water. That water either cuts them off from, or connects them
to, other lands, depending on your point of view: The term *insular*
(from the Latin *insula*, island) changed its meaning between 1611
("belonging and community") and 1755 ("isolation and alienation").
According to one calculation, Earth holds 680 billion islands,
"all of them different," writes Owe Ronstrom, an ethnologist at
the University of Gotland, who then reflects, "What is an island?
The obvious answer: a word. What are words? Beautifully small
and magically tensile forms, tools for thought and emotion. By
expressing ourselves, we give form to the world."

As real places, writes Pete Hay of the University of Tasmania
in the first issue of *Island Studies Journal*, islands "attract affection, loyalty, identification. And what do you get when you take

a bounded geographical entity and add an investment of human attachment, loyalty, and meaning?" he asks. "You get the phenomenon known as 'place.'"

The difference between *place* and *space* was codified in 1977 by geographer Yi-Fu Tuan: "Place is security, space is freedom: we are attached to the one and long for the other." We give a place meaning, he says, by knowing it thoroughly, through "smell, taste, and touch," through seeing and hearing, through emotion, and, perhaps most importantly, through reflection: "Thought tints all human experience," Tuan writes. "What can be known is a reality that is a construct of experience, a creation of feeling and thought."

Tuan seems to prefer freedom to security. Reviewing Tuan's *Cosmos and Hearth*, Herb Childress reads Tuan as saying that we—all humans—"are moving away from place toward space; and that this movement is a good thing." The hearth is "close-minded and illiterate," while the cosmos is "progressive, tolerant, and materially enriched" in Tuan's view. He teaches, Childress writes, "that it is inherently human, that it is inevitable, to leave the weary village behind and move into the 'sun and air.'" Childress finds that idea unsettling, as do I. Childress assigns it to Tuan's own unsettled existence: He "was born in China, moved to Australia at ten, to England at fifteen, and then to America in his early twenties, during which time he has studied at Berkeley, taught at the Universities of Indiana, Chicago, New Mexico, Toronto, Minnesota, and Wisconsin, and taken sabbatical or fellowship years in Hawaii, Australia, and California."

Childress compares the peripatetic Tuan to the poet Wendell Berry, who has lived all but four years of his life in Kentucky. "The more grounded, cyclical Berry, however, insists upon honoring 'local knowledge, memory, and tradition,' and will not let his hearth go without a hell of a fight." Childress calls this wisdom, and I agree—in the abstract. Unlike Berry I have no roots, no interest in the traditions of the Philadelphia suburbs where I was raised. I shrug off his notion that the accident of my birth defines my hearth. Yet I side with those who will not let local knowledge—of elf rocks or elm trees—go without a fight, those for whom the cosmos is not opposed to the hearth, but revealed by it.

I despaired when I learned, from Robert Macfarlane, that the editors of the 2007 *Oxford Junior Dictionary* had excised "the entries it no longer felt to be relevant to a modern-day childhood," including *acorn, beech, bluebell, catkin, fern, newt, pasture,* and *willow,* and replaced them with the more useful *broadband, bullet-point, chatroom, committee,* and *voice mail.* In response, Macfarlane began collecting nature words, and I vowed to learn some:

> *haze-fire:* luminous morning mist or haze rising from the ground

> *saltings:* salt marshes, usually on the seaward side of sea walls

> *fizmer:* rustling noise produced in grass by petty agitations of the wind

> *didder:* of a bog: to quiver as a walker approaches

quacky: of ground: springy, mossy

snow-bones: patches of snow seen stretching along ridges, in ruts or in furrows after a partial thaw

holm: river island; land formerly covered with water

Of course, I knew *holm*. It's an Icelandic word. It's also the surname chosen by the émigré great-grandfather of the Icelandic American writer Bill Holm, when his Icelandic patronym proved too unwieldly for his Minnesota neighbors. "Call me island," Holm writes to begin *Eccentric Islands.* "Or call me Holm. Same thing. It's one way to start, though like so many other human starts—or human books—it's not original. We stand on the shoulders of our ancestors no matter how many machines we invent. Only our memory and our metaphors carry us forward."

In his lyrical book about his homeland, *Rising Ground*, Marsden characterizes Tuan as "the chief cheerleader for 'place,'" but I disagree. I'm not only unsettled by Tuan's dualities, like Childress is; I'm concerned by his influence on modern geography. Publishing a twenty-fifth-anniversary edition of Tuan's *Space and Place*, the University of Minnesota press called it a "foundational work on human geography." Yet to me, Tuan's definition of place is too narrow—and too biased. For Tuan, clearly, man is the measure of all things. In a 1975 paper, he writes of "the central significance of the city" and of the city as "the one environment created exclusively for human use." It is "contrary to common sense," he argues, for anyone to believe that "sparsely settled farmlands are somehow more meaningful than cities, and wilderness areas more meaningful than farmlands." It's just a cliché, he believes. People want pretty pictures to hang on their walls. They don't really value farms and wilderness over cities. "Place is created by human beings for human purposes," he concludes. "To remain a place it has to be lived in. This is a platitude," he concedes, "unless we examine what 'lived in' means. To live in a place is to experience it, to be aware of it in the bones as well as with the head." And then, it seems to me, just as he has expanded *place* to encompass almost anywhere, including any wildernesses that we are "aware of," Tuan squeezes the word again into his artificial box: "Place, at all scales from the armchair to the nation, is a construct of experience; it is sustained not only by timber, concrete, and highways, but also by the quality of human awareness."

"By timber, concrete, and highways," but not by magic mountains or elves? Is the "soul clad in air," Snaefellsjokull, not also a place? Do we not experience the lava field at Galgahraun in our bones, as well as with our head, when we accept not only its lichens and buttercups and screaming arctic terns, but also its elf stories? Are these not "a construct of experience, a creation of feeling and thought"? As Tuan himself admits, "People tend to suppress that which they cannot express." And, "Artists are admired because, to a degree, they can objectify intimate feelings in a painting, a sculpture, or in words. Few people have this skill," he admits. "Sensitivity cannot be shared the way thoughts can."

It is the same point, though differently expressed, that folklorist Terry Gunnell makes by quoting the French philosopher Michel de Certeau. Stories "have the function of founding and articulating spaces," says Certeau in his 1984 book, *The Practice of Everyday Life*; that is, stories turn spaces into places. Places themselves, Certeau continues, can be defined as "fragmentary and inward turning histories, pasts that *others* are not allowed to read, accumulated times that can be unfolded . . . like stories in reserve." Comments Gunnell, "In other words, in the minds of those who lived among them, 'places' were all, essentially, composed of memories and stories; we might say that they were articulated by the stories that people told, by precisely those stories that are now gathering dust in the archives."

Without stories, places become spaces: open ground, empty lots, wasteland, waiting for "timber, concrete, and highways." Houses, cities, and roads can, of course, spark stories. But we need not privilege these, as Tuan seems to do, simply because they are new, nor relegate elf stories to the archives because they are old. Nor should we assume, like the people who laugh at Iceland's "loony elf-seers," that the new stories (of roads) are more true than the old ones (of elves). "For some, the expression 'it's just folklore' means that something is total fiction; in short, it is not a 'fact' (whatever 'facts' are)," Gunnell writes. When we dismiss the people of the past as ignorant, he continues, we are "blithely forgetting the 'fact' that most of our 'knowledge' about the world is based on information that has been passed on to us by others (from parents, teachers, television news readers, film directors, politicians, and computer technicians), material which we 'believe'/'trust' to be true (in spite of having read Orwell's *1984* and regularly encountered government 'spin'). In this regard, we are really not so different from the people of the past."

In the early 1800s, while the Brothers Grimm were collecting fairy tales in Germany and inspiring other nationalists to do the same, at a time when the great auk rookeries off Iceland's west coast were dwindling but not yet destroyed, Alexander von Humboldt was inventing nature. The turn of phrase is Andrea Wulf's from *The Invention of Nature*, where she writes, "At a time when other scientists were searching for universal laws, Humboldt wrote that nature had to be experienced through feelings." Facts per se were not so important; what mattered were the connections among them and Humboldt, says Wulf, "found connections everywhere." He "asked so many questions that some people thought him to be stupid." His pockets, they mocked, "were like those of a little boy—full of plants, rocks and scraps of paper. Nothing was too small or insignificant to investigate."

From Johann Wolfgang von Goethe, Humboldt got the idea that "nature and the imagination were closely interwoven," Wulf writes. From Immanuel Kant, the concept that "Humans were like citizens of two worlds, occupying both the world of the *Ding an sich* (the thing-in-itself) which was the external world, and the internal world of one's perception." The first "could never be truly known"; the second "was always subjective." And not only did our imagination color our perception of the world, but the world, Humboldt saw, worked its magic on our imagination: "Nature, he wrote, was in a mysterious communication with our 'inner feelings.'"

Humboldt had the eye of a painter and the heart of a poet. He was filled with wonder at "a world in which the coloured rays of an aurora 'unite in a quivering sea flame,' creating a sight so otherworldly 'the splendour of which no description can reach,'" Wulf writes. "At a time when imagination had been firmly excluded from the sciences, Humboldt insisted that nature couldn't be understood in any other way."

His books were bestsellers (one sold twenty thousand copies in a few months) and were translated from German into English, Danish, Dutch, French, Hungarian, Italian, Polish, Russian, Spanish, and Swedish. The concept he invented, of the web of life, is "the concept of nature as we know it today," Wulf says. It inspired Charles Darwin and Henry David Thoreau, Thomas Jefferson and Jules Verne, Samuel Taylor Coleridge (who suspended his disbelief) and George Perkins Marsh. It is the basis of the modern conservation movement and the science of ecology.

John Muir owned three of Humboldt's books: His pencil marks on nearly every page show how actively he read them. The National Park Service, which Muir fathered; the Sierra Club, which he co-founded; and his writings so full of "playful joy that he inspired millions of Americans, shaping their relationship with nature," writes Wulf—"It had all begun with Humboldt and with a walk. 'I only went out for a walk, and finally concluded to stay out till sundown,' Muir wrote after his return, 'for going out, I found, was really going in.'"

Nature is good for you, scientists are now saying. In one study reported by Florence Williams in her 2017 book, *The Nature Fix*, a fifteen-minute walk in the woods reduced the subjects' stress hormone levels. A forty-five-minute walk enhanced their ability to think, to remember, plan, focus, and dream. Access to green space improved the mental health of the poor; the sense of awe evoked by natural wonders made the rich more generous. "This book explores the science behind what poets and philosophers have known for eons: place matters," Williams writes. "Nature, it turns out, is good for civilization."

It can also make you happy. George MacKerron, an economist at the University of Sussex, amassed millions of data points by pinging twenty thousand iPhone-using volunteers (including Williams) at random times twice a day over a period of seven years and asking what they were doing and how happy they were. His "Mappiness" iPhone app recorded their GPS coordinates, from which he learned where they were and what the weather was like. His generally young, well-educated, and employed volunteers, he found, were "significantly and substantially happier outdoors in all green or natural habitat types than they are in urban environments." (And yes, Williams notes, he did factor in a "vacation effect.")

"Yet, remarkably," Williams notes, "the respondents, like me, were rarely caught outside. Ninety-three percent of the time, they were either indoors or in vehicles." Mappiness, says Williams, "is an indictment not only of the structures and habits of modern society, but of our self-understanding. As the writer Annie Dillard once said, how we spend our days is how we spend our lives. Why don't we do more of what makes our brains happy?"

Partly because we're taught not to. In *Landscapes of the Sacred*, theologian Belden C. Lane retells a story of Petrarch, the fourteenth-century Italian poet sometimes said to be the first person to climb a mountain just for the view. One bright day, delighting in being "free and alone, among the mountains and forests," as he wrote, Petrarch reached the peak, took in the view, then settled in to enjoy the book he had brought along, Saint Augustine's *Confessions*—and his delight turned to shame as he read: "Men go to gape at mountain peaks, at the boundless tides of the sea, the broad sweep of rivers, the encircling ocean, and the motions of the stars: And yet they leave *themselves* unnoticed; they do not marvel at themselves." Petrarch wrote, "I closed the book, angry with myself that I should still be admiring earthly things who might long ago have learned . . . that nothing is wonderful but the soul." Writes Lane, Petrarch "hurriedly left the mountain's crest, reflecting on how the world's beauty can divert men and women so easily from their proper concerns."

Their proper concerns. Think about that for a moment. Augustine lived in North Africa in the fourth century. His opinions shaped the medieval Catholic Church, as well as the Protestant Reformation. Petrarch, a founder of Renaissance humanism, is often called "the first modern man." The attitudes of these two men echo throughout modern Western thought.

"Even when our society concedes that fuzzy animals and pretty plants can be engaging for children, it does not grant that anyone should waste his or her time on such things after the age of puberty," complains Gary Paul Nabhan in *The Geography of Childhood.* "Our society's token nature-lovers are treated as overgrown but harmless juveniles, dillydallying away their time and money on matters undeserving of serious attention by mature adults." His complaint isn't new, he concedes. A Swedish botanist, visiting America in 1750, was alarmed to find natural history was "looked upon as a mere trifle, and the pastime of fools."

And now nature is not even considered "relevant" for children: *acorn* is replaced by *chatroom*, *bluebell* by *voice mail.*

We no longer even know how to talk about nature. In the United Kingdom, writes George Monbiot in *The Guardian*, "On land, places in which nature is protected are called 'sites of special scientific interest.' At sea, they are labeled 'no-take zones' or 'reference areas.' Had you set out to estrange people from the living world, you could scarcely have done better.

"Even the term 'reserve' is cold and alienating," he continues. "Think of what we mean when we use that word about a person." The word *environment* "creates no pictures in the mind." Calling plants or animals "resources" or "stocks" implies "they belong to us and their role is to serve us." Language has power, Monbiot reminds us. "Those who name it own it," he argues. His advice? "We need new words."

Or, perhaps, a new look at some very old ones, like *elf*.

"In Iceland, the center is the margin. Geography is inside-out. What is at the center is wilderness. What kind of self might these places reflect?" English professor Gillian Overing wondered in 1992.

I think I know the answer now. As Icelandic writer Audur Ava Olafsdottir notes, "To my knowledge, Icelandic is the only language that uses the same word to say home and the world." That word is *heima*.

Everyone Is an Artist

I n 1979, William Scott Wilson, an expert on ancient samurai culture, hiked up Mount Ontake with a Japanese friend. This ten-thousand-foot active volcano, which "dominates the spiritual landscape," has its own religion, called Ontake-kyo. "Over the centuries, Ontake-kyo developed from a mixture of ancient mountain worship, Shinto, and esoteric Buddhism," Wilson writes. Its "practice centers around prayers to the gods of the mountains, recitations of various sutras, and climbing the mountain itself." There's a restroom at the trailhead, with a prominent reminder to go there and not risk polluting the mountain and driving away the spirits who live there. "The practitioners of Ontake-kyo believe that the natural phenomena they personally experience on the mountain—the rocks, grasses, trees, and even the clouds and wind—are the abode and work of the gods and buddhas. This is a deeply felt and sincere belief, and not one to be taken lightly."

Busloads of pilgrims come in the summers. "The trails leading to the various summits are dotted with white-clad pilgrims, praying as they climb," writes Wilson. They make symbols with their fingers, they chant, and they clap their hands "to get the gods' attention." The four-and-a-half-hour climb, from the parking lot to the sulfur-reeking caldera of the volcano's crater, took Wilson past a coffee house, a small shop "where a priest sells various amulets, talismans, and scrolls depicting the gods of the mountain," shrines to various Shinto and Buddhist deities, and many places holy to the Brightness King of Unwavering Mind, an avatar of the Great Sun Buddha, who is "mystically related to . . . the sun goddess from whom the Japanese emperors descend. Thus," Wilson concludes, "almost every step on this mountain participates in a mysterious liminal realm."

I have never been to Japan. All I know of Ontake-kyo is what Wilson chooses to tell me, but it seems from what I've read that the Japanese make no excuses for their reverence of these gods of the mountain. They do not take lightly the "deeply felt and sincere" beliefs of practitioners of Ontake-kyo. They do not ridicule people who believe that rocks are the abode of buddhas as "loony elf-seers." What is the difference between a buddha and an elf? Aren't we talking, really, about vocabulary? Aren't each of these words—*elf, buddha*—an attempt to describe something that "cannot be caught in a net of words," as J. R. R. Tolkien says of Faërie, "for it is one of its qualities to be indescribable, though not imperceptible"?

A net of words itself is a flimsy, fantastical thing. Whence do these odd sounds come, and how do we agree on their relation to the world? To Tolkien's friend Owen Barfield, "The full meanings of words are flashing, iridescent shapes like flames—ever-flickering vestiges of the slowly evolving consciousness beneath them." Think of the words *spirit* and *inspiration*. In the oldest texts, a poet was possessed by an unseen *spirit*—some godlike being—who spoke through the poet's, the prophet's, the shaman's voice. Later, gods spoke through a lesser intermediary—a Muse, still invisible—who *inspired*, breathed a spirit, a thought, a word into the poet's mind when suitably invoked. Finally, this "breathing in" itself became a metaphor, though *inspiration* retains a sense of "diminished *self*-consciousness," writes Barfield, a sense that some other being, rather than you, is doing the thinking. "Inspiration! It was the only means, we used to be told, by which poetry could be written, and the poet himself hardly knew what it was—a kind of divine wind, perhaps, which blew where it listed and might fill his sails at some odd moment after he had whistled for it all day in vain." Today—which to Barfield was the 1920s—even that magic has been removed and "we are more inclined to think of inspiration as a mood—a mood that may come and go in the course of a morning's work."

A mood is all in your head. It's hormones, caffeine, lunch, the quality of last night's sleep (or sex). It admits no shapely Muses, no shamanistic possessions. It's a capitalist construct, writes art critic John Berger. Since the 1700s, the world has been "'opened up,' 'unified,' modernized, created, destroyed, and transformed on a scale such as had never occurred before" by capitalism, which is not only an economic system but a value system in which "self-interest, instead of being seen as a daily human temptation" that must be fought against, as it was in the Middle Ages, is "made heroic." The spiritual is marginalized, replaced at the center of our lives by the material—by what money can buy. And as we all know, money can't buy love, it can't buy happiness, it can't buy a way into heaven (cue the camel and the needle's eye), it can't buy much of anything that matters.

Worse, our self-centeredness is ruining what *does* matter: Earth. "The real culprit of the climate crisis is not any particular form of consumption, production, or regulation, but the very *way* in which we globally produce, which is for profit rather than for sustainability," writes Benjamin Y. Fong, a professor of psychology and religion at Arizona State University. "It should be stated plainly: It's *capitalism* that is at fault."

Steven Hartman, lead author on a 2017 study of why the Viking colony in Greenland collapsed in the fifteenth century, agrees. "The great environmental predicament of our age is not primarily an ecological crisis, though its ramifications are far reaching within ecological systems; rather it is a crisis of culture. Bound into this predicament is a global overdependence on fossil-fuel energy within an economic system (free-market capitalism) that rarely bears the true costs of human labor, resource consumption, and biodiversity loss, to name but a few of the *wicked* problems of the twenty-first century." He and his colleagues do not define *wicked*. They continue, "The processes by which societies negotiate environmental challenges and respond to threats are neither natural nor a matter of scientific understanding in the classic sense. They are cultural."

How do we cope? Partly by returning to that earlier definition of inspiration, and opening ourselves to the unseen, the unnoticed, the useless, and the inhuman, what Berger calls "the *beyond*," whatever does not "fit into materialist explanations." Art, says Berger, is by definition "a meeting-place of the invisible, the irreducible, the enduring, guts, and honour."

It is also "a two-way process. To draw is not only to measure and put down, it is also to receive. When the intensity of looking reaches a certain degree, one becomes aware of an equally intense energy coming towards one." It's not a matter of question and answer, but "a ferocious and inarticulated dialogue. To sustain it requires faith. It is like a burrowing in the dark, a burrowing under the apparent." He can't explain it, he admits, but "I simply believe very few artists will deny it. It's a professional secret."

The resulting work of art is not an object, anthropologist Tim Ingold explains, but an invitation. "The work invites the viewer to join the artist as a fellow traveller, to look *with* it as it unfolds in the world," he writes. The point of art is not to look back, not to stop time in the now, but to press on with life, "not to reach a terminus but to keep on going."

A stone is not an object either, argues Ingold. It, too, is an invitation to travel, to press on. He offers, as proof, this simple experiment: Pluck a stone from a river. Set it on a windowsill until it is dry. What happened? "Without any intervention on your part, it has changed." Its shape is the same, but its color is not. "Indeed it might look disappointingly dull." I have done this. I have jars of dull rocks that I wish I hadn't pocketed on rainy or riverside walks. (Some I've repatriated.) Home and dry, they are, as Ingold puts it, somehow less "stony." They feel different. They sound different when rattled together in my hand. How can that be? "Stoniness,"

Ingold explains, "is not in the stone's 'nature,' in its materiality. Nor is it merely in the mind of the observer." The stone cannot be understood apart from the medium it is bathed in—water, air. It cannot be understood apart from "the manifold ways in which it is engaged in the currents of the lifeworld." Stoniness is not an attribute, but a history.

Or many histories. In her beautiful meditation on nature, *A Land*, from 1951, Jacquetta Hawkes writes, "Life has grown from the rock and still rests upon it; because men have left it far behind, they are able consciously to turn back to it. We do turn back, for it has kept some hold over us." Kings, she notes, are still crowned on the Stone of Scone. "The Church, itself founded on the rock of Peter, for centuries fought unsuccessfully against the worship of 'sticks and stones,'" and yet look at our churchyards: "Who, even at the height of its popularity, ever willingly used cast-iron for a tombstone?"

"What can a stone do?" riffs Hugh Raffles in the journal *Cultural Anthropology*: "A stone can endure, it can change, it can harm, it can heal. It can make you rich, it can make you poor, it can become an enemy, a friend, and a teacher. It can carry your memories and your dreams. It can build empires and bury cities. It can reveal the history of the universe. It can open and close the gates of philosophy. It can change the course of nature. It can change its own nature. It can empty the world of time." He's talking of silicon (the basis of computer chips), of uranium, of gold, of volcanic basalt, of all stones. He has a favorite stone, from a beach in Oregon: "When the right light hits it, it glows from within."

Look at a stone. Really look at it, commands Rachel Corbett in her book *You Must Change Your Life*, and you'll understand the philosopher Theodor Lipps's concept of empathy, his explanation for "why art affects us so powerfully": Face the rock and "stare deep into the place where its rockness begins to form." Keep looking until your own center "starts to sink with the stony weight of the rock" forming inside of you. "It is a kind of perception that takes place within the body," Corbett says, "and it requires the observer to be both the seer and the seen. To observe with empathy, one sees not only with the eyes but with the skin."

To the poet Rainer Maria Rilke (the subject, along with sculptor Auguste Rodin, of Corbett's book and famous for the line "You must change your life"), such "indescribably swift, deep, timeless moments of this godlike in-seeing" were "my very greatest feeling, my world-feeling, my earthly bliss."

To the Scottish writer Nan Shepherd, "Simply to look on anything, such as a mountain, with the love that penetrates to its essence, is to widen the domain of being in the vastness of non-being." When one combines such seeing with walking, "hour after hour, the senses keyed," Shepherd asserts in *The Living Mountain*, "one walks the flesh transparent." You become, "not bodiless, but essential body." Shepherd says, "I have walked out of the body and into the mountain. I am a manifestation of its total life, as is the starry saxifrage or the white-winged ptarmigan." It is why, she believes, the Buddhist climbs a mountain, why the Japanese climb Mount Ontake. It is why I climb Helgafell and hike the path to Little Lava: "The journey is itself part of the technique by which the god is sought," Shepherd writes. "It is a journey into Being; for as I penetrate more deeply into the mountain's life, I penetrate also into my own."

I keep on my windowsill the three dry, dusty stones that I plucked from the glacial riverbed on my long horseback ride in 2009. Gray now, they were once jet black. Rounded, but not one is a perfect sphere. They are ordinary pebbles, pocked and spotted, little cratered moons of basalt, I think, though I don't really know or care to classify them. I corral them in a rusty horseshoe to keep them from rolling off the windowsill. They are a symbol to me of the door that is not a door to the Otherworld that is not another world.

"'In Iceland, seventy-five per cent of the time that the sun is up the shadow is longer than the object causing it,'" the Icelandic Danish artist Olafur Eliasson told Cynthia Zarin, who profiled him for *The New Yorker*. Zarin writes, "With his hands, he made an arc in the air, then brought them down to a skimming stop—the only time Eliasson uses body language to describe something is when he speaks about Iceland. 'In Iceland, everything is such a drama. A little rock in a field casts a long shadow,'" Eliasson told Zarin. "'One could draw more or less compelling lines between the history of identity and the history of sensational spaces.'"

The philosopher J. E. H. Smith uses Iceland's rocks, instead, to introduce environmental ethics. "A student in rural Iceland, of sheep-farming stock, had her guard down, or didn't yet have a guard. She didn't know how to talk to foreigners . . . ," he writes in "The Moral Status of Rocks," "or perhaps felt there was something she had to get across to foreigners, or to this foreigner, who showed an interest in her country. She said, in the hope of conveying to me the whole ethical-spiritual outlook of her country in a single concrete example: *In Iceland we are taught not to smash rocks.*"

In 2007, the American artist Roni Horn created the Library of Water in an empty building in the town of Stykkisholmur on the Snaefellsnes peninsula. In 1994, she explained to an interviewer why Iceland is her muse. As published in Phaidon's *Roni Horn*, she said: "Iceland is primarily young geology. Young geology is very unstable. In a literal sense, Iceland is not a very stable place. Iceland is always becoming what it will be, and what it will be is not a fixed thing either. So here is Iceland: an act, not an object, a verb, never a noun." In her 2020 collection, *Island Zombie*, she continues the thought: "I come here to place myself in the world. Iceland is a verb and its action is to center."

The writer Ursula K. Le Guin could be talking about Iceland, the Iceland of Eliasson and Smith and Horn and me, and not an imaginary Otherworld when she says, in "World-Making" in 1981, "To make a new world you start with an old one, certainly. To find a world, maybe you have to have lost one. Maybe you have to be lost. The dance of renewal, the dance that made the world, was always danced here at the edge of things, on the brink, on the foggy coast."

On the public radio program "Speaking of Faith," host Krista Tippett interviewed the Irish poet and philosopher John O'Donohue shortly before his death in 2008. For O'Donohue, "the visible world is the first shoreline of the invisible world." He paraphrases Martin Heidegger, saying, "as a human being, you are the place in which the universe becomes visible to itself, becomes conscious of itself." And that universe is "always larger and more intense and stranger than our best thought will ever reach." To be fully human, then, you must keep your imagination alive. "Everyone is an artist," he says. "I mean everyone is involved, whether they like it or not, in the construction of the world . . . There is no fixed world out there."

And so, we come full circle to Ragnhildur Jonsdottir, an Icelandic artist with long silver hair and gray-blue eyeglasses who speaks to elves who live in rocks, and whose place within this company of artists, writers, philosophers, and anthropologists all pondering words and worlds, gods and stones, I feel is assured, and whose vision, I am convinced, can provide a way for us all to press on.

I didn't think so the first time I met her. I had to take the journey, have the conversations, clean my windows. I had to open the doors in my mind—and walk through them.

I first met Ragnhildur in October 2015, at Iceland Affair, a small festival held in Winchester Center, Connecticut. The spirit behind this one-day celebration of all things Icelandic—livestock, candy, landscape, singing—is a local woman named Gerri Griswold. Her Facebook page is littered with selfies taken in the "crapper" at Logan Airport or the big bathtub in her backyard (censored by soap bubbles). She has a pet pig. She's passionate about bats and porcupines, which she rehabilitates for the White Memorial Conservation Center. Even her friends call her "peculiar." According to a press release she wrote for Iceland Affair, Gerri fell "hopelessly in love with Iceland on her first trip in May 2002"; she has since visited fifty-one times and counting. To fund (or fuel) her Iceland habit, she established Krummi Travel, offering high-end tours that focus on interactions with Icelanders. The company's name brilliantly encapsulates Gerri's rule-busting approach to life: *Krummi* is a fond nickname for ravens in Icelandic, but it is pronounced pretty much like "crummy." Tongue-in-cheek is a gross understatement for Gerri Griswold.

In 2015, she invited Ragnhildur, me, and four others to lecture for forty minutes apiece in the musty upstairs auditorium of the Winchester Center Grange. In front of an audience of fifty to a hundred people, I spoke on Icelandic horses. The others spoke on Iceland's rescue service, Arctic foxes, the volcano that had just quit erupting, and the country's bizarre geology. Ragnhildur spoke on elves. Gerri had not asked Ragnhildur to speak in order to ridicule the loony elf-seer. That's not Gerri's style. Yet I squirmed, watching Ragnhildur give a PowerPoint presentation on Iceland's elves. There was a fatal clash, I thought, between form and content, between Ragnhildur's soft voice and long silver hair, her whimsical drawings of an elf named Frodi (from the Icelandic for wisdom; the name Tolkien turned into Frodo), and the mechanics of computers and cables, the aggressively whirring projector fan, the static photos on the dull, matte screen standing a little lopsided on its tripod. The way the darkness behind the podium swallowed her up. I felt sorry for her.

There was a party at Gerri's house the next day. I sought out Ragnhildur, or perhaps it was she who wanted to meet me. At any event, when we stood face-to-face I saw not a woman I could feel sorry for, but a woman so secure in her knowledge, and so willing to share it, that she glowed. Her graceful posture and sly, sideways smile reminded me of Cate Blanchett's, playing the elf queen. PowerPoint was about as important to her as peanut butter. She knew the technology—any technology—would be ineffective.

She knew she couldn't *make* us believe in elves. But she was game to try. I was ashamed of myself. In silent apology, I gave her copies of two books I'd written about another Icelandic heroine of mine, Gudrid the Far-Traveler. Ragnhildur could not accept the gift without giving me one in return, so sent me home with a guide, in Icelandic, to the elves of her local town park and a dual-language booklet she had illustrated called *What Does It Take to See an Elf?* The booklet was written, she said, by Frodi the Elf.

It took me a while to read it. Months. Even after having met Ragnhildur, it was too easy to laugh at an Icelander publishing a handbook on how to spot elves. How touristy! In spite of my interest in Icelandic folklore—my file drawer stuffed with news clippings on elf sightings going back to 1982, my bookshelf full of folktales in both Icelandic and English translation—I picked up and put down *What Does It Take to See an Elf?* several times.

Eventually, I reached page 2:

> To see us elves, you only need three things: A touch of joy in your heart, a permission from the grown up inside of you to allow your inner child to "go out and play," and an elf willing to be seen.

My inner child responded. As Andrew Lang says in *The Blue Fairy Book*, "He who would enter into the Kingdom of Faërie should have the heart of a little child." Tolkien, though he thought Lang's wording too sentimental, agreed. "Children are meant to grow up," he writes, "and not to become Peter Pans." But growing up does not mean losing our sense of wonder. It does not mean suppressing our desire "to survey the depths of space and time" or "to hold communion with other living beings." That sense of wonder, he explains, "represents love: that is, a love and respect for all things, 'inanimate' and 'animate,' an unpossessive love of them as 'other.' This love will produce both truth and delight. Things seen in its light will be respected, and they will also appear delightful, beautiful, wonderful, even glorious."

I turned to page 3 of Frodi's book. What does it take to see an elf? Nothing too esoteric, it turns out. "Find a rock you feel drawn to. Sit down and be comfortable." Look at the rock. Notice its shape, its texture. Is there moss growing on it? Or lichen? Are there any other plants around? What colors are they? Do they have a smell? Do you feel the breeze? Are there any sounds? Did you see a movement out of the corner of your eye? Keep still and wait—it might be an elf coming out to play. "Allow yourself to enjoy the adventure."

But here's the passage that finally opened my eyes: "It is also fine if you think all this is imaginary."

Acknowledgments

———

M any people, both Icelanders and Americans, helped me write this book. All were storytellers. On my first trip to Iceland in 1986, and on nearly every trip thereafter, I have been welcomed to Helgafell by Hjortur Hinriksson, his wife Kristrún (until her untimely death), and their seven children: Jóhanna, Ásta, Gummi, Hinrik, Ragga, Ósk, and Óskar. Their friendship, as I hope this book makes clear, changed my life. Thanks also to Ásta's daughter, Kristrún, for sending me her school term-paper, "Saga Helgafells," in 2015—it was the best Christmas card ever.

My love of Iceland was fostered by Kristín Vogfjörð, Pétur Orri Jónsson, and Gunnar Stefánsson, who as graduate students at Penn State University in 1986 helped me plan my first trip to Iceland and admitted me into their family networks. Pétur's mother, Sólveig, provided my first Icelandic home, and his brother, Vésteinn (Venni), later rented me his apartment. Venni also introduced me to Þórður Grétarsson, who helped me plan many adventures over the years and who shared my encounter with a volcano in 2010 (and again in 2021). Pétur's uncle, Gunnar; Kristín's mother, Élin; Gunnar's mother, Þyri; and Þórður's parents, Grétar and Guðný (Gigi), were my first and best guides to Iceland's nature and culture. On a later trip, Gunnar's brother Pétur and his friend, Anna Gyða, took me to beautiful Litla Hraun; Anna Gyða arranged my family's stay there for a summer and introduced me to the neighbors at Snorrastaðir, Haukur and Ingibjörg, who changed my life again by helping me buy my first Icelandic horse.

It was also in 1986 that I met Vilhjálmur Knudsen and was infected by his passion for volcanoes. Thanks to Haraldur Sigurðsson, Magnús Johannsson, and Anna María Ágústsdóttir, as well as to Kristín Vogfjörð again, for deepening my understanding of Iceland's volcanic landscape.

Svandís, Eyjólfur, Hjalti, Åse, and the crew at Íshestar took me for a truly memorable horse trek over Kjölur in 2009.

Steinunn Kristjánsdóttir and Terry Gunnell generously shared their knowledge of Iceland's monasteries and folklore with me, and gave me copies of many of their published and unpublished books and papers.

On numerous occasions over the last thirty years I've been helped professionally by anthropologist Gísli Pálsson, whether I needed a ride to an archaeological site, a place to stay, a book from the library, the loan of a jeep, or an editing job to support my travels. I hope I've been able to return some of those favors. Thanks, too, to Guðbjörg Sigurðardóttir, who has always been there when I needed a home, a meal, practical advice, or the cultural insights only an Icelander can provide.

Patrick Stevens, curator of the Fiske Icelandic Collection at Cornell University has, as usual, gone above and beyond the call of a librarian, photographing for me pages from Jón Árnason's rare 1852 collection of Icelandic folktales (which, of course, is in the Fiske Collection).

Sigrún Þórmar and her colleagues at Snorrastofa graciously provided lodging and use of the library at Snorri Sturluson's estate, Reykholt (and earned my sincere gratitude by stocking my books on Iceland in their gift shop).

My travel companions Jennifer Anne Tucker, Ginger McCleskey, Gabe Dunsmith, and Nina Casby gave me an extra set of eyes to see Iceland with. Thanks to Ginger and Nina, too, for their insightful comments on a draft of this book, along with those of writers Denise Brown and Pat Shipman and artist Claire Van Vliet. Thanks also to Claire and to Jean Ervasti for editing some of my photos.

This book was truly born when Gerri Griswold introduced me to Ragnhildur Jónsdóttir at Iceland Affair in Winchester Center, Connecticut, in 2015, and the collection of travel essays I had been working on for many years was hijacked by Iceland's elves. Thanks to my husband, Charles Fergus, for supporting me through the long writing process, and for recognizing me each time I returned from my Otherworld. And finally, thanks to my agent, Michelle Tessler, for persistently championing my unconventional manuscript, and to editors Claiborne Hancock and Victoria Wenzel for finding it "just quirky enough."

Notes

—∞∞∞—

1. THE ELF LOBBY

Find Sagnagrunnur at http://sagnagrunnur.com/en/. Terry Gunnell describes the project in "Sagnagrunnur: A New Database of Icelandic Folk Legends in Print," *Folklore: Electronic Journal of Folklore* 45 (2010): 151–162; he explained it to me on August 4, 2016.

The trolls appear in J. R. R. Tolkien's *The Hobbit* (New York: Houghton Mifflin, 1966), chapter 2; Linda Ásdísardóttir wrote about Tolkien's Icelandic au pair in "Barnfóstran frá Islandi og Tolkien-fjölsklydan," *Morgunblaðið* (February 2, 1999).

Peter Davidson writes about Kjarval in *The Idea of North* (London: Reaktion Books, 2005), 165.

I walked with Ragnhildur Jónsdóttir at Gálgahraun on June 21, 2016. The photo of her "planking" illustrated Alda Sigmundsdóttir's blog *The Iceland Weather Report* (October 21, 2013). Rannveig Magnúsdóttir's "Passion for Lava—The Struggle to Save Gálgahraun Lavafield," on savingiceland.org (October 21, 2013), discussed road safety; see also "Iceland's Roads Rate Low on Safety" by Jelena Ciric, *Iceland Review* (March 21, 2018).

Ryan Jacobs interviewed Ragnhildur in "Why So Many Icelanders Still Believe in Invisible Elves," *The Atlantic* (October 2013). News of the "elf lobby" was reported by Jenna Gottlieb for the Associated Press (December 22, 2013) in "Iceland's Hidden Elves Delay Road Projects." Arit John referred to "loony elf-seers" in "Iceland's 'Elf Lobby' Isn't Real, According to Icelanders" for *The Wire* (December 23, 2013). The "impact on elves" was reported by *Iceland Monitor*, the English-language website of *Morgunblaðið*, in "Elves Make Compromise with Road Administration" (May 3, 2016). The moving of the elf church was reported by *Morgunblaðið* (March 3, 2015) as "Álfarnir sáttir á nýjum stað."

NOTES

2. ICELANDERS BELIEVE IN ELVES

"Elf Rock Restored after Its Removal Wreaks Havoc on Icelandic Town" appeared on *Iceland Monitor* (August 30, 2016). The elf surveys are discussed by Valdimar Tr. Hafstein, "The Elves' Point of View: Cultural Identity in Contemporary Icelandic Elf-Tradition," *Journal of Folktale Studies* 41 (2000): 87–104; and by Terry Gunnell in "Legends and Landscape in the Nordic Countries," *Cultural and Social History* 6 (2009): 305–322, and "Modern Legends in Iceland," a paper he presented on June 25, 2009, at the 15th Congress of the International Society of Folk Narrative Research in Athens, Greece, and shared with me in manuscript, as well as in more depth in "'Það er til fleira á himni og jörðu, Hóras': Kannanir á íslenskri þjóðtrú og trúarviðhorfum 2006–2007," in *Rannsóknum í félagsvísindum* (2007): 801–812, and "Heima á milli: Þjóðtrú og þjóðsagnir á Íslandi við upphaf 21 aldar," in *Rannsóknir í félagsvísindum* (2009): 899–908; we also spoke about them on August 4, 2016. On UFOs, see Lee Spiegel, "48 Percent of Americans Believe UFOs Could Be ET Visitations," *The Huffington Post* (September 11, 2013).

The story of Staðarfell is linked to Vigfús Gíslason in the Sagnagrunnur database; this translation is by Jacqueline Simpson, "The Fire at Stadarfell," in *The Penguin Book of Scandinavian Folktales* (London: Penguin Books, 1994).

Iceland's elves are mentioned by Alex Ross in "Björk's Saga," *The New Yorker* (August 23, 2004); Brad Leithauser, "Iceland: A Nonesuch People," *Atlantic Monthly* (September 1987); Robert Wernick, "Sagas Are Still Alive and Kicking for Icelanders," *Smithsonian* (January 1986); Michael Lewis, "Wall Street on the Tundra," *Vanity Fair* (April 2009); Brian Stelter, "Vanity Fair Article Draws Outcries from Iceland," *The New York Times* (April 6, 2009); Jonas Moody, "Vanity Fair's Fishy Tales from Iceland," *New York* (March 18, 2009); Matt Eliason, "An American in Reykjavík: Do Icelanders Actually Believe in Elves or Is the Joke on Us?" *Iceland Magazine* (September 26, 2014); Jessica Pan, "Elves Fuck, and Dress Better Than You: What I Learned at Elf School in Reykjavik," Fly Girl (November 6, 2015) at jezebel.com; and Sarah Lyall, "Building in Iceland? Better Clear It with the Elves First," *The New York Times* (July 13, 2005).

3. OTHERWORLDS

Stefan Jonasson speaks about elves in "Stumbling Upon Hólahólar" and "The Defeat of Elías Kjærnested" (May 1, 2016) and "The Truth about Elves" (February 15, 2017) in *Lögberg-Heimskringla*.

On gravity and quantum mechanics, see Amanda Gefter, "Newton's Apple: The Real Story," *Culture Lab* (January 18, 2010) at www.newscientist.com; Carlo Rovelli, "This Granular Life: An Extract from *Reality Is Not What It Seems*," *Aeon* (January 23, 2017); Carlo Rovelli, *Seven Brief Lessons on Physics* (New York: Riverhead Books, 2016), chapters 1 and 2; Paul Davies, *Other Worlds: Space, Superspace, and the Quantum Universe* (London: J. M. Dent & Sons, 1980; rpt. Penguin Books, 1990), 75, 90; Joseph Silk, Joel Primack, Lisa Randall, Tasneem Zehra Husain, and Mary-Jane Rubenstein were published in the "Cosmos" edition of *Nautilus* (January 2017). The encyclopedias I checked were Wikipedia (as of August 2017) and the 15th edition of the *Encyclopedia Britannica* (1980). Alan Burdick reported on muons in the "Science Times" newsletter of the *New York Times* (April 9, 2021); see also Dennis Overbye, "A Tiny Particle's Wobble Could Upend the Known Laws of Physics," *The New York Times*, April 7, 2020 (updated April 9, 2021), 1.

4. THE ISLAND THAT LIKES TO BE VISITED

Rebecca Solnit's, "Summer in the Far North," appeared in *Mother Jones* (June 13, 2013); *The Faraway Nearby* (New York: Viking, 2013) was reviewed by Robin Romm for the *New York Times* (August 16, 2013).

For J. R. R. Tolkien's essay, see *Tolkien On Fairy-stories*, expanded edition, with commentary and notes by Verlyn Flieger and Douglas A. Anderson (London: HarperCollins, 2008; rpt. 2014). On J. M. Barrie, see Alexander Woollcott's review of Mary Rose, "Importing Tears and Laughter," in *Everybody's Magazine* (December 1920); Rosalind Ridley, *Peter Pan and the Mind of J. M. Barrie: An Exploration of Cognition and Consciouness* (Newcastle upon Tyne, UK: Cambridge Scholars Publishing, 2016); and Chris Frith, "'J. M. Barrie Was a Close Observer of Human and Animal Behaviour': Interview with Rosalind Ridley," *The Psychologist* (January 2017): 54–57.

I interviewed Haraldur Sigurðsson on June 24, 2009. The story of Helgafell comes from *Eyrbyggja saga*, chapters 9–11. On Gudrun's grave, see W. G. Collingwood and Jón Stefánsson, *A Pilgrimage to the Saga-Steads of Iceland* (W. Holmes, 1899), 92. On raven lore, see Hjálmar R. Barðarson, *Birds of Iceland* (Reykjavík, 1986), 233. The verse from *The Lay of Grimnir* is stanza 20 of the Eddic poem *Grímnismál*.

5. THOUGHT AND MEMORY

W. H. Auden is quoted by Matthías Jóhannessen in "A Brightly Burning Light," *Iceland Review* 1 (1987); see also Auden and Louis MacNeice, *Letters from Iceland* (New York: Paragon House, 1990). Eric Weiner wrote about "thin places" in "Where Heaven and Earth Come Closer," *The New York Times* (March 11, 2012).

On saga sites, see Carol Hoggart, "A Layered Landscape: How the Family Sagas Mapped Medieval Iceland," *Limina* 16 (2010); Emily Lethbridge, "The Icelandic Sagas and Saga Landscapes: Writing, Reading, and Retelling Íslendigasögur Narratives," *Gripla* 27 (2016): 51–92; and Tim Ingold, *Being Alive: Essays on Movement, Knowledge, and Description* (Oxfordshire, UK: Routledge, 2011). On chaos, see S. Leonard Rubinstein, *Writing: A Habit of Mind* (Dubuque, IA: Wm. C. Brown, 1972).

For the history of Helgafell, I am indebted to Hermann Pálsson's *Helgafell: Saga höfuðbóls og klausturs* (Reykjavík: Snæfellingaútgáfan, 1967) and to "Saga Helgafells," a 2015 school paper by Kristrún Kjartansdóttir, the granddaughter of my friend Hjörtur Hinríksson of Helgafell. Hermann Pálsson and Paul Edwards describe the writing of the sagas in their introduction to *Eyrbyggja Saga* (Toronto: University of Toronto Press, 1973). Lena Liepe writes about the Helgafell manuscripts in *Studies in Icelandic Fourteenth Century Book Painting* (Reykholt, Iceland: Snorrastofa, 2009) and "Image, Script, and Ornamentation in the 'Helgafell Manuscripts,'" in *From Nature to Script: Reykholt, Environment, Centre, and Manuscript Making*, edited by Helgi Þorláksson and Þóra Björg Sigurðardóttir (Reykholt, Iceland: Snorrastofa, 2012), 245–271. I spoke with Steinunn Kristjánsdóttir about her work on August 3, 2016. See her papers "Skriðuklaustur Monastery: Medical Centre of Medieval East Iceland?" *Acta Archaeologica* 79 (2008): 208–215; "The Tip of the Iceberg: The Material of Skriðuklaustur Monastery and Hospital," *Norwegian Archaeological Review* 43, no. 1 (2010): 44–62; and her field report, with Vala Gunnarsdóttir, *Kortlagning klaustra á Íslandi: Helgafell* (Reykjavík,

2014). On "Munkr-skard," see Frederick Metcalfe, *The Oxonian in Iceland* (Longman, Green, Longman, and Roberts, 1861), 288–290.

6. WALKING WITHERSHINS

The witch at Helgafell and the Burnt Place appear in *Laxdæla saga*, chapters 76 and 37, respectively. The gods' anger is mentioned in *Kristni saga* (The Saga of Christianity), chapter 12. The eruption at Eldborg is recorded in *Landnámabók*, chapter 68. Svan's fog spell is in *Brennu-Njals saga*, chapter 12. The witch Ljot appears in *Vatnsdæla saga*, chapter 26. George Steuart Mackenzie is quoted in *The Iceland Traveller: A Hundred Years of Adventure* by Alan Boucher (Iceland Review, 1989), 139; William Lord Watts by L. J. Downer, "Travellers' Tales," in *Iceland and the Mediaeval World: Studies in Honor of Ian Maxwell*, edited by Gabriel Turville-Petre and John S. Martin (Melbourne, 1974), 70. Tolkien's description of Mordor appears in book 4, chapter 2 of *The Lord of the Rings*.

On volcanoes, see Oren Falk, "The Vanishing Volcanoes: Fragments of Fourteenth-Century Icelandic Folklore," *Folklore* 118 (April 2007): 1–22.

On witches, see Astrid Ogilvie and Gísli Pálsson, "Weather and Witchcraft in the Sagas of Icelanders," in *The Fantastic in Old Norse/ Icelandic Literature: Preprint Papers of the 13th International Saga Conference* (Durham, UK: Durham, 2006), 734–741; and Jack Zipes, *The Irresistible Fairy Tale: The Cultural and Social History of a Genre* (Princeton, NJ: Princeton University Press, 2012), 57–60, 77–78. Richard Green discusses fata, strega, and Reginald Scot in *Elf Queens and Holy Friars: Fairy Beliefs and the Medieval Church* (Philadelphia: University of Pennsylvania Press, 2016), 195–197.

On magical vision and stories as spells, see Nan Shepherd, *The Living Mountain* (1940), reprinted in *The Grampian Quartet* (Edinburgh: Canongate, 1996), 8; Susan Greenwood, *The Anthropology of Magic* (Oxford: Bloomsbury Academic, 2009; rpt. 2012), 1, 31, 63; Arthur Frank, *Letting Stories Breathe* (Chicago: University of Chicago Press, 2010), 2–3, 37, 41; and Daniel Smith et al., "Cooperation and the Evolution of Hunter-Gatherer Storytelling," *Nature Communications* 8 (2017): 1853. Ursula K. Le Guin was interviewed by Jonathan White in *Talking on the Water: Conversations about Nature and Creativity* (San Antonio, TX: Trinity University Press, 2016), 104–106.

On how stories shape the world, see Robert Macfarlane, *Mountains of the Mind: Adventures in Reaching the Summit* (New York: Random House, 2003), 18–19, 74–75, and *The Old Ways: A Journey on Foot* (New York: Viking, 2012), 152. Tim Ingold writes about boots in *Being Alive* (New York: Routledge, 2011), 16–17, 35–36.

On the Anthropocene, see Ben Rawlence, "The First Rule of Book Club Is . . . ," *New York Times Book Review* (January 29, 2017), and Robert Macfarlane, "Generation Anthropocene: How Humans Have Altered the Planet for Ever," *The Guardian* (April 1, 2016); Paul Crutzen is quoted by Macfarlane. See also Sianne Ngai, "Stuplimity: Shock and Boredom in Twentieth-Century Aesthetics," *Postmodern Culture* 10, no. 2 (January 2000).

7. WINDOWS

My husband and I chronicled our summer in the abandoned house in a pair of books: *Summer at Little Lava: A Season at the Edge of the World* by Charles Fergus (New York: Farrar, Straus, & Giroux, 1998), and *A Good Horse Has No Color: Searching Iceland for the Perfect Horse* (Mechanicsburg, PA: Stackpole Books, 2001).

On escapism and fantasy, see Pico Iyer, *The Art of Stillness: Adventures in Going Nowhere* (New York: Simon & Schuster, 2014), 66, 74; Laura Miller, *The Magician's Book: A Skeptic's Adventures in Narnia* (New York: Little, Brown, 2008), 182; Tom Shippey, *Tolkien: Author of the Century* (New York: Houghton Mifflin, 2001), xxv; Ilan Stavans, *Quixote: The Novel and the World* (New York: W. W. Norton, 2015), 139; and Kevin Pask, *The Fairy Way of Writing: Shakespeare to Tolkien* (Baltimore, MD: Johns Hopkins University Press, 2013), 1, 19, 65. Samuel Johnson on realism and Edmund Burke on Homer are quoted by David Sandner in *Critical Discourses of the Fantastic, 1712–1831* (Burlington, VT: Ashgate, 2011), 42–44, 57–58. J. R. R. Tolkien's comments on the writing of "On Fairy-stories" are quoted by Edward James in "Tolkien, Lewis, and the Explosion of Genre Fantasy," in *The Cambridge Companion to Fantasy Literature* (Cambridge: Cambridge University Press, 2012), 62–78; for the essay itself, and its most recent editors' comments, see the expanded edition by Verlyn Flieger and Douglas A. Anderson (New York: HarperCollins, 2008; rpt. 2014), 9, 14, 22, 51–52, 59–60, 67, 147.

C. S. Lewis's speech "On Three Ways of Writing for Children" appears in the collection *Of Other Worlds: Essays and Stories* (New York: Harcourt Brace Jovanovich, 1967), 22–34. Robert Macfarlane combines Tolkien and Burke in *Mountains of the Mind* (New York: Random House, 2003), 243.

8. SEEING IS BELIEVING

The Winter of Marvels appears in *Prests saga Guðmundar góða*, chapter 4. The tale of blessing the cliff is filed in the Sagnagrunnur database under the keyword *bjargsig*. Bishop Oddur Einarsson writes on elves in "Qualiscunque Descriptio Islandiae," translated by Richard Firth Green in *Elf Queens and Holy Friars* (Philadelphia: University of Pennsylvania Press, 2016), 13.

Mott T. Greene comments on seeing in *Natural Knowledge in Preclassical Antiquity* (Baltimore, MD: Johns Hopkins University Press, 1992), 144, and on Hesiod's Theogony and the individuality of volcanoes, 46, 52–53, 56, 88.

Charles Gross cites Andrew Marvell and outlines historical theories of sight in "The Fire That Comes from the Eye," *Neuroscientist* 5, no. 1 (1999): 58–64. Tim Ingold discusses the senses in *Being Alive* (New York: Routledge, 2011), 128. On blurring and change blindness, see Chris Frith, *Making Up the Mind* (Hoboken, NJ: Blackwell Publishing, 2007), 40–42. On problems of scale, see Miguel P. Eckstein et al., "Humans, but Not Deep Neural Networks, Often Miss Giant Targets in Scenes," *Current Biology* 27 (September 25, 2017): 2827–2832.

On novelty, analogy, and culture, see Diane Ackerman, *An Alchemy of Mind: The Marvel and Mystery of the Brain* (New York: Scribner, 2004), 47–51, 218; Elizabeth and Paul Barber, *When They Severed Earth from Sky: How the Human Mind Shapes Myth* (Princeton, NJ: Princeton University Press, 2004), 1, 9–11, 97, 107–108, 158; Moshe Bar, "The Proactive Brain: Memory for Predictions," *Philosophical Transactions of the Royal Society: Biological Sciences* 364, no. 1521 (May 12, 2009): 1235–1243; and Richard Nisbett, *The Geography of Thought: How Asians and Westerners Think Differently . . . and Why* (New York: Free Press, 2003), xiii, xvi–ii. Nisbet's experiments were described by Nicolas Geeraert in "How Knowledge about Different Cultures Is Shaking the Foundations of Psychology," *The Conversation* (March 9, 2018).

Ármann Jakobsson connects dragons and fear in Old Norse legends in "Why Be Afraid? On the Practical Uses of Legends," from *Á Austrvega: Saga and East Scandinavia*, vol. 1 (Gävle, Sweden: Gävle University Press, 2009), 35–42. Tim Ingold writes of St. Benedict and Francis Bacon in "Dreaming of Dragons: On the Imagination of Real Life," *Journal of the Royal Anthropological Society* 19 (2013): 734–752.

On animism, see Susan Greenwood, *The Anthropology of Magic* (Oxford: Bloomsbury Academic, 2009; rpt. 2012), 133–135; and H. Frankfort et al., *The Intellectual Adventure of Ancient Man: An Essay on Speculative Thought in the Ancient Near East* (Chicago: University of Chicago Press, 1946; rpt. 1977), 4–6.

9. THE VOLCANO SHOW

I visited the Fimmvörðuhals eruption site on Eyjafjallajökull on March 30, April 1–2, and April 4, 2010. For Tolkien's dragons, see *Tolkien On Fairy-stories*, edited by Verlyn Flieger and Douglas A. Anderson (London: HarperCollins, 2008; rpt. 2014), 55. On Iceland's volcanic landscape, see Þorleifur Einarsson, *Geology of Iceland: Rocks and Landscapes* (Reykjavík: Mál og menning, 1994).

Parts of my 1990 interview with Vilhjálmur Knudsen were published as "The Volcano Show: Film Maker Vilhjálmur Knudsen Continues a Fiery Family Tradition," *News from Iceland* (March 1991), 8; I interviewed him again on March 31, 2010.

On painting versus filmmaking, see John Berger, *Ways of Seeing: Based on the BBC Television Series* (London: Penguin Books, 1972), 7–9, 16, 18.

10. SEND CASH, NOT ASH

The Icelandic Meteorological Office published all their data on Eyjafjallajökull's 2010 eruption online at www.vedur.is. I interviewed Kristín Vogfjörð on April 6, 2010; versions of our discussion were published in *The Penn Stater* (July/August 2010) and on pennstatermag.com (June 22, 2010).

News reports cited include "Airline Losses from Ash Spiral over $1 Billion," *The New York Times* (April 19, 2010); "Hellfire: Volcano

That Shut Down the World," *New York Post* (April 18, 2010), 1; Rosanne D'Arrigo, "How Volcanoes Can Change the World," CNN .com (April 16, 2010); "750 Tonn á sekúndu" (April 18, 2010) and "Öskubylur næstu mánuðina" (April 19, 2010) in *Morgunblaðið*; and "Ash Fall Turns Iceland into 'Another Planet'" (April 16, 2010) and "Iceland Eruption: The Birds Fly into the Ash and Die" (April 17, 2010) on *Iceland Review Online*; "Send Cash, Not Ash!" *Pressan* (April 15, 2010); and Ýrsa Sigurðardóttir, "Send Cash—Not Ash," murderiseverywhere.blogspot.com (April 19, 2010). On the eruption in general, see also S. R. Gislason et al., "Characterization of Eyjafjallajökull Volcanic Ash Particles and a Protocol for Rapid Risk Assessment," *PNAS* 108, no. 18 (May 3, 2011).

On Snorri Sturluson, see my *Song of the Vikings: Snorri and the Making of Norse Myths* (London: Palgrave Macmillan, 2012). On volcanoes in Old Norse literature, see Oren Falk, "The Vanishing Volcanoes," *Folklore* 118 (April 2007): 1–22; Jan Bergström, "Incipient Earth Science in the Old Norse Mythology," *GFF: Journal of the Geological Society of Sweden* 111, no. 2 (1989): 187–191; and Mathias Nordvig, *Of Fire and Water: The Old Norse Mythical Worldview in an Eco-Mythological Perspective*, PhD dissertation, Aarhus University (2013).

The Icelandic annals entry for 1341 is translated by Falk, other annal entries are translated by Elisabeth Ashman Rowe, both from unpublished work shared with me. *Völuspá* (The Song of the Seer) appears in the medieval collection known as *The Poetic Edda*, as well as in Snorri Sturluson's *Edda* (or the *Prose Edda*), which also includes the story of Thor's fight with the giant Hrungnir. My translation of *Haustlöng* is adapted from Peter Hallberg, *Old Icelandic Poetry* (Lincoln: University of Nebraska Press, 1975). I discussed the myth in "Volcanoes in Snorri's Edda: A New Reading of the Fight between Thor and Hrungnir," a paper presented at the 48th International Medieval Congress at Kalamazoo, Michigan, on May 9, 2013.

On the economic crash, see Arthur L. Centonze, "Case Study: Iceland's Financial Meltdown," *Journal of Financial Education* 37 (Spring/Summer 2011): 131–166, and Michael Lewis, "Wall Street on the Tundra," *Vanity Fair* (April 2009).

On Iceland's ad campaign, see the Inspired by Iceland YouTube channel and Andrew Sheivachman, "Iceland and the Trials of 21st Century Tourism," Skift.com (June 2016).

11. ELF STORIES

Eygló Svala Arnarsdóttir reported "Icelandic MP Moves Elves' Boulder to His Home" for *Iceland Review* (May 15, 2012) and the follow-up story, "Do You Believe in Elf Stories?" (May 18, 2012). Terry Gunnell comments on the power of stories in "The Power in the Place: Icelandic *Álagablettir* Legends in a Comparative Context," which he shared with me in draft form in August 2016.

"The Red-Headed Whale" is recorded in the Sagnagrunnur database as Rauðhöfði 97; the alternate version, "Redhead," appears in *Elves, Trolls, and Elemental Beings: Icelandic Folktales II*, translated by Alan Boucher (Reykjavík: Iceland Review Library, 1977), along with "The Sheriff's Lady of Burstarfell." On the history of the great auk, see Hjálmar R. Barðarson, *Birds of Iceland* (Reykjavík, 1986), 18–26; also *An Awkward Extinction: The Great Auk and the Loss of Species* by Gísli Pálsson (Princeton, NJ: Princeton University Press, forthcoming), which I read in manuscript. The Elf Lady's Cloth is treasure #Þjms 3465 in Iceland's National Museum.

On the *baðstofa*, see Ida Pfeiffer, *A Visit to Iceland and the Scandinavian North (1845)* (London, 1852; rpt. Waking Lion Press, 2006), 50. Uno Von Troil is quoted by Alan Boucher, *The Iceland Traveller: A Hundred Years of Adventure* (Reykjavík: Iceland Review, 1989), 216. Jónas Jónasson is quoted by Einar Ó. Sveinsson, *The Folk-Stories of Iceland* (1940; rpt. London: Viking Society for Northern Research, 2003), 68.

On folklore and nationalism, see Terry Gunnell, "Daisies Rise to Become Oaks: The Politics of Early Folklore Collection in Northern Europe," *Folklore* 121 (2010): 12–37. On Konrad Maurer's influence see also Árni Björnsson, *Wagner and the Volsungs: Icelandic Sources of Der Ring des Nibelungen* (London: Viking Society for Northern Research, 2003), 14.

I interviewed Agnar Helgason of Decode Genetics on July 22, 2005, and wrote about his work in *The Far Traveler* (Boston: Harcourt, 2007), 101–102; for an update, see S. S. Ebenesersdóttir et al., "Ancient Genomes from Iceland Reveal the Making of a Human Population,"

Science 360 (June 1, 2018): 1028–1032. On Iceland in the Middle Ages see Gunnar Karlsson, *The History of Iceland* (Minneapolis, MN: University of Minnesota Press, 2000). On Norway and the Hansa League, see Michael Pye, *The Edge of the World: A Cultural History of the North Sea and the Transformation of Europe* (New York: Pegasus Books, 2015), 221–241. "With laws shall our land be built" appears in *Brennu-Njals saga*, chapter 70.

Gunnell quotes Guðbrandur Vigfússon's introduction to the 1862 collection of Icelandic folktales. On their cultural importance, see May and Hallberg Hallmundsson, *Icelandic Folk and Fairy Tales* (Reykjavík: Iceland Review Library, 1987), 7, and Guðmundur Páll Ólafsson, *Iceland the Enchanted* (Reykjavík: Mál og menning, 1995), 125.

12. DOORS

For Tolkien's door, see *Tolkien On Fairy-stories*, edited by Verlyn Flieger and Douglas A. Anderson (London: HarperCollins, 2008; rpt. 2014), 48. For the history of *The Book of Land-Taking*, see Hermann Pálsson and Paul Edwards, *Landnámabók: The Book of Settlements* (Winnepeg, Canada: University of Manitoba Press, 1972), 3–4; the story of Fluga appears in chapter 202. I rode *Kjölur* with *Íshestar* June 27–July 5, 2009.

Robert Macfarlane writes about the children's doors, and those of Muir and Graham, in *Landmarks* (London: Hamish Hamilton, 2015), 315–320; he comments on Weber and disenchantment, 24. See also Egil Asprem, *The Problem of Disenchantment: Scientific Rationalism and Esoteric Discourse, 1900–1939*, PhD thesis (Amsterdam: University of Amsterdam, 2013), 1; Richard Jenkins, "Disenchantment, Enchantment, and Re-Enchantment: Max Weber at the Millennium," *Max Weber Studies* 1 (2000): 11–32; and Michael Saler, "Rethinking Secularism: Modernity, Enchantment, and Fictionalism," *Immanent Frame* (December 20, 2013) at blogs.ssrc.org. Wittgenstein and Charles Taylor are quoted by Saler.

Gillian Overing expands on "the center is the margin" in *Landscape of Desire: Partial Stories of the Medieval Scandinavian World* (Minneapolis: University of Minnesota Press, 1994), coauthored with Marijane Osborn.

13. THE HOUSE OF THE STEWARD

On elves as "old-fashioned," see Valdimar Tr. Hafstein, "The Elves' Point of View," *Journal of Folktale Studies* 41 (2000): 87–104; Terry Gunnell's introduction to *Hildur, Queen of the Elves and Other Icelandic Legends*, translated by J. M. Bedell (Northampton, MA: Interlink Publishing Group, 2007), 12; and Gunnell's unpublished draft, "The Power in the Place: Icelandic *Álagablettir* Legends in a Comparative Context," in which he discusses the work of Bjarni Harðarson. Ragnhildur Jónsdóttir and I met with Gunnell on August 4, 2016. Jesse Byock and Davide Zori write of Church Hill and the Hill of the Hidden Folk in "Interdisciplinary Research in Iceland's Mosfell Valley," *Backdirt: Annual Review of the Cotsen Institute of Archaeology at UCLA* (2013): 124–141.

Icelandic folkways were collected by Jónas Jónasson frá Hrafnagili in *Íslenzkir Þjóðhættir* (Reykjavík: Ísafold, 1961); several of these examples were highlighted by Sara McMahon in "Head-Butting Sheep Predicted Heavy Winds: How to Foretell the Weather," *Iceland Magazine* (August 1, 2014).

Find Sagnagrunnur at http://sagnagrunnur.com/en/; Gunnell describes the project in *Folklore: Electronic Journal of Folklore* 45 (2010): 151–162; Feargus O'Sullivan tests it in "Mapping Where to Find Elves in Iceland's Proposed New National Park," *CityLab* (March 17, 2016).

On nature spirits, see Peter Foote and David M. Wilson, *The Viking Achievement* (Westport, CT: Praeger Publishers, 1970), 392. On the negative effects of Iceland's settlement, see P. C. Buckland et al., "Holt in Eyjafjallasveit, Iceland: A Paleoecological Study of the Impact of Landnám," *Acta Archaeologica* 61 (1990): 252–271 ("desert"; "landscape of ruins"); Andrew Dugmore and Orri Vésteinsson, "Black Sun, High Flame, and Flood: Volcanic Hazards in Iceland," in *Surviving Sudden Environmental Change: Answers from Archaeology*, edited by Jago Cooper and Payson Sheets (Boulder: University Press of Colorado, 2012); and Thomas McGovern et al., "Landscapes of Settlement in Northern Iceland: Historical Ecology of Human Impact and Climate Fluctuation on the Millennial Scale," *American Anthropologist* 109, no. 1 (2007): 27–51 ("stranded").

The sermon against "foolish" women is from E. O. Sveinsson's *The Folk-Stories of Iceland*, translated by Benedikt Benedikz (London: Viking Society for Northern Research, 2003). The story of the steward in the stone is from *Kristni saga* and *Þorvalds þáttr ens víðförla*. The image of the elves packing their bags comes from the *Þáttr Þiðranda ok Þórhalls*; this translation is by Sian Grønlie from "Miracles, Magic, and Missionaries: The Supernatural in the Conversion *Þættir*," in *The Fantastic in Old Norse/Icelandic Literature: Preprint Papers of the 13th International Saga Conference*, edited by John McKinnell et al. (Durham, NC: Centre for Medieval and Renaissance Studies, 2006), 298, where she also discusses desanctification.

Lynn Townsend White Jr. blamed Christianity in "The Historical Roots of Our Ecological Crisis," *Science* 155 (March 10, 1967): 1205. Snorri Sturluson writes about Iceland's *landvættir* in *Ólafs saga Tryggvasonar*, chapter 33, in the collection *Heimskringla*. Paul Beekman Taylor spoke of his collaboration with W. H. Auden in "Auden's Icelandic Myth of Exile," *Journal of Modern Literature* 24, no. 2 (2000–2001): 213–234.

On the Ásatrú religion, see Michael Strmiska, "Ásatrú in Iceland: The Rebirth of Nordic Paganism?" *Nova Religio: The Journal of Alternative and Emergent Religions* 4, no. 1 (2000): 106–132; J. D. Tómasson, *Soul of the North: An Introduction to Ásatrú* (Burlington, VT: Huginn & Muninn Publishing, 2020); and *Vísir* (January 2, 1973), 3.

14. A KIND TROLL

Ragnhildur Jónsdóttir and I met in Hvalfjörður on June 8, 2017. On the ambiguity of *troll* and *elf*, see Sandra Ballif Straubhaar, *Old Norse Women's Poetry: Voices of Female Skalds* (Woodbridge, UK: D. S. Brewer, 2011), 101; Ármann Jakobsson, "Beware of the Elf! A Note on the Evolving Meaning of *Álfar*," *Folklore* 126 (August 2015): 215–223; Jacqueline Simpson, "On the Ambiguity of Elves," *Folklore* 122 (April 2011): 76–83; and John Lindow, *Trolls: An Unnatural History* (London: Reaktion Books, 2014), 14–17, 21. The story of King Sveigdir appears in *Ynglinga saga*, chapter 12, in Snorri Sturluson's collection *Heimskringla*; it is discussed by Lindow in "Supernatural Others and Ethnic Others: A Millennium of World View," *Scandinavian Studies* 67 (1995): 8–31, where he also discusses virtuosity and sex. Sighvatr Þórðarson's verse, from the poem "Austfararvisur," is translated by Anders Winroth in *The Conversion of Scandinavia: Vikings, Merchants, and Missionaries in the Remaking of Northern Europe* (New Haven, CT: Yale University Press, 2012), 148.

Terry Gunnell discusses elf worship in "The Season of the *Dísir*: The Winter Nights, and the *Dísablót* in Early Medieval Scandinavian Belief,"

Cosmos 16 (2000): 117–149. J. R. R. Tolkien introduces his elves in *The Lord of the Rings*, book 1, chapter 3, and describes them further in book 2, chapters 1, 7, and 8.

On the word *elf*, see Jacqueline Simpson's 2011 paper (listed above) and Noel Williams, "The Semantics of the World *Fairy*: Making Meaning out of Thin Air," in *The Good People: New Fairylore Essays*, edited by Peter Narvaez (New York: Garland, 1991), 457–478.

On William of Auvergne, the English sermon of 1400, and witch hunts, see Richard Firth Green, *Elf Queens and Holy Friars* (Philadelphia: University of Pennsylvania Press, 2016), 1, 6, 8, 14. On Joan of Arc, see the entry by Herbert Thurston in *The Catholic Encyclopedia*, vol. 8 (New York: Robert Appleton Company, 1910). Carolyne Larrington discusses Thomas the Rhymer in *The Land of the Green Man: A Journey through the Supernatural Landscapes of the British Isles* (London: I. B. Tauris, 2015), 51–56. For Chaucer, I used Albert C. Baugh's *Chaucer's Major Poetry* (Hoboken, NJ: Prentice-Hall, 1963); for Shakespeare, *The Riverside Shakespeare*, edited by G. Blakemore Evans et al. (Boston: Houghton Mifflin, 1974).

Tolkien defines fairies in *Tolkien On Fairy-stories*, edited by Verlyn Flieger and Douglas A. Anderson (London: HarperCollins, 2008; rpt. 2014), 28–29. Gísli Pálsson shared a transcript of his and Hugh Raffles's 2015 interview with elf-seer Erla Stefánsdóttir with me in August 2016. Erla also described elves to Ármann Jakobsson, who defines the New Age elf in "Beware of the Elf!" 219–220. Rich Warren wrote "Learn about Iceland's 'Hidden People,' Trolls, and More at Elf School in Reykjavik" for the *Chicago Tribune* (August 21, 2017). Gunnell quotes the work of Júlíana Magnúsdóttir in "Heima á milli: Þjóðtrú og þjóðsagnir á Íslandi við upphaf 21 aldar," in *Rannsóknir í félagsvísindum* (2009): 899–908; the translation is my own.

15. WONDER

On Asbjorn's death and "troll space," see Ármann Jakobsson, *The Troll Inside You: Paranormal Activity in the Medieval North* (Santa Barbara, CA: Punctum Books, 2017), 17–19, 49.

On religion and cognitive science, see Mary Ann Lieberg's interview with Andrew Newberg, "The Neurotheology Link: An Intersection between Spirituality and Health," *Alternative and Complementary Therapies* 21 (February 2015): 13–17; Eugene G. D'Aquili and Andrew B. Newberg, "The Neuropsychological Basis of Religions, or Why God Won't Go Away," *Zygon* 33 (June 1998): 187–201; Stewart Guthrie, "A Cognitive Theory of Religion," *Current Anthropology* 21 (1980): 181–203; and M. Andersen, U. Schjoedt, K. L. Nielbo, and J. Sørensen, "Mystical Experience in the Lab," *Method and Theory in the Study of Religion* 26 (2014): 217–245.

On belief, see Rodney Needham, *Belief, Language, and Experience* (Oxford: Basil Blackwell, 1972), 4, 37, 41–44, 47–49, 52–53 (on David Hume), 56–57 (on Stuart Hampshire); Jonathan A. Lanman, "In Defence of 'Belief': A Cognitive Response to Behaviourism, Eliminativism, and Social Constructivism," *Issues in Ethnology and Anthropology N.S.* 3, no. 3 (2008): 49–62. Jesse Prinz discusses wonder in "How Wonder Works," *Aeon* (June 21, 2013).

On the science of the brain, see Lisa Feldman Barrett, "Emotional Intelligence Needs a Rewrite," *Nautilus* 51 (August 3, 2017); "Navigating the Science of Emotion," in *Emotion Measurement*, edited by Herbert L. Meiselman (Amsterdam: Elsevier, 2016), 31–63; "The Predictive Brain," *Edge* (July 14, 2017); "The Secret History of Emotions," *Chronicle of Higher Education* (March 10, 2017); and "What Emotions Are (and Aren't)," *The New York Times* (August 2, 2015).

Jules Evans quotes Philip Pullman and discusses his own book, *The Art of Losing Control: A Philosopher's Search for Ecstatic Experience* (Edinburgh: Canongate, 2017), in "Dissolving the Ego," *Aeon* (June 26, 2017). On Jill Bolte Taylor's experience, see *My Stroke of Insight: A Brain Scientist's Personal Journey* (New York: Viking Penguin, 2006), 41, 43, 69, 76–77, 103, 127–128, 147.

16. A SOUL CLAD IN AIR

The tale of the glacier's guardian spirit is from *Barðar saga Snæfellsás*. Halldór Laxness's *Christianity at Glacier* was translated by Magnús Magnússon (Reykjavík: Helgafell, 1972).

On the glacier, see Haraldur Sigurðsson, *Snæfellsjökull: Art, Science, and History of an Icelandic Volcano* (Stykkishólmur, Iceland: Vulkan, 2017), 7, 8, 18, 49, 100 (quoting Árni Þórarinsson); and Rúna Guðrún Bergmann, *The Magic of Snaefellsjokull: Legends, Folklore, and Mystique* (Reykjavík:

Isis-Iceland Publishing, 2014), 11, 73–76, 79, 100. On Kjarval, see Peter Davidson, *The Idea of North* (London: Reaktion Books, 2005), 165.

On magic mountains, see Philip Marsden, *Rising Ground: A Search for the Spirit of Place* (Chicago: University of Chicago Press, 2016), 70–71; and William Scott Wilson, *Walking the Kiso Road: A Modern-Day Exploration of Old Japan* (Boulder, CO: Shambhala, 2015), 113.

Barbara Dancygier cites Neil Philip's retelling of *The Arabian Nights* in *The Language of Stories: A Cognitive Approach* (Cambridge: Cambridge University Press, 2012), 4, 203.

17. A SENSE OF PLACE

Peter Davidson quotes William Morris and Mariusz Wilk in *The Idea of North* (London: Reaktion Books, 2005), 47–48, 168; in the translation of Wilk, I've Americanized *jumper* to *wool sweater*. Nan Shepherd's poem "Achiltibuie" is published in Roderick Watson's introduction to her collection, *The Grampian Quartet* (Edinburgh: Canongate, 1996), viii.

On edges and islands, see Jane Ledwell, "Afraid of Heights, Not Edges: Representations of the Shoreline in Recent Prince Edward Island Poetry and Visual Art," a paper presented at the Islands of the World VII conference at the University of Prince Edward Island, Charlottetown, PEI, in 2002; Pete Hay, "A Phenomenology of Islands," *Island Studies Journal* 1 (2006): 19–42; Owe Ronström, "Island Words, Island Worlds: The Origins and Meanings of Words for 'Islands' in North-West Europe," *Island Studies Journal* 4 (2009): 163–182.

On place and space, see Yi-Fu Tuan, "Place: An Experiential Perspective," *Geographical Review* 65, no. 2 (April 1975): 151–165, and *Space and Place: The Perspective of Experience* (1977; rpt. Minneapolis: University of Minnesota Press, 2001), 3, 6–9, 18; Philip Marsden, *Rising Ground* (Chicago: University of Chicago Press, 2016), 24–25; and Herb Childress, "Book Review," *Environmental and Architectural Phenomenology Newsletter* 10 (Fall 1999): 4–6.

On words and metaphor, see Robert Macfarlane, *Landmarks* (London: Hamish Hamilton, 2015) and "The Word-Hoard: Robert Macfarlane on Rewilding Our Language of Landscape," *The Guardian* (February 27, 2015); Bill Holm, *Eccentric Islands: Travels Real and Imaginary* (Minneapolis: Milkweed Editions, 2000); and Terry Gunnell, "Legends and Landscape in the Nordic Countries," *Cultural and Social History* 6, no. 3 (2009): 305–322.

Andrea Wulf describes Alexander von Humboldt's work and influence in *The Invention of Nature: Alexander von Humboldt's New World* (New York: Knopf, 2015), 3, 5, 34–35, 91, 129, 133, 245–246, 248, 328, 334. Florence Williams describes the "Mappiness" project and other health benefits of nature in *The Nature Fix: Why Nature Makes Us Happier, Healthier, and More Creative* (New York: W. W. Norton, 2017), 1–4.

On "our proper concerns," see Belden C. Lane, *Landscapes of the Sacred: Geography and Narrative in American Spirituality* (Mahway, NJ: Paulist Press, 1988), 187–188; Gary Paul Nabhan, "Going Truant," in *The Geography of Childhood: Why Children Need Wild Places*, edited by Nabhan and Stephen Trimble (Boston: Beacon Press, 1994), 35–58; and George Monbiot, "Forget 'the Environment': We Need New Words to Convey Life's Wonders," *The Guardian* (August 9, 2017).

Gillian Overing spoke about the center and the margin in "Place and Self: Social, Legal, and Spatial Boundaries in the Sagas," a lecture I attended at the 27th International Congress on Medieval Studies (1992) in Kalamazoo, Michigan. She and Marijane Osborn expand on the question in *Landscape of Desire: Partial Stories of the Medieval Scandinavian World* (Minneapolis: University of Minnesota Press, 1994). Auður Ava Ólafsdóttir spoke in the video, "Iceland Keeps Us Creative: Icelandic Authors on Icelandic Literature," on the Iceland Writers Retreat website, http://www.icelandwritersretreat.com/iceland -keeps-us-creative-icelandic-authors-icelandic-literature/ (January 9, 2018).

18. EVERYONE IS AN ARTIST

William Scott Wilson examines Ontoke-kyo in *Walking the Kiso Road* (Boulder, CO: Shambhala, 2015), 113–116. Tolkien speaks of words and wonder in *Tolkien On Fairy-stories*, edited by Verlyn Flieger and Douglas A. Anderson (London: HarperCollins, 2008; rpt. 2014), 32, 34, 58. For more on words, read Owen Barfield, *Poetic Diction: A Study in Meaning* (1928; rpt. New York: McGraw-Hill, 1964), 72–75, 109.

On the process of art, see John Berger's essays "Miners," "A Professional Secret," and "The Soul and the Operator" in *Keeping a Rendezvous* (New

York: Pantheon, 1991), 9, 130–131, 230–231; and Tim Ingold, "The Textility of Making," *Cambridge Journal of Economics* 34 (2010): 91–102.

On capitalism and climate change, see Benjamin Y. Fong, "The Climate Crisis? It's Capitalism, Stupid," *New York Times* (November 20, 2017); and Steven Hartman et al., "Medieval Iceland, Greenland, and the New Human Condition: A Case Study in Integrated Environmental Humanities," *Global and Planetary Change* 156 (2017): 123–139.

On stones, see Tim Ingold, *Being Alive* (New York: Routledge, 2011), 16, 21, 32; Jacquetta Hawkes, *A Land* (1951; rpt. Boston: Beacon Press, 1991), 100; Hugh Raffles, "Twenty-Five Years Is a Long Time," *Cultural Anthropology* 27, no. 3 (August 2012): 526–534; Rachel Corbett, *You Must Change Your Life: The Story of Rainier Maria Rilke and Auguste Rodin* (New York: W. W. Norton, 2016), as excerpted in Maria Popova, "The Invention of Empathy: Rilke, Rodin, and the Art of 'Inseeing,'" *Brain Pickings* (December 14, 2016); Nan Shepherd, *The Living Mountain*, as reprinted in *The Grampian Quartet* (Edinburgh: Canongate, 1996), 97, 83–84; Cynthia Zarin, "Seeing Things: The Art of Olafur Eliasson," *The New Yorker* (November 13, 2006), 79; Justin E. H. Smith, "The Moral Status of Rocks," jehsmith.com (May 21, 2013); Roni Horn, in "The Phaidon Folio: 'Iceland Could Have Been Anywhere': Roni Horn on How to Be Present amidst Shifting Landscapes," *Artspace* (July 14, 2017); and Roni Horn, *Island Zombie* (Princeton, NJ: Princeton University Press, 2020), 55.

On making the world, see Ursula K. Le Guin, "World-Making," in *Dancing at the Edge of the World: Thoughts on Words, Women, Places* (New York: Grove Press, 1989), 48. Krista Tippett's interview with John O'Donahue, "The Inner Landscape of Beauty," was first aired on *Speaking of Faith*, Minnesota Public Radio (February 28, 2008); it is archived at *On Being with Krista Tippett:* onbeing.org/programs/john-odonohue-the-inner-landscape-of-beauty/.

Tolkien writes of wonder as love in the preface to *The Smith of Wootton Major*, excerpted by Verlyn Flieger in *A Question of Time: J. R. R. Tolkien's Road to Faërie* (Kent, OH: Kent State University Press, 1997), 246.

To see an elf, follow the directions in *What Does It Take to See an Elf? A Book by Fróði the Elf*, published by Ragnhildur Jónsdóttir (Garðabær, Iceland: Álfagarðarinn, 2012).